D1823182

# Full–Stack JavaScript Development:

## Develop, Test and Deploy with
## MongoDB, Express, Angular and Node on AWS

## Eric Bush

"The only way of discovering the limits of
the possible is to venture a little way past
them into the impossible."
- Arthur C. Clarke

REDSKY PRODUCTIONS LLC

Copyright © 2016, Eric Bush

All rights reserved. No part of this book may be reproduced, stored in a retrieval system, or transmitted in any form or by any means, without the prior written permission of the author, except in the case of brief quotations embedded in evaluation articles or reviews as accompanied by proper references to the book.

Every effort has been made in the preparation of this book to ensure the accuracy of the information presented. However, the information contained in this book is sold without warranty, either expressed or implied. Neither the book's author, nor publisher, nor its dealers and distributors will be held liable for any damages caused or alleged, resulting directly by or indirectly by this book.

The views expressed herein are the sole responsibility of the author and do not necessarily represent those of any other person or organization.

Cover artwork: Licensed from fotolio.com. Author: BillionPhotos.com

Author photo: Taken by Niels Arnason photography (http://nielsarnason.com)

Please send any comments to the author at jsdevstack@outlook.com.
You can also follow the author's blog at http://jsdevstack.com/ to learn more about full-stack JavaScript development and tools.

Paperback ISBN-10: 0-9971966-0-2
Paperback ISBN-13: 978-0-9971966-0-3

e-book ISBN-10: 0-9971966-3-7
e-book ISBN-13: 978-0-9971966-3-4

# Contents

# Acknowledgements

This book really revolves around the phenomenal technology of Node.js. I am in awe of Ryan Dahl for his having conceived of it in the first place and especially for his having built it on top of some great work by others. Thank you Ryan! I want to thank all those who have collaborated on the modules that make Node such a capable platform. This is open-source at its best.

I would also like to thank TJ Holowaychuk for his contribution to node through his work in creating the Express web framework. This really does a great job organizing and simplifying the code needed to implement a Rest Web API.

I want to thank the brilliant people behind all of the Amazon Web Services infrastructure. From those who envisioned it in the first place, to those who build it and also those who run it 24 hours a day.

Another great piece of technology is that of MongoDB. I want to thank those who write and maintain MongoDB and also thank mLab for their making it easy to host MongoDB in a PaaS environment.

The Angular framework has come along at a great time. This is another great member to add to the "super hero" lineup of technologies. I acknowledge all of the effort that is ongoing to build, maintain and evolve it.

I owe a huge thanks to my editor, Maura van der Linden, for applying her editing skills to the project. This allowed me to concentrate on the content of the book and be assured that she would make everything presentable.

I am grateful to my friend Jeff, who welcomed me into his home and treated me as a brother when I needed a place to stay for a while. I wish I were talented enough on guitar to keep up with your musical keyboard skills.

I express my love and thanks to my family. The happiest times in my life have been with them. No work I have done in my profession has ever been as rewarding as what we have accomplished together in our family.

# Preface

Many people will turn to the first few pages of a book to determine whether or not it will meet their needs. If you are just now reading this paragraph in order to make a decision about whether you want to invest the time and money necessary to build up your skills in the area of full-stack development, I will state to you that you are doing well to have found this book.

Let me give you a bit of a marketing pitch about why you need to pursue investing in full-stack skills with this book. Technology trends come and go, but what this book covers is really here to stay. The JavaScript technologies that this book covers have come together in a unified stack using the same programming language. With this book, you will not only learn about these technologies, but will also gain a longer lasting foundational understanding of what the architectural designs are that utilize them.

If you are even remotely interested in JavaScript development, I advise you to stick with it and it will pay off. You will have to study hard but it will be worth it. There is a huge development community behind it and you will be in good company. Many developers and top companies are finding success doing full-stack JavaScript development today.

**Level of skill required**
I have written this book for all levels of experience. If you are a beginner and need to learn some of the basic concepts of three-tier architecture, I have you covered. I always lead off with some material that covers the basic concepts that are involved in the architecture. I do this so that when you get to the actual code implementation, you have this insight and are not just haphazardly writing code.

I have put myself in your shoes and have given you the information that you really need that no one else is giving you. It took me a long time to pull it all together. One of my goals was to give you knowledge that will help you get, and keep a job.

If you are already familiar with the basics of the MEAN stack, this book can get you to the next stage and actually lead you towards some professional enterprise-level development. I make sure to dive deep into each topic and show real implementation and deployment details. This book is not just a copy-and-paste of the API documentation of each framework.

You do need to have some basic understanding of JavaScript in order to be effective in learning what this book contains. If you don't already know the basic JavaScript language concepts, you can use online content to learn them or you can buy a book on it, if needed. Those of you who consider yourselves experts in MEAN development may still get some valuable information out of my unique content in this book. It may just pay for itself in saving you time trying to figure out ways to test and secure your application.

Half the battle of learning a new technology is learning the add-ons and tools required to get it all working. This is where this book will really come in handy. I don't just dump a lot of code on you, but I also have taken the time to explain the development process and what tools you can use along the way.

**Two books to consider**

I have written two books at the same time. This book utilizes AWS for its implementation. This is also the more complete of the two books, as it contains substantial foundational instruction, such as details on security measures and information on how to perform functional, load and UI automation testing. The other book I wrote focuses on a Microsoft Azure implementation. It is titled "Using Microsoft Azure DocumentDB in a Node.js Application". The other book is basically just what is contained in the first third of this book, but it uses DocumentDB instead of MongoDB. The other book contains no foundational instructional material on Node.js or Angular.

**Choices**

This is certainly a great time to be a software developer. One of the things that makes it so great is the myriad of open-source projects available to leverage. There are frameworks that exist to help you with every layer of your architecture from the back-end services to the front-end GUI.

There are literally hundreds of options for technologies that could be used in your development of a full-stack JavaScript application. I will help you get started by narrowing things down to some of the essentials that are needed to get off the ground. I will also cover more advanced topics on building quality enterprise applications.

I had to make some tough decisions on which frameworks and tools to utilize in this book and have done so based on the following criteria:

1. **It must be simple and quick to get value from.**
2. **It must have wide adoption, with committed support for growth and future relevance.**
3. **It must have broad platform reach.**

After experiencing what is covered in this book, you can turn around and evangelize full-stack JavaScript development as a reality today. It is great already and will only get better.

Happy coding,
Eric Bush

# About the Author

Eric Bush began his professional career programming embedded microcontrollers in assembly language. He then worked on client-server development for what were known as workstation computers developing CAD software. When Windows came along, Eric was right there, developing some of the first desktop applications for Windows. After that he transitioned back to client-server applications for Windows Server. Finally, he made the move to .Net based cloud enterprise development in 2009 and is now focused on full-stack JavaScript technologies, centered on Node.js in the cloud.

Eric has worked for some well-known companies including Microsoft, Tektronix, Mentor Graphics, Nike, Intel and Boeing.

His last project at Microsoft was the development of the global support feature in the Microsoft Azure portal. That software architecture is constructed of many business and data storage backend systems that all coordinate together to feed information to the support agents that engage with customers. Before that, he worked in the Windows Server group and helped launch the System Center Operations Manager (SCOM) product.

He is now an independent consultant and is putting his considerable breadth and depth of knowledge into training and consulting to help companies implement full-stack JavaScript architectures. Contact Eric via email if you want to have him and his associates deliver some training. His company can provide training on Node.js and full-stack application designs.

You can email Eric at jsdevstack@outlook.com.

Follow his blog at http://jsdevstack.com/ for more information on full-stack JavaScript development.

# Introduction

This book presents the technologies and engineering best practices that span across all of the layers of a software development architecture. The core of this book focuses on specific JavaScript frameworks used to implement each architectural layer. Everything is based on the MongoDB, Express, Angular, and Node (MEAN) development stack. I will walk you through the design and development of a sample application to teach you some best practices in architecting, coding, testing, securing, deploying and managing a RESTful Web Service.

This introduction section will define several key terms and also introduce you to the sample application. This is important content you need to understand before going deeper into the materials presented in the rest of the book.

## What is a development stack?

A development stack is the collection of languages and technologies used to construct the overall application. These are the technologies you would piece together from bottom to top and is independent from what software architecture you choose. This book utilizes a particularly popular set of technologies referred to as the MEAN development stack. The MEAN acronym stands for the technology platforms of MongoDB, Express.JS, AngularJS and Node.js. These are called platforms, or frameworks, because they take code or some form of markup and execute it at a higher level of abstraction above the operating system level.

The MEAN stack only specifies four technologies but, in reality, there are many more technologies that come into play. Node.js, in particular, is a framework that really gets its capabilities from modular plug-ins that extend its basic capabilities. You will learn about many of the important extensions that can be utilized to extend the capabilities of Node.js.

*Note: AWS does have DynamoDB as a NoSQL database technology choice. I have chosen to develop with MongoDB instead because of its rich set of capabilities and its popularity. MongoDB is still hosted in AWS as a PaaS service, even though it is not provided directly by AWS.*

## The three–tier architecture

No matter what you are constructing, it is a good idea to modularize and build in layers so that you can more easily assemble everything together. For example, if you were building a house, you would not build it as one jumbled-up mess. Instead, you would first lay a foundation and eventually construct the attic and roof. Each of the needed modules would fit together: flooring, walls, heating, plumbing, electrical, etc. Software construction can be thought of in a similar way.

# Introduction

Architecting software in layers and writing code as modules (also referred to as components) helps with testing, debugging, and incorporating future enhancements. The latest buzzword in the area of software construction is "microservices." You may also have heard of the older, yet still relevant, concept of a service-oriented architecture (SOA).

One proven approach to developing a software application is to divide it up into three distinct layers. The three layers, or tiers, are named data, service, and presentation. Definitions of each layer and an assessment of where each MEAN development stack technology should fit into those layers are listed below. While this gives you the briefest of introductions to each of these, the three parts of this book go through the details of each.

- **The Data Layer (MongoDB):**
  This layer is where you persist your data in a DBMS. Data can be stored, retrieved, updated, or deleted. MongoDB is a document-based database and has a JavaScript API to interact with, as well as a management console UI using mLab.

- **The Service Layer (Node.js+Express.js):**
  This layer is where a web service API is exposed as the doorway to all your business logic and ultimately to the data stored in the data layer. It performs workflows that require more complicated computations and sequencing of operations. These might be event-driven paths or code that is scheduled to run periodically. Node.js was specifically designed for the writing of scalable server-side web applications. Express.js is used as an add-on module to Node.js to simplify the building of a web service layer with support for request routing and sending back of responses.

- **The Presentation Layer (AngularJS/HTML):**
  This layer provides the capability to display and enter data for human interaction. This could be on a computer or mobile device of some type. Angular.js provides a declarative style where your display code binds your data in both directions.

You can utilize patterns such as model view controller (MVC) within a three-tier architecture. You will see this depicted in an upcoming figure.

*Note: In my opinion, the middle service layer choice of Node.js is something foundational to this JavaScript based development stack and could not be swapped out. The other choices of MongoDB, and Angular could be swapped out and replaced with some other similar technology choices. For example, since MongoDB is accessed through a Node module, you could easily find another solution using whatever database you prefer and find it similar in its API construction. Angular is the highest layer and could be replaced with any number of frameworks that allow you to make HTTP web requests to reach the Node service layer and do the data binding.*

# Using JavaScript everywhere

I am sure you understood from the title that 100% of the development done in this book is done in JavaScript. There are considerable benefits with having one single coding language used in all three architecture layers. For one thing, the code will all look the same and be similarly refactored and maintained. You can also benefit from using the same testing framework across layers.

JavaScript has a huge amount of momentum with lots of online resources like articles and open-source code. Become good at searching online before building your application.

JavaScript Object Notation (JSON) will be used as the data-interchange format. This is an excellent fit with a JavaScript application.

# Using public cloud infrastructure

Every piece of code and all data storage should be hosted on public cloud infrastructure. This gives you characteristics like fast deployment, low cost, and elastic scalability. This book shows you how to construct an application that hosts everything in AWS.

Cloud hosting infrastructure can be split into three categories: IaaS, SaaS, and PaaS. The "aaS" part of each acronym stands for "as a Service".

In **IaaS**, the "I" is for "Infrastructure" and means you can utilize the lowest level virtual machines (VMs or containers) and have complete control of what operating systems and software you deploy on them.

In **SaaS**, the "S" is for "Software" and indicates a complete offering such as Salesforce.com, Azure SharePoint, or Amazon WorkMail. Think of this as being applications that formerly would have been installed and accessed only on your machine, but that now can be accessed from anywhere.

In **PaaS**, the "P" is for "Platform" and this variation makes your life a bit easier as a developer. It still gives you the flexibility you need over machine deployment and scaling, but it frees you from the day-to-day maintenance of machines. You could go through the added work of using IaaS to install and manage your own Node.js service, or use a PaaS service instead that is much simpler to setup and operate. After all, you want to spend your time on application development and not on DevOps.

***Note****: With Elastic Beanstalk as your hosting PaaS, your deployment updates can be "rolling" so that your service is never taken down. From the AWS management console, you can also set up a maintenance window during which AWS will automatically perform any needed OS updates.*

# Microsoft Visual Studio Code

If you are out in the real world trying to make a living by writing software, the reality is that you have to be able to combine many technologies at once and target many different platforms. Central to this is the code editor that you choose to use. Visual Studio Code (VS Code) is a great tool for entering your code. This is the tool utilized throughout this book to write code with. You can certainly choose whatever code editor you like and are not required to use VS Code.

VS Code does offer a rich editing environment as well as integrated features for source code control and debugging. VS Code also has the capability to launch tasks using tools like Gulp, without needing to jump to a command line prompt. These tools can be used to automate build and test steps that you run frequently.

Using VS Code, you can create a project, run it locally on your machine and have access to IntelliSense, debugging, and app publishing. VS Code can be installed on Mac OS X, and Linux, as well as on Windows.

If you are starting from scratch and don't have any development tools installed yet, go ahead and install the following:

✓ Visual Studio Code.
✓ Git. This is used for source code control, but it can also be the means of deploying to AWS through GitHub and other tools.
✓ Node.js from https://nodejs.org/. Get a stable version that is labeled LTS.

# The NewsWatcher sample application

This book is written using a really nice sample application to illustrate all of the topics. That way, you understand how everything can come together across all three layers of an application development stack. I will now walk you through the capabilities and architecture of the sample application called NewsWatcher.

The basic capability of NewsWatcher allows a user to set up keywords to scan and filter news stories with for viewing.

It is important to spend a short amount of time on the vision for what NewsWatcher will do for its users. There needs to be a vision statement and also some sketches of what it should look like. A rough plan for the development can be laid out from there by creating a prioritized backlog of features.

Here is the vision statement that I put together for NewsWatcher:

**Vision/Value proposition Statement**
> *Users of NewsWatcher will get the news personally served up to them. NewsWatcher will be their trusted advisor to alert them and save important information without their needing to constantly scan endless feeds of news stories. Users can do things like adjust filters to get just the news they are interested in, see what their friends are looking at, and share comments about news stories.*

This vision statement is the longer term goal of what to shoot for and would take many iterations to realize. From this vision statement, I was able to distill the vision down into a list of features that can be iterated over. Here is what I came up with for NewsWatcher. I also added in some requirements and may have snuck in a bit of implementation detail.

**Prioritized feature list that fulfills the vision:**
1. I can set up multiple news filters to hold news stories.
2. I can give my filter a title to identify it.
3. I can set up keywords for each filter with Boolean operations of AND and OR. For example, "Treatments AND insomnia", "Dogs OR Cats".
4. The filters are periodically scanned by the NewsWatcher backend service to search for news stories that match from a central pool of collected stories from a news service provider. Client-side processing will be freed up. Finding of stories proceeds even while devices are turned off or unable to connect to the internet. The server-side runs a periodic pull of stories from a news feed service.
5. News stories in folders can be scrolled through and clicked on to take me to the story content. The ten most recent stories are shown for each filter.
6. Upon opening NewsWatcher, I see the news folders list.
7. I can click on and open a news folder to see the stories in it.
8. Stories in filter folders can be saved to an archive folder.
9. I can delete individual saved stories I select.
10. I can delete the filter itself with all of its stories.
11. All my account settings are stored server-side, but cached on the device client-side also.
12. I can delete my NewsWatcher account.
13. There are global shared news stories in which I can share a story to be seen by all NewsWatcher users. All other NewsWatcher users can see and comment on these stories. Stories will be kept for a week before being deleted. A maximum of thirty shared stories can exist; new ones will bump older ones off before the week is up. Any given user is limited to sharing five stories a week. There can be thirty comments per story kept. Offensive language in comments is blanked out.

14. With a signed-in account, I can view my news on whatever device I am logged in with.
15. The login expires and requires me to log in again periodically.
16. Two-factor authentication requires a text message code to be entered.
17. I can set actions on news folders to alert or email me when new entries are found.
18. I can set limits for when news alerts are sent to me. For example, wait at least ten minutes between alerts.
19. I can set times during the day when I don't want news alerts sent to me.
20. I can set NewsWatcher to only download stories to my device when I am connected to Wi-Fi.
21. I can use a search entry box to do a search of all loaded stories.
22. I can designate the order I want to see the filters in.
23. I can email stories to others or share them via Twitter and Facebook.

This book will only get a start on some of the core functionality in order to produce a Minimal Viable Product. Not everything will make it into the initial iteration, but it is nice to have a backlog ready to draw from.

**Wireframe prototype**
The following wireframe images were created in PowerPoint. PowerPoint has a great set of storyboard templates you can use to piece together and make realistic looking wireframe prototypes.

To create a PowerPoint prototype image:
1. Open PowerPoint and create a blank slide.
2. Click the **Storyboarding** tab, then click **Storyboard Shapes** on the ribbon to open the **Storyboard Shapes** library.
3. Start creating your prototypes by dragging shapes from the **Storyboard Shapes** library to your slide.

*Note: If you are using PowerPoint 2013, you need to have installed Visual Studio 2013 or later, or the Team Foundation Server Standalone Office Integration 2015 on the same machine to create and modify storyboards. PowerPoint 2016 is installed with everything you need for this feature to work.*

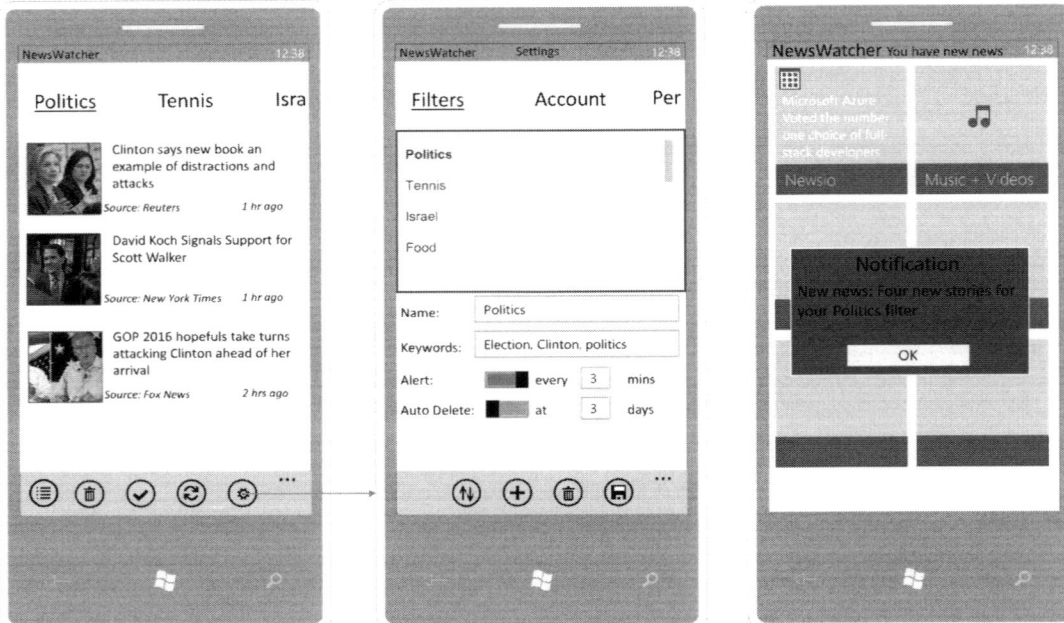

*Figure 1: NewsWatcher wireframe*

## A peek at the result

Here are a few screen shots of what the actual UI ended up looking like. Of course, it doesn't look quite like the wireframes prototypes. Any good design evolves.

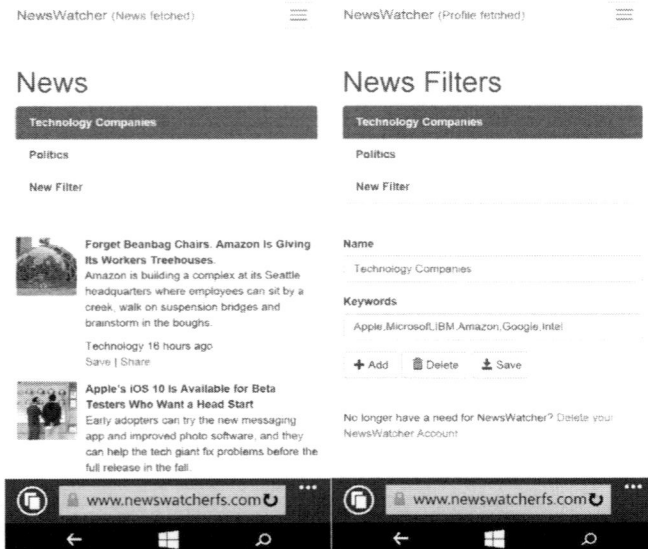

*Figure 2: NewsWatcher actual resulting UI on a mobile phone*

# Introduction

You can try the completed sample app out on your mobile device or desktop browser by going to https://www.newswatcherfs.com.

All of the code for the sample application can be found on GitHub. You can download a ZIP file from https://github.com/eljamaki01/NewsWatcherAWS.

**A peek at the architecture and deployment topology**
The three-tier architecture of NewsWatcher is depicted in the following diagram. The arrows show what parts of the architecture call what other parts.

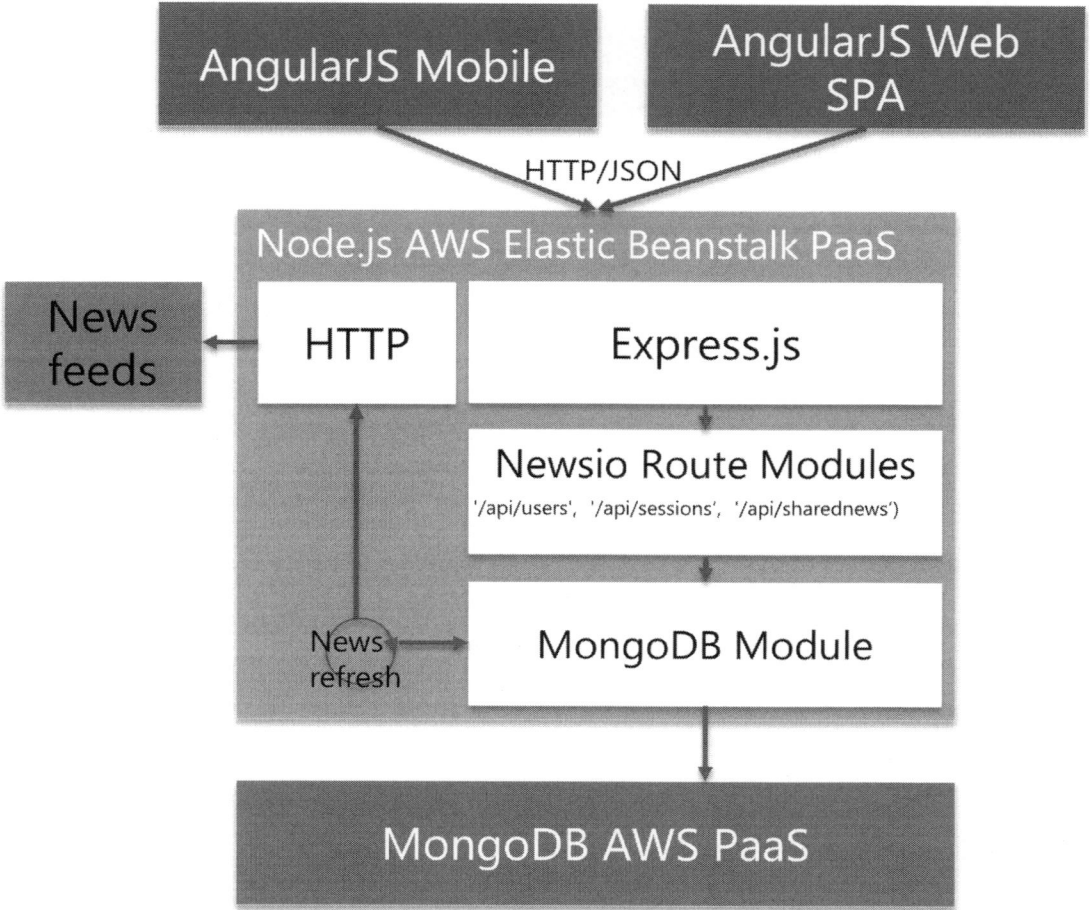

*Figure 3: NewsWatcher architecture diagram*

The machine topology required to implement a three-tier application can vary widely and may actually change over time. This is because the topology is really a function of the scaling you are needing to achieve. You would certainly not start off with a topology that could scale

11

to millions of users. It would be unnecessarily complicated to setup and maintain. Even though you pay for what you need, some things would be in place that will still cost you money that you would otherwise not need.

The following diagram gives you a look at a starting point for an architecture topology that would give you a fair amount of room to scale up the number of users you support.

**NewsWatcher Service Topology (US East – N. Virgina)**

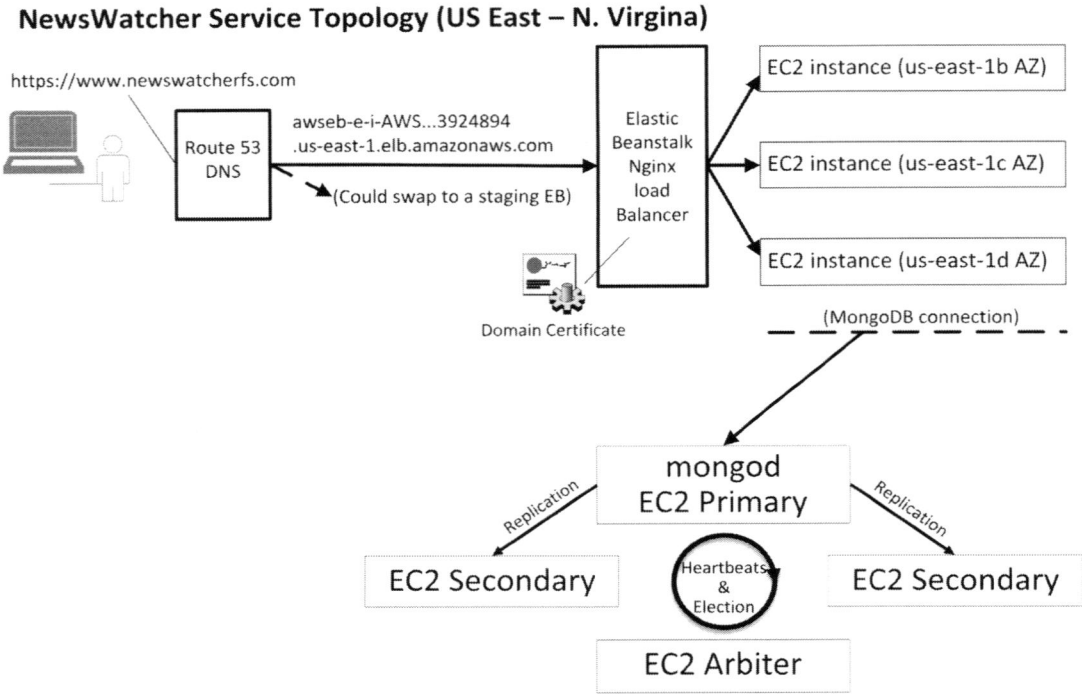

*Figure 4: NewsWatcher service hosting topology*

# PART I: The Data Layer (MongoDB)

The first part of this book will now teach you what a data layer is and how to implement one using MongoDB hosted as PaaS in AWS through the use of mLab.

The very first step of creating a data layer involves the modeling of the types of data you will want to store. After that, I will teach you what MongoDB is, and how it can be used to implement a data model.

To finish out the first part of the book, you will actually construct a data layer that will support the needs of the NewsWatcher sample application. You will end up with a fully capable data layer that can then be utilized as you move on and build the service layer of the application architecture in the second part of this book.

In order to give full coverage to the topic, I will cover what it means to manage the day-to-day operations of a MongoDB deployment.

# Chapter 1: Fundamentals

This chapter presents the concepts of a backend data storage system. I will show you what one is composed of and what capabilities are essential. After looking at backend storage systems in general, I will delve into the specifics of MongoDB and show how it fits into the NewsWatcher architecture to fulfill the backend data storage requirements.

*Note: This book is about full-stack development and is not meant to be an administrator's guide for any part of the infrastructure being used. For example, I will cover what it takes to develop programs with MongoDB, but topics like what it takes to administer the service are out of scope for this book. Please see MongoDB's and mLab's help resources for more information on administrative topics.*

# 1.1 Definition of the Data Layer

The data layer of a software application architecture provides for the persistent storage of information. Anything of importance can be stored there such as: customer account information, inventory, orders, auditing logs, tax computation tables, and anything else that can conceivably be stored in electronic form.

The term database management system (DBMS) is used to describe the commercial offerings that implement a data layer at the lowest level. Each available DBMS has capabilities that differentiates it from the others. MongoDB from MongoDB, Inc. is one such DBMS system that is developed as an open-source project. See https://www.mongodb.com/ for their various offerings and capabilities. MongoDB Atlas is a commercial PaaS offering from MongoDB Inc. You will also find other companies, such as mLab (https://mlab.com/) that also host certain versions of MongoDB in a PaaS environment.

## DBMS capabilities

DBMS implementations can be placed into several general categories. One possible way to categorize them is as follows: relational, key-value, hierarchical, object-oriented, or document-based. Some DBMSs can also be said to be of the "NoSQL" type. Each category exists for a specific reason and you would want to look at your specific needs and choose the particular DBMS technology that fulfills your needs the best.

A DBMS will provide the physical storage medium where the data resides and should even withstand a power failure. In a cloud hosted DBMS, data eventually makes its way to being stored on non-volatile cloud storage drives in a secure data center. Data storage might even be geo-replicated to distant data centers for redundancy and load-balancing performance.

# PART I: The Data Layer (MongoDB)

The data storage and data access features provide for the creation, retrieval, updates, and deletion of data. The acronym "CRUD" is commonly used to refer to these operations. As well as data storage, a DBMS will typically provide the following features:

- Data storage
- Attribution
- Auditing
- Authorization
- Data access
- Encryption
- Notification
- Programmability
- Schematization
- Security
- Transformation
- Validation

Even though the DBMS itself provides some type of programmatic access, there is often an additional layer on top that is referred to as a Data Access Layer (DAL). There are both community written and commercial DALs available, or you can even write your own. The DAL will create an abstraction layer that hides the complexities of the particular data storage technology and may even allow you to switch to a different backend DBMS without affecting the upper layers of your application.

A DAL can greatly simplify your access by creating an object structure that might not even exist in the actual data storage system itself. For example, some DBMSs don't provide schematization of data. If you need that, you can get it through a custom DAL. The following image shows all of the sub-layers within the data layer:

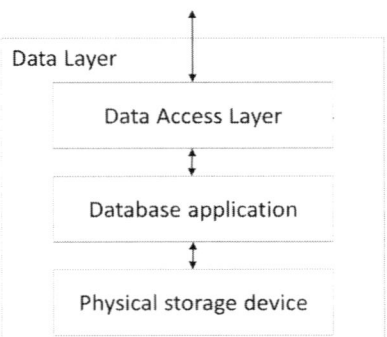

*Figure 5: Data Layer with sub-layers*

# 1.2 Data layer design process

Before just randomly storing data in your data layer, you need to create models for what that data should look like. There is a lot of design work required in order to be able to organize your data in an efficient way. You will need to diagram out a model for your data to help you understand all of the nuances of the records with their properties and relationships. Knowing what information you would like to store is the first step to take. With that information determined, you can model the structural form of the data.

Often the data in a data layer outlives the applications that were written to expose it. User interfaces come and go, but backend data systems seem to live on. It can sometimes be hard to go back and modify your data storage after you have started using it, so take your time and design it for future growth.

*Note: Even when the lifetime of the DBMS is finally reached, the data you have may still remain valuable. If you decide to migrate to a newer DBMS technology, the data can be exported from your old DBMS and then be re-imported into your new DBMS. Most systems provide capabilities to import and export data in bulk. Some systems even provide an ongoing syncing capability for the transfer and transformation of the data.*

## Data layer planning

The following questions are useful to go through as you work through the initial data layer design. The answers to these questions should be carefully determined. Utilize experts along the way before rolling anything out into a production environment.

Data layer planning questionnaire:
- Is the data shared? If so, how is it shared between customers, applications, and processes?
- Is multi-tenant storage ok? What isolation of data is necessary?
- What are your data security and privacy requirements?
- Will you be storing data that is classified as high business impact (HBI) or any personally identifiable information (PII)? If the data is compromised, what are the legal ramifications?
- Do you need data access roles to control access to the data?
- Are there any periodic processing jobs to run that will access the data?
- Do you require transactional capabilities?
- Will parallel access to a single record cause concurrency issues? Is there some type of locking or serialization of access required? Would request queuing or optimistic concurrency control (OCC) suffice?

# PART I: The Data Layer (MongoDB)

- What is the service level agreement (SLA) requirement for each CRUD operation? What are the access volume and rates per time period? Will there be bursts of activity or is the activity evenly distributed across each day?
- What is the size of the data? How many records and how large will they become?
- How many users will access the data? What will be the needed data capacity per customer?
- Do you anticipate that the structure of your data will change?
- Can writes be asynchronous or do you need immediate synchronous acknowledgment on a write?
- Do you need to keep a record of each data access, such as keeping an audit trail of accesses and changes?
- Will you be running data mining and analysis over the data?
- Is there a strict data schema that needs to be validated against?
- What are the record types, contents and relationships?
- What system dependencies are involved? What is taking this data as a dependency? How is the data fed back and forth and how is it combined and verified?
- Are you storing media data that is typically in file form such as photos, movies etc.?

# 1.3 Introducing MongoDB

MongoDB is classified as a NoSQL database. That simply means that it is non-relational and non-schematized. There is no central schema catalog or data record structure definition required. Database records can be more or less free-form. Don't get too worried about the unstructured nature of MongoDB, you will learn how to set up a data model and how to validate data before it is stored in your data layer.

MongoDB is also classified as being document-based. MongoDB is a document-based database because it conceptually stores JavaScript Object Notation (JSON) documents. I say conceptually, because it does not actually store JSON documents directly, but instead stores an internal binary representation of one. Documents are stored in Binary JSON (BSON) form.

*Note: If you look at the database offerings of AWS, you will find several choices for data storage in the cloud, including DynamoDB, RDS/Aurora, Redshift and S3. Each offering exists to fulfill different requirements and each has its own advantages.*

Document-based storage with MongoDB really hits a sweet spot for modern application needs. It gives you the best of both scaling and performance. All of this is done in an easy to manage environment, because it is a PaaS-hosted service that runs on AWS infrastructure.

You don't deploy MongoDB PaaS through AWS directly, but go through a company such as mLab. Through their management portal, you sign up to use MongoDB and then mLab deploys it for you to AWS infrastructure on your behalf.

## Benefits of MongoDB with mLab

Figure 5 in the prior section showed an illustration of the data layer. This included three different sub-layers. The great news is that you get all three built-in with MongoDB. Here are some compelling features to consider when evaluating the benefits of MongoDB, especially through the mLab offering that uses AWS infrastructure:

- **Elastic storage capacity:** You simply dial up and down your storage capacity by moving to a higher performance plan or by adding more databases. You can delete databases that are no longer needed and then not be charged for them anymore. You can configure your resources through code or through the mLab management portal. There is practically unlimited growth for "pay-as-you-grow" storage capacity.
- **Elastic performance:** You simply move your performance up or down by selecting a different plan. To achieve higher throughput, you can pay for the highest performance tier and get a sharded cluster.

- **PaaS:** MongoDB on AWS through mLab is a PaaS offering. All the machine jostling of software and hardware upgrades are invisible to you.
- **APM:** Monitoring, alerting, scale management and backups keep you in control.
- **Auto-Replication:** Data is automatically stored in redundant copies. The replications are there for your safety, to ensure availability through failover. You can also set up automatic backups to happen.
- **Security:** MongoDB has a native audit log to track all database operations. For added security, you can have an SSL connection to your database if you pay for a higher end plan. MongoDB has an encrypted storage engine to protect data (not currently available through mLab).

The mLab MongoDB offering on AWS is ready to meet all of your business and customer needs. It has a great feature set and is increasing its capabilities all of the time.

# Try it out

If you really wanted to, you could download MongoDB and run it on your local machine. You could also do the work to set up a VM or use a Docker container with MongoDB with IaaS in the cloud. My preference is to use MongoDB as a cloud-hosted PaaS solution. mLab is a company that makes it easy to sign up for a plan that then hosts MongoDB on your choice of Amazon, Microsoft Azure, or Google cloud services. This is the approach I have used for this book. You would have to do your own research if you wanted to depart from that. The rest of this book is written with this approach in mind.

It takes just a few clicks to install and be up and running with MongoDB as a hosted service in AWS. You then don't need to worry about the daily details of managing the software updates and machine hardware maintenance to keep it up and running. For example, there is no need to waste any time dealing with hardware failures, such as the replacement of drives or network cards.

You also enjoy the benefit of having machine replication, scaling, load-balancing, failover and backup. With the scaling of MongoDB, you only pay for the storage and performance you desire. You pay for what you use and can easily scale down when you no longer need data storage or performance.

You are freed up to concentrate on the aspects of your application that deliver value to your customer and increase ROI for your company. This is the huge benefit of PaaS cloud infrastructure.

*Note: MongoDB Inc. has their Atlas PaaS offering which will also deploy infrastructure to AWS for you. So far, they do not have a free offering, and they don't have a rich management portal experience yet. This offering should be a great choice in the near future.*

# Pay for performance

As previously mentioned, you only pay for what you need. As with other AWS cloud infrastructure, if you have an immediate need, you can pay for higher performance machines to run MongoDB. Thankfully, there is a free option through mLab for your initial investigations.

You can also pay for your scaling needs by purchasing a plan that comes with a higher storage allotment and is configured with what is called a replication set cluster for high-availability and auto-failover. If you need to scale up to more storage, you can keep adding databases as needed.

You also have the flexibility to pay for more than one plan at the same time and put data on the more expensive plan that needs the highest throughput, while other data can be on the less expensive plan of storage. You can even change a database back and forth from one plan to another as your needs change.

In some cases, a plan transition will actually require downtime, as you need to do a data backup and a restore. For example, this downtime would happen if you transition from a free plan to some paid plan. You can have a rolling database replacement happen with no downtime when switching back and forth with certain paid plans. See mLab's documentation for more details.

# MongoDB structure

With your mLab account, you can create one or more databases. These databases do not have any data in them but serve as the containers for what are called collections. Databases hold collections and they also hold your indexes and user accounts. Collections are what contain your data in the form of BSON documents.

Each database can have a set of users with specific permissions. You can control the users of your database and give individuals read access or also write access. This does not mean that everyone that connects to MongoDB through the NewsWatcher app needs their own user account. There are ways to allow general programmatic access through your service layer. Specific data access is controlled through your own middle-tier login mechanism. That will be covered later in this book.

There is a special admin account created with your mLab account that has certain privileges that cannot be granted to any other account. This is the account you start off with upon creation of a database.

The following illustration is an overall visual representation that shows the different resources that are part of the MongoDB managed platform service and how they relate to each other:

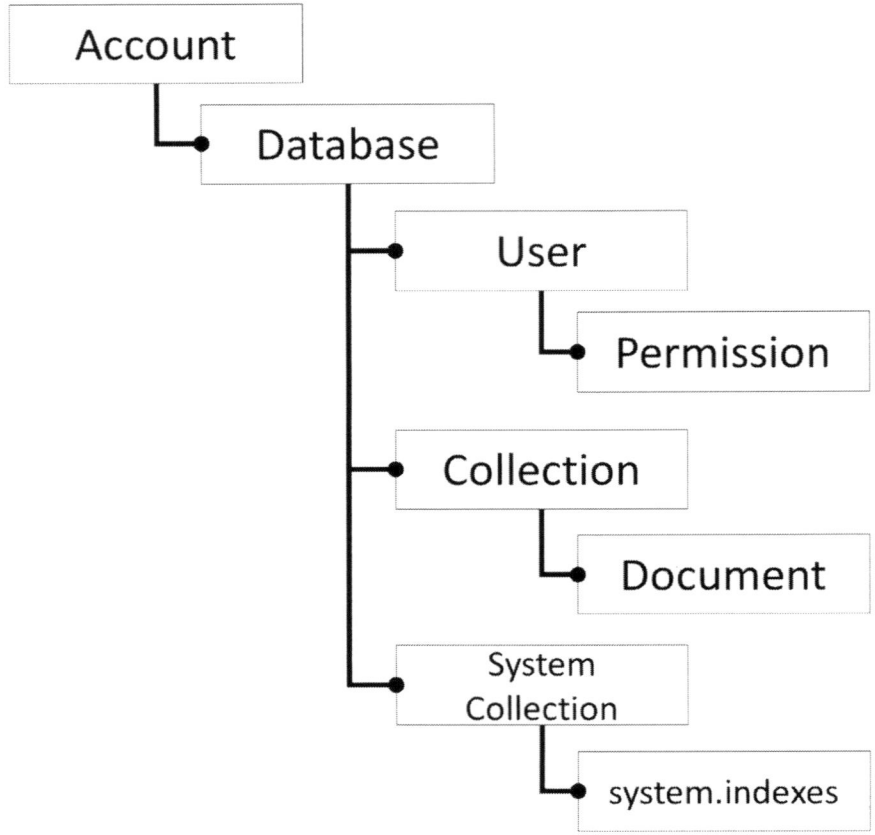

*Figure 6: MongoDB resources*

# 1.4 The MongoDB Collection

A collection is the container for storing documents and is the main resource with which interactions happen programmatically. You can create JavaScript functions for operating on the data in the collection in your Node.js server-side code.

Collections are a convenient way to separate out data in a MongoDB database. They collectively share whatever the limit of total storage is for the plan you are paying for.

To write data into a collection, you could log into the mLab management portal and add in any documents by hand. Most likely, though, you will want to use one of the APIs available to do that.

# 1.5 The MongoDB Document

Every database ever invented is fundamentally designed to store data as a set of records. Each individual record contains information that is useful for later retrieval. For example, in AWS S3, a record takes the form of data with its descriptive metadata. In a relational database, the record is in the form of a row in a table. With that, you might have a table of customers where each row represents a single customer with their name, age, and email as part of their record.

In MongoDB, a single record is represented by a document in a collection. The following image illustrates how you can have multiple collections, each with multiple documents in them:

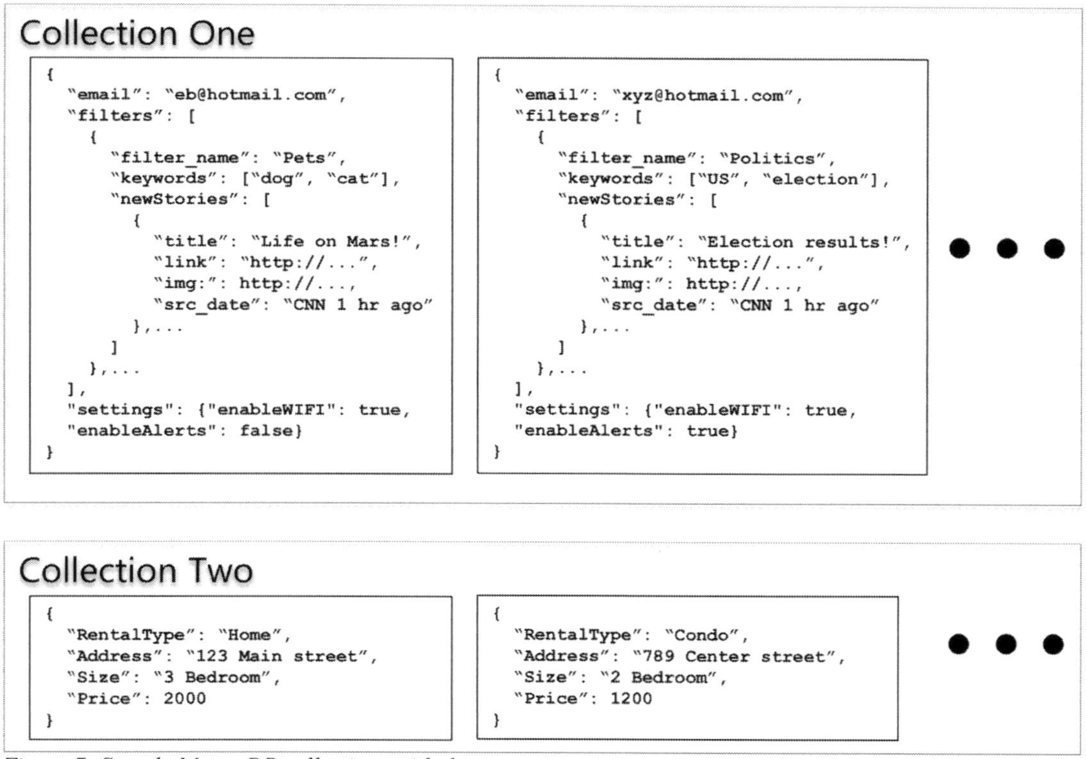

*Figure 7: Sample MongoDB collections with documents*

Documents, in this example, are represented as JSON with top-level curly braces enclosing each document. This is how they are shown textually, even though they really do not appear that way in the database itself.

This simple concept of storing documents in a document-oriented database has many advantages. For example, JSON is very simple to formulate and consume in code. Another benefit is that it can contain complex hierarchical data in its embedded structures and arrays.

# Datatypes in a document

The primitive data types supported in a MongoDB JSON document are the same ones that are available in JSON. These are:

- Array
- Boolean
- Null
- Number
- Object
- String

In addition, there is an extended syntax in JSON that can take the augmented BSON datatypes and preserve them. Some of the added data types of BSON are: Date, Binary data and 64-bit integer.

You will eventually be accessing MongoDB through your code and will be using JavaScript objects with their supported datatypes. I will give you a few tips here, as there are some interesting issues you might run into.

One of these issues is with the storage of binary data, especially media data such as photos and movies. Media data cannot realistically be inserted into a JSON file. You could use the BSON binary data type, but the main problem you would encounter would be that the maximum BSON document size is 16 megabytes. A movie would simply not fit into one single document. It is really best to store binary data in a separate storage system, such as AWS S3, and reference it from a MongoDB document.

Another issue is the representation of currency values, such as US dollars and cents. The problem comes when you attempt to perform floating point precision storage and arithmetic operations, such as might be required for investment calculations. If Node.js were to calculate and print $0.1 + 0.02$, the result would be 0.12000000000000001. You are not even safe in using the MongoDB 64-bit floating point datatype. This is due to the rounding errors inherent in CPUs in how they represent floating point numbers.

One solution is to multiply all your monetary values by a constant scaling factor. For example, if you were going to store the value of $1.99, don't store 1.99, but instead multiply that by 1000 and store an integer value of 1990. Then you can perform math on those integer values and convert back for display when needed.

# The JSON document

One distinguishing characteristic of a document-based database is that it can store complex hierarchical objects without any predefined schema definition. This means that every document in a collection could have a different structure. This could be considered both an advantage and a disadvantage.

There are many advantages to having a schema-less database. The obvious one is that you don't need to specify the JSON format in advance. There is no need to specify datatypes or place restrictions on them. It is simply a matter of creating the JSON with the name/value pairs that you desire and then inserting that into a collection. Here is a simple JSON document:

```
{
  "_id": {
    "$oid": "56ce1f0ed154d0d526b60338"
  },
  "myNumber": 99,
  "myString": "Hi there",
  "myBool": true
}
```

*Note: I refer to the name/value pairs in the JSON Document as "properties", since its syntax is so close to the syntax of the property in a JavaScript object literal. The MongoDB online documentation, however, uses the term "fields" to describe these name/value pairs.*

If you open of the mLab management portal and look at some documents, they are presented to you in the textual JSON form. In this chapter, documents will also be presented in that textual JSON form since when you experiment with the mLab management console you see JSON documents in that form. Once you get to the chapter on Node.js and are using the API to programmatically interact with MongoDB, I will be showing you JavaScript and the object literal syntax. Just be aware of that switch. As an example, the object literal syntax equivalent of the prior JSON example would be as follows (assuming MongoDB will provide the id property for us upon insertion):

```
var mydoc = {
  myNumber: 99,
  myString: "Hi there",
  myBool: true
};
```

*Note: There is one restriction on JSON documents in order to make them work in MongoDB. The restriction is that the property names in a single document must not be duplicated. This make sense because, if you were to query and ask for a given property and it existed twice, that would be a little confusing. In reality, the core MongoDB storage system that stores*

*BSON does not make this restriction, but the Node.js module API that accesses it will consider this necessary and enforce it.*

To help you understand what a document can contain, let's pretend you are running a business that sells books over the internet. The following example document represents what you might want to use in a collection that holds customers of your online bookstore. Each customer document would hold information associated with that customer. You would want to store information about what books they had purchased. You would also want to store their personal contact information. All of this can be placed in one single document:

```
// Customer Document
{
  "_id": "77",
  "name": "Joe Schmoe",
  "age": 27,
  "email": "js@live.com",
  "address": {
    "street": "21 Main Street",
    "city": "Emerald City",
    "state": "KS",
    "postalCode": "10021-3100"
  },
  "booksPurchased": [
    {
      "title": "Agile Project Management with Kanban",
      "ISBN10": "0735698953",
      "author": "Eric Brechner",
      "pages": 160,
      "publicationDate": "20150326",
      "category": "Software Engineering"
    },
    {
      "title": "The Merriam-Webster Dictionary",
      "ISBN10": "087779930X",
      "author": "Merriam-Webster",
      "pages": 939,
      "publicationDate": "20040701"
      "category": "English"
    }
  ]
}
```

It is important to remember that a single document should only contain the information for that one unique record. This means that you would not want to have two customers in a single document. That would get confusing. In the example above, there is a single customer in the document. Their book order data is also embedded in the document.

As previously mentioned, documents do not need to be completely uniform. This means that one document can contain properties that another document might not ever have and both can exist in the same collection. For example, if you had a collection that contained products for the fictitious bookstore, it would obviously have books in it. It might also have magazines, maps, and puzzles in it as well. The details for these products would need to be somewhat different.

Documents in a collection might each have some common properties such as price, title, description, and weight. For each product type there would be some unique properties. A puzzle, for example, might have a property that states what the recommended age is for that puzzle. The following example shows a collection with documents that have both common and unique properties. Note how the document for a book differs slightly from the document for a puzzle, yet both can exist in the same collection.

```
// Bookstore products
{
   "type": "BOOK",
   "title": "Agile Project Management with Kanban",
   "ISBN10": "0735698953",
   "author": "Eric Brechner",
   "pages": 160,
   "publicationDate": "20150326",
   "category": "Software Engineering"
},
{
   "type": "BOOK",
   "title": "The Merriam-Webster Dictionary",
   "ISBN10": "087779930X",
   "author": "Merriam-Webster",
   "pages": 939,
   "publicationDate": "20040701"
   "category": "English"
},
{
   "type": "PUZZLE",
   "title": "Balloons in sky",
   "company": "ZipZap Toys",
   "age": "3-5 years old"
}
```

Just because documents can contain heterogeneous or diverse content does not mean that you always will want to have collections set up that way. You may decide to have all your collections contain uniformly structured documents. I will later cover circumstances that will help you make these type of design decisions.

*Note: I would advise you to stay away from multidimensional, jagged, and non-uniform array element properties. Otherwise, you may find yourself later looking through your data and not remembering how you had set it up.*

# A common property of all documents

Each document has an `_id` property. When a document is created, it will always have a unique id associated with it so that it can be identified. This serves as the primary key. You can set its value yourself, or else MongoDB will set a value in it for you of type ObjectId. If you set it yourself, it can be of any type other than an array. It must be unique across all documents in that collection.

If you ever need to directly access a document, you can access a document quickly using the `_id` as the quickest way to query for it.

# Referencing external data

So far, you have seen that MongoDB allows for storage of JSON documents. As you know, the basic datatypes available with JSON can be used to represent lots of information you wish to store.

As already mentioned, the one thing that JSON datatypes are not suited for, is the representation of large binary data. For example, you would not really be able to store large media content such as photos, music, or video in a document. To overcome this limitation, you can create a property that is a reference to where the actual media content is externally stored. You would use a Universal Resource Indicator (URI) to indicate its location, and also create a parallel property that describes the type of data it consists of: text, image, binary data, etc. That way, your code can interpret it correctly.

The external referenced data can be any data you would like. It is up to you to set the type and then treat it as such when you retrieve it. Be sure to handle any needed deletion of your external data if it is supposed to be cleaned up when documents referencing it are deleted.

*Note: This chapter stated that MongoDB, as a document-based database, does not enforce any schema. MongoDB does have a capability where you can specify what properties should exist and what restrictions should be on them for documents. I do not utilize this capability in this book as it is not yet supported in the mongodb NPM Node.js module. I do later mention that you can use a Node.js module such as joi to validate your schema. The validation MongoDB performs is also not as strict a definition as you have with a relational database. Relationship key specification is also not available as with a relational database with the ability to also enforce referential integrity.*

# Chapter 2: Data Modeling Fundamentals

A data model defines the structure of records that are to be stored in a database. This includes information on how the different types of records relate to each other.

Just because a document-based database is not a relational database does not mean that it doesn't have structure or relationships between document types. Specifying a data model in MongoDB consists of specifying what the JSON documents are, which collections they exist in, and how they relate to each other. It could simply be a mental model that you will be consciously following. I will however instruct you on how to use validation code to make sure any data going in conforms to expectations, but nothing beyond that.

It is helpful to design your document structures in advance so that you can look at all aspects of your data. You can match your data storage needs against the characteristics that a MongoDB database offers and do your data modeling accordingly. Sketching out your data model will be an important step in the creation of your data layer.

To visualize your data model, you can use whatever diagram format or tool you like. You can even scribble it out on a piece of paper. Ultimately, for MongoDB, it all needs to be represented in JSON form when you implement it. Let's now cover some of the big design decisions that need to be made with a document-based DBMS.

# 2.1 Referencing or Embedding Data

You may have heard the term "normalization" used in the context of a relational database design. This means that you have done the work to separate out the data into multiple related record types. Relational database records each contain keys to identify them and to act as references between each other. A relational DBMS has mechanisms to specify and enforce the integrity of these references to some extent.

Normalization requires the separating out of data into different record types and relating them to each other. For example, you might have two types of records in your database, one that represents people and another that represents the pets that are owned by the people. There would be a key to relate an owner to one or more of their pets. The following illustration shows this normalized structure:

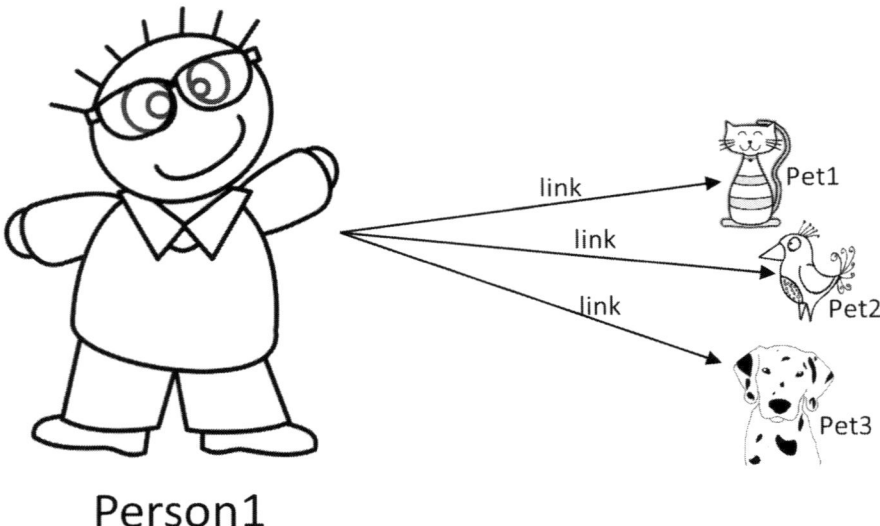

**Person1**

*Figure 8: Normalized structure*

In a relational DBMS, you set up the keys to relate the record types to one another. The relational DBMS provides functionality to be able to query and join the records together. This means you can query the database to return a person and all of the pets they possess through a single query operation.

Let's now bring this conversation into the MongoDB world. In MongoDB, you could have separate person and pet documents in the same collection. Keep in mind that there is no concept of a schema for a collection, and no concept of relational keys or cross-document join queries. You would be required to design your own properties on each document in order to relate pets to their owners. With people and their pets separated out across MongoDB documents, you have achieve a normalized database model.

A normalized model, however, is not necessarily the best way of storing data in a document-based database. You really want to think more about how to denormalize your data. Denormalized data means that everything is all bundled together.

To denormalize and bundle pets together with a person, you would simply place pets as an array property that is embedded in each person document. Imagine stuffing all of the pets in the pocket of the person. This way, people and their pets are always found together. In this way there are no more relational links required. You also do not need a join operation if you denormalize your data. In fact, the classic relational join operation is not even supported in MongoDB. The following visualization shows how the person and pets travel together:

*Figure 9: Denormalized structure*

As was mentioned, document-based databases like MongoDB do not support joins of records such as cross-table joins of a relational database. This is because cross-document joins really do not make sense in document-based databases. This means that you need to get comfortable with keeping your database designs denormalized. Denormalization is more efficient and works best in a document-based database. What you do, is make use of array and embedded object properties in your JSON.

In the previous chapter, I showed you a JSON document representing a customer of an online bookstore company. What was shown was actually a denormalized data pattern. Each customer document contained information about the customer, but it also contained information about each book they had purchased. You will end up with larger and more complex documents when you denormalize your data.

Even if you end up with large, complex documents using MongoDB, the querying capability supports retrieval of just the portions of the documents that you want. For example, if you kept pets embedded in a person document, you can still do a query to just return the pets of a given owner. You do not need to return the complete person document if you do not want to. Perhaps you just want to know the pets and do not want to retrieve contact info, billing info, or whatever else is a part of the person document.

In summary, you can remember that relational database normalization has you separate out your data into different distinct record types and has you set up keys as reference links between them. On the other hand, denormalization with document-based databases, has you keep as much bundled together as possible by embedding data that is related.

# 2.2 When to use Referencing

It is obviously not going to work too well if you always embed all of your data and end up with huge documents. You need to make decisions as to what properties will be embedded in a document and what would make more sense to pull out into separate document types for referencing.

You can still keep all of your different document types in one collection. There are, however, reasons why different document types should be kept in separate collections or maybe even separate databases. I will cover more on that topic later.

## Performance implications

Your data model design will have an impact on the performance of all database operations. For example, the performance of reads and writes could improve if you spread data out into separate documents. Doing this results in decreased data transfer amounts and in more efficient document updates as well.

The downside of referencing data from one document to another is that it will be slower if you need to combine the data and present it together at any point in time. Imagine the code required to piece together a person with their pets if pet documents were kept separate.

Let's go back to the online bookstore example. Imagine that you have two document types: customers and books. With these documents, you keep track of all the books your customers have individually purchased. If you keep only the book IDs in the customer document, certain queries would run slower, such as listing a customer with the book titles they ordered. For each customer, you have to look through the `booksPurchased` array property and then do individual fetches of data for each book id listed. Here is how this normalized model looks:

```
// Customer documents
{
    "_id": "77",
    "type": "CUSTOMER_TYPE",
    "name": "Joe Schmoe",
    "age": 27,
    "email": "js@gmail.com",
    "address": {
        "street": "21 Main Street",
        "city": "Emerald City",
        "state": "KS",
        "postalCode": "10021-3100"
    },
    "booksPurchased": ["0735698953", "087779930X"]
}
```

```
// Book Documents
{
   "_id": "7865",
   "type": "BOOK_TYPE",
   "ISBN10": "0735698953",
   "title": "Agile Project Management with Kanban",
   "author": "Eric Brechner",
   "pages": 160,
   "bookReviews": [
      {
         "reviewer": "Joe Schmoe",
         "comments": "Wish I had this years ago!",
         "rating": 4
      },
      {
         "reviewer": "Jane Doe",
         "comments": "Forever a classic. ",
         "rating": 5
      }
   ]
}


{
   "_id": "7866",
   "type": "BOOK_TYPE",
   "ISBN10": "087779930X",
   "title": "The Merriam-Webster Dictionary",
   "author": "Merriam-Webster",
   "pages": 939,
   "bookReviews": []
}
```

Imagine that you want to query and find all books that are over 500 pages in length and that were purchased by a particular customer, Joe Schmoe. To do this, the query must first search the collection to find the Joe Schmoe document and then, for every book ID listed in the Joe Schmoe document, look up that book document and see if the `pages` property value is over 500, and then finally return those documents. This involves a join operation.

In relational databases, this can be done in a single query. In MongoDB it has to be done in separate queries and involves code to piece everything together if needed.

This is not necessarily a bad thing and is just part of what you need to do in a document-based database when you separate out data into related documents. But then again, remember that denormalization relieves you from doing these join operations across documents. You will later see that there is a compromise that can be made between the two options.

# When to reference

Let's cover the basic scenarios that would influence you to split data across documents with a normalized design that uses references. The following are some of the common reasons to do this:

- **The data is rarely used in queries:**

  For example, the address property in the customer document could be taken out and placed into a separate document if it is decided that it is rarely needed. If you find that you rarely reference certain properties in a document, then you might see this as a sign that those properties belong in a separate document, or even in a separate collection that can be referenced as needed. Just remember that you are gaining the faster interaction with the primary data in this case at the expense of slower data retrieval processing to join it together later.

- **The data is shared in common across documents:**

  The book detail is certainly data that would be duplicated across customers. If you had thousands of customers that each had a Merriam-Webster Dictionary, it would not be necessary to keep duplicating all of the data for that book. With duplicated data, one big problem is if one of the properties of a book needs to be altered, it would mean altering it across all the duplicates instead of in one central document. In this case it would be wise to keep the properties in a separate book document if they are shared and updated frequently.

- **The data has a mutual or cross-reference relationship:**

  The information in the `bookReviews` property really originates from the customers that submit the reviews, but each review is also specific to a single book. The question arises — should the book reviews exist with the book being reviewed, or with the customer giving them? You might not want to update the individual book document and keep adding to it every time a new customer adds a review. Nor do you want to fetch all of the book reviews every time you fetch the document for a book. This is where you can make the case for the book reviews to be in their own separate document and then referenced by both the customer and the book documents.

- **The data will grow very large:**

  The `bookReviews` property is an array that might grow to have a large number of entries. For example, an array property of a document cannot grow unbounded. Remember that there is a 16 megabyte limit on the size of an individual document in MongoDB.

# 2.3 Reference Relationship Patterns

At one point I showed you a customer document that contained a list of the ids of the books a person purchased. That allowed you to keep documents for the actual book details separated out. This is one of several patterns you can find useful for referencing data.

I will stress again though, that this is totally under your control to implement. MongoDB does not provide any built in recognition of any relationships. MongoDB will not verify the referential integrity of the data as a relational DBMS might do. It is up to you to realize this. If a given book is deleted from a collection, you also need to delete all the references to it. For example, if you had a `booksPurchased` array entry of 777 in a customer document, there is nothing in MongoDB that is verifying that a book document with that id of 777 actually exists.

Here are some common patterns that can be used for referencing data across documents in MongoDB:

- **One-to-One:** This is where you would split out one piece of infrequently accessed data. For example, you could pull out the address information of a customer and put it into its own document. This diagram illustrates a one-to-one pattern:

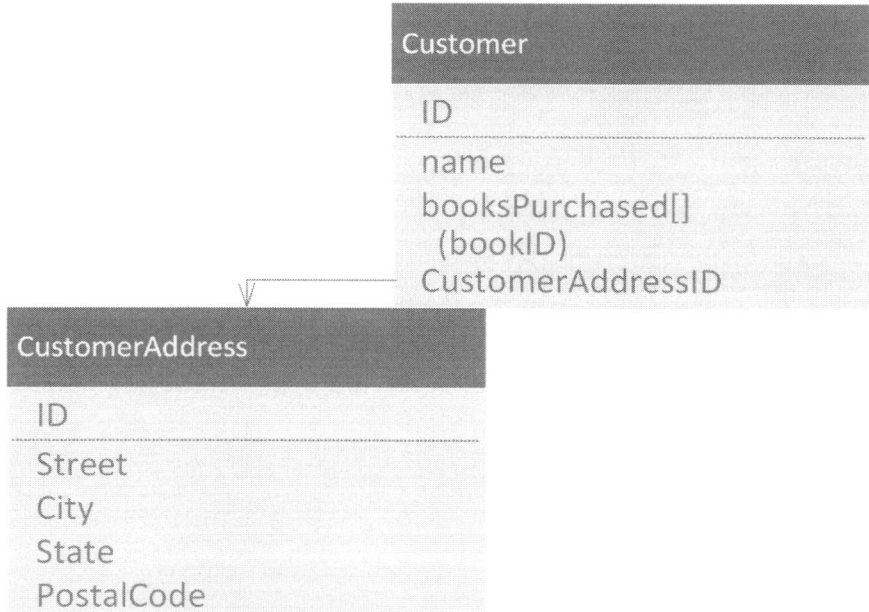

*Figure 10: One-to-one relationship pattern*

- **Many-to-One:** This is where one document might be referenced by many other documents. This is the example you have already seen where a single book can be referenced by multiple customers. Each entry in the `booksPurchased` array has an ISBN10 ID to reference the book document with. This diagram illustrates a many-to-one pattern:

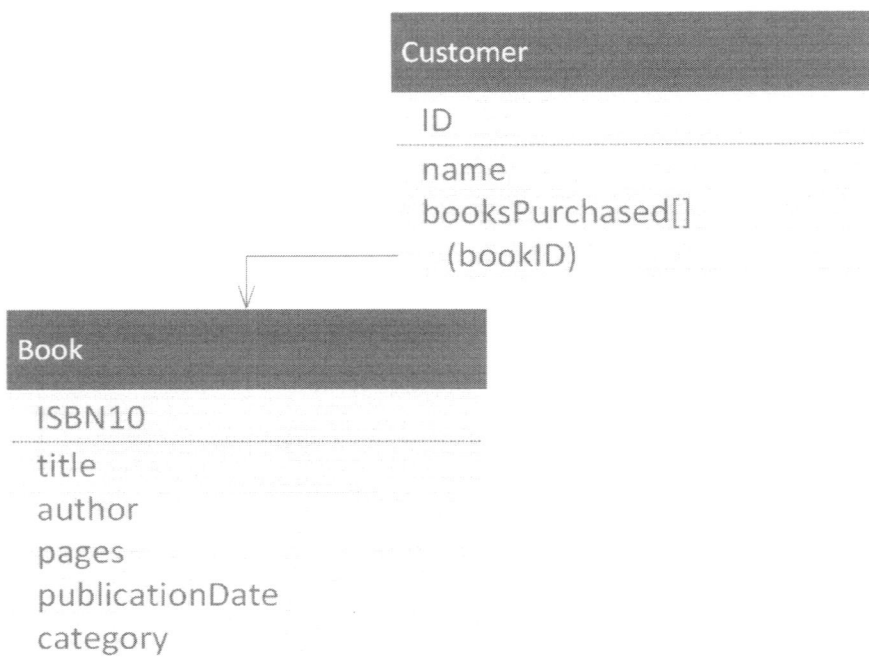

*Figure 11: Many-to-one relationship pattern*

- **Many-to-Many Association:** This is where you have two separate document types where neither references the other, but instead there is a third document type that can tie the two together through an association. This third document can also contain information relevant to that association. For example, you might have a document for purchases that records the details of the transaction of a book purchase. Thus you have many purchase documents that reference many customer and book documents. This diagram illustrates a many-to-many association pattern:

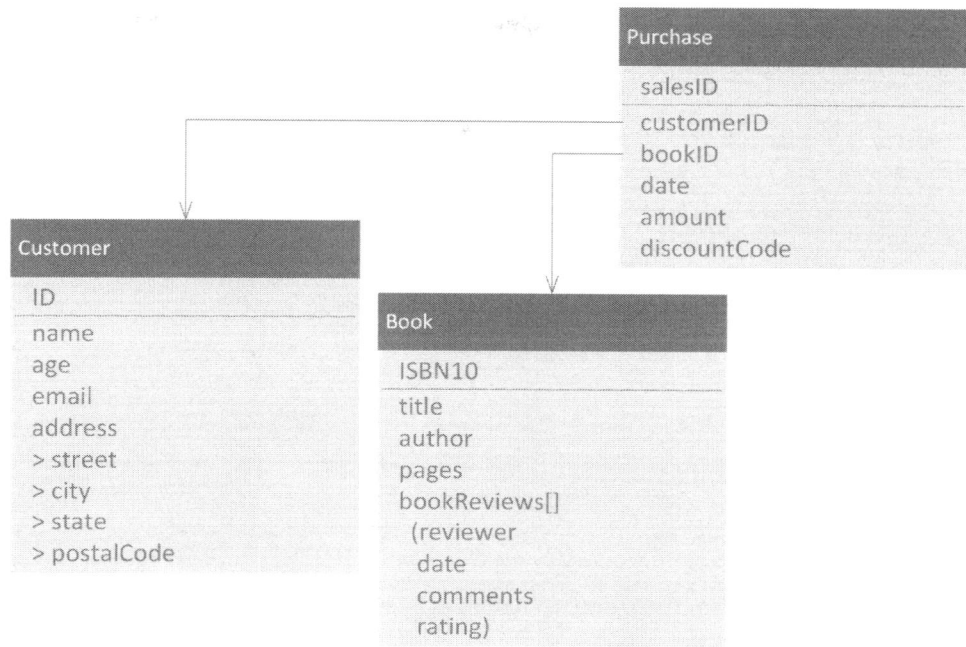

*Figure 12: Many-to-many association pattern*

Many-to-many relationships can have documents referencing each other in a circular manner. Try not to get that complicated, as it presents many difficult data integrity issues and complicates the service layer implementation.

*Note: It is useful to create a visual diagram of your document types as you go through your data model design process. You are then able to more clearly see the structure and relationships. Several diagram standards have been created over the years to visually represent objects in object-oriented languages and for representing records in databases. All you really need is a simplified visual representation of JSON objects in your data model. You can draw a rectangle shape for each document type and list all the properties inside as I have shown in the previous illustrations. I have chosen to have the ID property exist above a line. Those properties below the line are the rest of the document properties. I have chosen to use a greater than sign to show sub-object properties. An array element entry is shown in parenthesis if it is an object and it is understood there would be zero or more of these in an actual instance of the document. You might also want to list the data type of each property out to the right of the name.*

# 2.4 A Hybrid Approach

You are now ready to learn about a hybrid approach that can give you the best of both the techniques of referencing as well as embedding data. Why not combine the two concepts in a sort of compromise? For example, if you find that you often need to list the titles of the books that a customer owns, you can duplicate a portion of that information across documents. This means you store the book id and also the title, even though that is duplicated information. The following is an example of what the documents would look like with this hybrid approach:

```
// Customer Documents
{
   "_id": "77",
   "name": "Joe Schmoe",
   ...
   "booksPurchased": [
      {
         "ISBN10": "0735698953",
         "title": "Agile Project Management with Kanban"
      },
      {
         "ISBN10": "087779930X",
         "title": "The Merriam-Webster Dictionary"
      }
   ],
   ...
},
...

// Book Documents
{
   "ISBN10": "0735698953",
   "title": "Agile Project Management with Kanban",
   "author": "Eric Brechner",
   "pages": 160,
   "publicationDate": "20150326",
   "category": "Software Engineering"
},
...
```

You can see that the compromise was to keep the title duplicated across document types, as the title is frequently needed. The rest of the properties are kept separated out. Be aware that you would want to synchronize any duplicated properties that existed. For example, if you need to make a change to the `title` property in the book document for a given book, you would want to have some background process that would search out all occurrences of that book in the customer documents and update the title in those as well. It is unlikely that a book title associated with an ISBN number would ever change.

# 2.5 Differentiating Document Types

You might have several different document types existing in a single collection. One reason you would want to store all of your document types in one single collection is that Web API connection access works on a single collection basis.

With all document types in the same collection, you need a way of differentiating them from each other so that queries can find each specific type. One way to solve this is to include a type property in each document. Let me use the previous illustration of a collection that has documents for persons and documents for pets. Person documents would be declared with: `"type": "PERSON_TYPE"` and pet documents would be declared with `"type": "PET_TYPE"`. For example:

```
// Person and Pet types in same Collection
{
   "type": "PERSON_TYPE",
   "_id": 1,
   "name": "Ian",
   "Pet club membership": true,
   "pets": [12, 24],
},
{
   "type": "PET_TYPE",
   "_id": 12,
   "name": "Kirby",
   "breed": "Cavalier dog",
},
{
   "type": "PET_TYPE",
   "_id": 24,
   "name": "Kaitlyn",
   "breed": "Siamese cat",
}
```

This allows a query to narrow down results to just returning the document type you want and then you can add in whatever further criteria you are looking for.

# 2.6 Running Out of Space in a Database

There are ways to deal with cases where the number or size of documents becomes a problem. Think about what would happen if you keep adding documents to a collection that existed on a single primary SSD? Obviously, at some point, you are going to reach the storage space limit that is set for a single database you are paying for. This does not necessarily mean that you need to separate out and reference data across document types in separate collections. You can still keep data embedded.

The method for achieving storage capacity scaling is through what is called sharding. This means your collection is more of a logical concept and is spread across multiple SSDs. The unit of scaling is with the MongoDB concept of a replica set. A given document must only be found in one replica set of the sharding cluster. The nice thing is that MongoDB hides that from you, and your query and update does not even realize what is going on.

For customer documents, you could have a sharding hashed ID that distributes customer documents out across different replica set storage. In a later chapter, I will discuss this type of data partitioning. Don't worry if you do not fully understand this concept yet.

# 2.7 Access Control

There are several ways to interact with MongoDB documents. One is through the mLab management portal UI and the other is through API access, such as in Node.js code. Of course, there is also the Mongo shell, but that is not used in this book and is out of scope. If you want to learn more about the Mongo shell, please refer to MongoDB's documentation.

From the mLab management portal, a user account must be added to the mLab account to provide authentication for a user. You can give them read-only privileges, if you need that restriction in place. Account administration through the portal is really not central to the topic of this book, so if you need more information, please refer to mLab's management portal documentation.

The other type of access is done programmatically through a MongoDB API, such as one that is provided for Node.js developers. The details of this will be explained in the Node.js content later in this book.

The NewsWatcher sample application client UI will go through the middle-tier service layer where interaction happens with the database. The middle tier will then be able to authenticate on behalf of the user.

# Chapter 3: Querying for Documents

You may have heard of SQL (Structured Query Language) as the language used to query records in relational databases. You submit SQL queries to your DBMS and receive back the resulting records. MongoDB definitely supports querying, but it does not use SQL. Instead, it has its own query syntax.

The actual MongoDB database has a single means of programmatic interaction to accomplish things like a query. Everything on top of that is done through a TCP/IP connection that has a well-defined wire protocol for the operations that it supports. There are around nine operations you can make with this protocol. All you need to know is that other people have done the work to abstract away the complexities of using this protocol through specific language drivers you can use. This book will be concerned with using the Node.js driver. The following diagram shows the overall access layers:

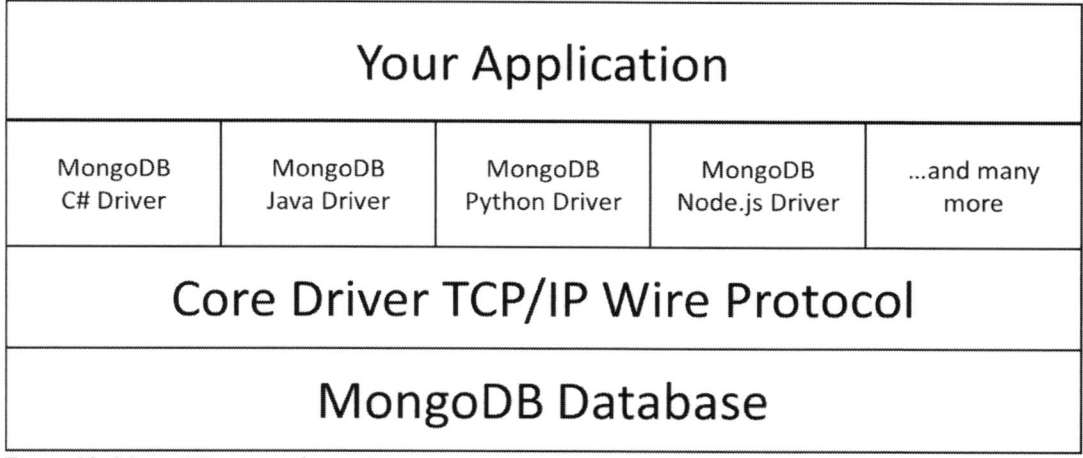

*Figure 13: MongoDB access abstraction*

In the service layer part of this book, I will show you how to use the MongoDB Node.js driver for operations like create, read, update, and delete (CRUD). This current chapter will only cover the specifics of the querying syntax for operations in general.

Regardless of which of the CRUD operations you perform, you need to specify your query criteria as part of that request. You can actually explore this topic now, because you don't need to write any code to try out your queries. You can use the mLab management portal UI to try them out and experiment with the syntax as you like.

# Example documents

Carefully review the example JSON documents shown below. They will be used with examples showing how to construct your queries. You can imagine these documents being used by an online bookstore. There would obviously be a lot more data available than what is in this example:

```
// Customer Documents
{
  "_id": "77",
  "name": "Joe Schmoe",
  "age": 27,
  "email": "js@gmail.com",
  "address": {
    "street": "21 Main Street",
    "city": "Emerald City",
    "state": "KS",
    "postalCode": "10021-3100"
  },
  "rewardsPoints": 99,
  "booksPurchased": [
    {
      "id": "1098",
      "title": "Agile Project Management with Kanban"
    },
    {
      "id": "1099",
      "title": "The Merriam-Webster Dictionary"
    }
  ]
},
{
  "_id": "78",
  "name": "Jane Doe",
  "age": 37,
  "email": "jd@gmail.com",
  "address": {
    "street": "100 S Bridger Blvd",
    "city": "Paradise",
    "state": "UT",
    "postalCode": "84328"
  },
  "rewardsPoints": 0
}
```

```
// Book Documents
{
   "_id": "1098",
   "title": "Agile Project Management with Kanban",
   "ISBN10": "0735698953",
   "author": "Eric Brechner",
   "pages": 160,
   "format": "Paperback",
   "price": 27.66,
   "publicationDate": "20150326",
   "category": "Software Engineering",
   "bookReviews": [
      {
         "reviewer": "Joe Schmoe",
         "date": "20140321",
         "comments": "Wish I had this years ago!",
         "rating": 4
      },
      {
         "reviewer": "Jane Doe",
         "date": "20150923",
         "comments": "Forever a classic.",
         "rating": 5
      }]
},
{
   "_id": "1099",
   "title": "The Merriam-Webster Dictionary",
   "ISBN10": "087779930X",
   "author": "Merriam-Webster",
   "pages": 939,
   "format": "Paperback",
   "price": 11.26,
   "publicationDate": "20040701",
   "category": "English",
   "bookReviews": [
      {
         "reviewer": "Joe Schmoe",
         "date": "20100101",
         "comments": "A terrific volume to keep handy.",
         "rating": 4
      },{
         "reviewer": "Jane Doe",
         "date": "20120817",
         "comments": "Wish it came in an audio book format.",
         "rating": 2
      }]
}
```

In this chapter, I will introduce you to the basics of the query syntax. I won't cover each and every aspect of it, as it is fairly robust and much of it is beyond the scope of this book. One topic I will only briefly mention, is the topic of using the MongoDB aggregation features. For more information on that topic and other supported syntax intricacies, refer to MongoDB's documentation.

*Note: You cannot just create a query and assume that it will end up being efficient. The execution time of a query can vary greatly. To address performance issues, you either have to create indexes that can speed up your queries, or think about a more efficient way of modeling your data. I will cover the topic of index creation later.*

## Syntax overview

In a later chapter, you will be querying a collection using functions such as `find()` or `findOneAndDelete()`. These are functions that come with the Node.js mongodb module. The first parameter of these functions is the query criteria that specifies the matching to take place across all of the documents in a collection. If you are familiar with SQL, this is similar to what a WHERE clause does. Here is an example query using the `find()` function with a greater than operator in the query criteria. This query will return all of the documents in the collection whose age property contains a value greater than 35:

```
db.collection.find({age: {$gt: 35}});
```

For the function call above, there is the possibility that the query criteria does not match anything and that no documents will be returned. On the other hand, if there are a lot of returned documents, then you need to use the Node.js driver capability to fetch results in batches. You will see how to actually access the results of the `find()` function in code later in this book.

Besides the query criteria I just showed you, there are also criteria you can provide for what is called the projection criteria. The projection criteria determines the properties that will be returned from each document. Here is another example using the same `find()` function, but this time with an optional second parameter added to specify the projection:

```
db.collection.find({age: {$gt: 35}}, {name: 1, age: 1});
```

This query will find all documents in the collection whose age property contains a value greater than 35, but only the name, age and _id properties of those documents will be returned. _id is always returned, unless you specify otherwise.

As mentioned, the second parameter in this query is the projection criteria. This is where you list the properties you want returned. The number following the colon determines if the property is wanted (included), or if it is not wanted (excluded). I will explain more about this soon.

I will keep using the example of the bookstore customer documents, but for now, just pretend they only have four properties each. The following diagram of the previous query shows the two criteria in the function call and how they act on the data to determine the output:

*Figure 14: Criteria flow*

You can see that the query criteria determines what documents pass through to the result set. The projection criteria selects what properties you want for each document in the result set.

Now I can go into the details of both the query and the projection criteria operations. You can log into your mLab account, add a database, add a collection and some documents, and then try out some queries on your own.

# 3.1 Query Criteria

The query criteria is actually optional on a function such as the `find()` function. It is, however, something you will almost always be using. If you call `find()` without any query criteria parameter, every single document in the collection will be returned.

The query criteria is a test that is applied to the collection to see what documents are to be included as part of the result set. If you really want to, you can narrow down the result to return a single document. For example, you can query by the `_id` property with an equality test. The `_id` property is unique, so each document can be uniquely identified with it. Here is an example of code to query by `_id`. The result it returns is also shown:

```
// Query
db.collection.find({_id: {$eq: "77"}}, {address.state: 1});

// Results
{
   "_id": "77",
   "address": {
     "state": "KS"
   }
}
```

# PART I: The Data Layer (MongoDB)

You don't need to write any code at the moment to try this out, but can try out queries in the mLab management portal. In the UI, navigate to a collection and then use the drop down menu on that page to select **[new search]**. This allows you to experiment with the different types of queries I will be showing here. Just be aware that the UI uses JSON syntax while the code you will be using later looks a bit different because it is written in JavaScript. Here is what the mLab management portal UI looks like if you are trying out a query:

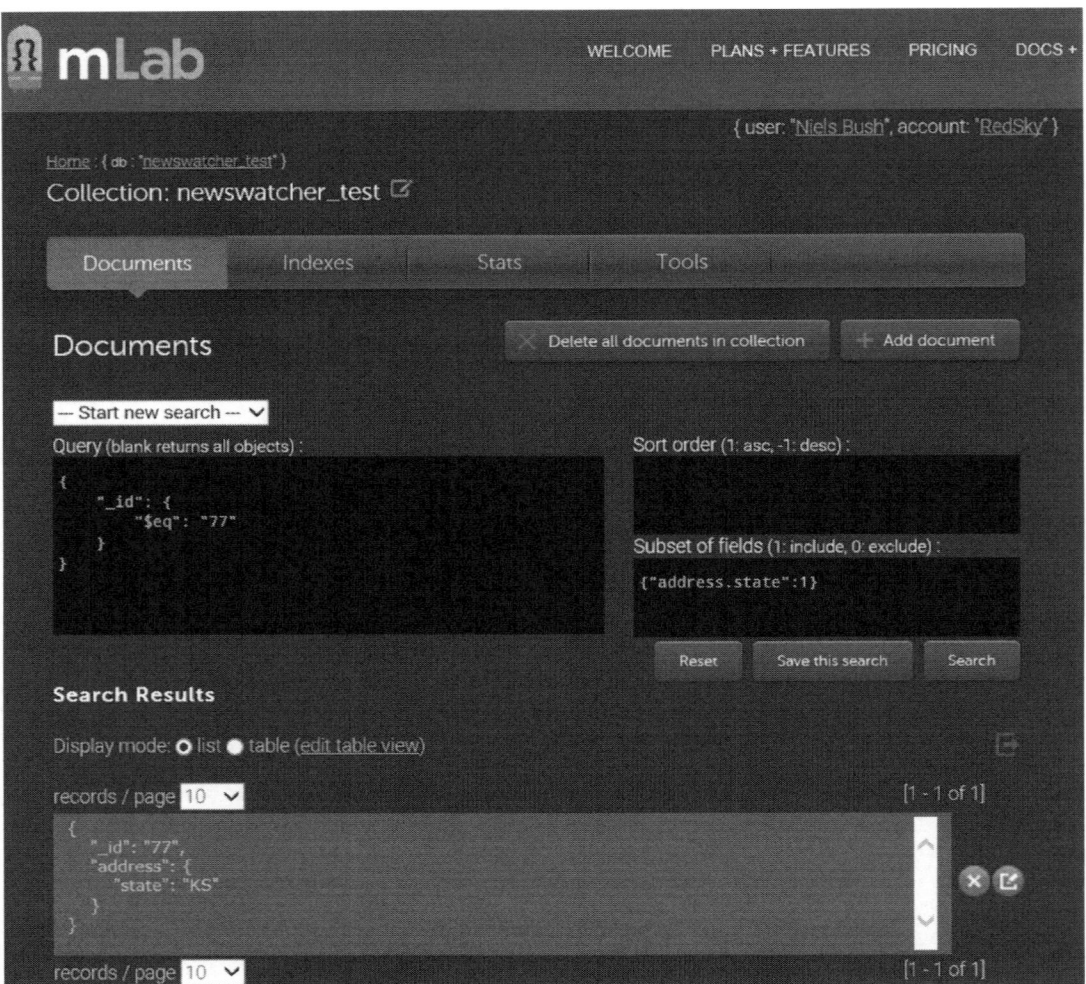

*Figure 15: mLab management portal collection querying page*

Each query criteria can utilize one or more operators. The example above uses the `$eq` operator. The real power of the query is in the use of the criteria operators. I'll now go over what those are and show you some examples.

# Criteria operators

You have seen operators such as `$gt` and `$eq` used in the examples in this chapter. Those operators stand for greater than and equal to. There are many more operators that you can use in your query criteria to filter documents. The following operators are currently supported:

- **Comparison**
  - `$eq`
  - `$gt`
  - `$gte`
  - `$in`
  - `$lt`
  - `$lte`
  - `$ne`
  - `$nin`
- **Array**
  - `$all`
  - `$elemMatch`
  - `$size`
- **Bitwise**
  - `$bitsAllClear`
  - `$bitsAllSet`
  - `$bitsAnyClear`
  - `$bitsAnySet`
- **Element**
  - `$exists`
  - `$type`
- **Evaluation**
  - `$mod`
  - `$regex`
  - `$text`
  - `$where`
- **Geospatial**
  - `$geoIntersects`
  - `$geoWithin`
  - `$near`
  - `$nearSphere`
- **Logical**
  - `$and`
  - `$or`
  - `$nor`
  - `$not`

Each of the operators uses its own unique syntax. The $eq operator uses the following syntax:

```
{ <name>: { $eq: <value> } }
```

The `name` is a property that you want to test. It can be a top-level property, or it can be a property within the hierarchy of the JSON. You use a string, number or other value matching the data type of the property for the `value`. Here is an example that tests a second-level property, sometimes referred to as an embedded document field in MongoDB documentation:

```
{"address.state": {"$eq": "UT"}}
```

You can even specify a property of an element in an array property. If you look at the example document, you see that `booksPurchased` is an array and `id` is a property of one of the elements of that array. In the example below, the returned document is the complete document, as the query criteria is only used to find a document match and then no projection criteria is being used.

```
{"booksPurchased.id": {"$eq": "1098"}}
```

Here are a few operators from some of the categories to give you an idea of how they work. For more detailed information on each of the operators, see MongoDB's documentation.

**Comparison**

With the comparison operators, you need to first select the property name you are interested in testing. This is then followed by the comparison operator and finally the value you want for that comparison test. The only exception to this is with the $in and $nin operators, which use an array and not a single value.

I'll use the same example I have shown you previously, which is doing a query for a single document by its _id value:

```
{"_id": {"$eq": "77"}}
```

To just test the equality of a property, you can shorten the syntax to the following:

```
{"_id": "77"}
```

You can use more than one comparison operator at a time, such as you would need to do to test ranges of values. All operator tests need to pass in order for a given document to be included in the results set. Here is an example that queries for books that have between 100 and 200 pages:

```
// Query
{
   "pages": {
      "$gt": 100,
      "$lt": 200
   }
}
```

**Logical**

The logical operators let you string together several tests in a row to perform the desired logical testing. The syntax for the logical operator $and is:

```
{$and: [ { <expression1> }, { <expression2> } , ... , { <expressionN> } ]}
```

The logical operator syntax starts with a boolean operator such as $and. It then contains an array of expressions that can be made up of individual comparison operators that we have seen previously.

The following query looks for books that are less than 200 pages in length and which are also in the Software Engineering category.

```
// Query.
{"$and": [{"pages": {"$lt": 200}},
          {"category": {"$eq": "Software Engineering"}}]}

// Results. Assuming you also have a projection criteria of {"_id": 1}
{
   "_id": "1098"
}
```

If you are only carrying out this one level of boolean operation, then you don't really need the $and operator. Instead you can just list the conditions one after another. Here is the same example query without the $and operator:

```
// Query.
{"pages": {"$lt": 200}, "category": {"$eq": "Software Engineering"}}

// Results. Assuming you also have a projection criteria of {"_id": 1}
{
   _id": "1098"
}
```

Here is a query that uses both the $and and the $or operators. I'll use the complete expanded text formatting of the query as it is easier to read. This example queries for books that have less than 200 pages and are either in the category of Software Engineering or Science Fiction.

# PART I: The Data Layer (MongoDB)

```
// Query.
{
  "$and": [
    {
      "pages": {
        "$lt": 200
      }
    },
    {
      "$or": [
        {
          "category": {
            "$eq": "Software Engineering"
          }
        },
        {
          "category": {
            "$eq": "Science Fiction"
          }
        }
      ]
    }
  ]
}

// Results. Assuming you also have a projection criteria of {"_id": 1}
{
  "_id": "1098"
}
```

If you find your query has a lot of $or operations to match on many different values for the same property, then you can use the $in operator. The value to match can even be a regular expression. The following example shows how easy it is to use this to list all the possible matches:

```
// Query using IN
{
  "category": {
    "$in": [
      "Software Engineering",
      "Science Fiction"
    ]
  }
}
```

## Element
The element operators $exists and $type are for selections based on whether a property exists and if it is of a certain datatype. The following example shows the syntax for $exists:

```
{ name: { $exists: <boolean> } }
```

A typical use for $exists would be to use this operator inside another operator. In this example, you want to make sure the document has the publicationDate property. It may be that a book has a price set, but has not been published yet, so the publicationDate property is not there yet.

```
{"$and": [{"price": {"$lt": 30}}, {"publicationDate": {"$exists": true}}]}
```

**Evaluation**

If you struggle to get exactly what you want in your query, you might find the evaluation operators are just what you need. Here is an example that shows the use of a regular expression with the option set for a case-insensitive test. This example will find all books that have a title that starts with the word "agile" no matter the letter casing:

```
{
    "title": {
        "$regex": "^agile",
        "$options": "i"
    }
}
```

You might have a document with large amounts of text that you want to search for specific words or phrases. You can use the $text operator in this case. To use it, you need to first create an index of type text on the properties you want to use it on. For example, you could create the index on the title property and then search for books that contain certain words in their title.

```
{"$text": {"$search": "MongoDB"}}
```

For those rare occasions where you just cannot get what you want through all of the available operators, you can resort to writing JavaScript using the $where operator. Here is a test that can check to see if a person has purchased more than a single book. This requires JavaScript, because the length property of the booksPurchased array is only accessible through the API returned object.

```
{"$where": "this.booksPurchased.length>1"}
```

You cannot presently try this query out from the mLab management portal, but it will work in code and is actually used in this book's sample code.

# Object and array properties

So far, the examples shown have been testing properties that are single values, such as a string or a numeric data type. But what if you have a document that has a property in it that is an array of strings? What if you have an object property? Even better, what if you have a property that is an array of objects?

The `address` object property in the bookstore customer example document ends up as an embedded document in MongoDB BSON. You can do a search for an exact match on an embedded document and specify individual names to match as shown in a previous example.

For arrays, you can do an exact match on the full contents of the array, or just on specific values existing somewhere within the array. If the array holds objects, you can search for the element entry and sub-property off of that. Here is a previous example query that was doing this:

```
{"booksPurchased.id": {"$eq": "1098"}}
```

Just as you can test multiple single property values, you can do that for arrays of properties. Let's say you wanted to search for books with book reviews by Joe where he gave a four-star rating. Here an example of how that would look:

```
{
    "bookReviews.reviewer": "Joe Schmoe",
    "bookReviews.rating": 4
}
```

For a simple array of strings, you could match for that exact array. To search for documents where one string entry in an array exists, you could do an equality test. Here is an example document with a property that is an array of strings:

```
{
    "favoriteColors": ["green", "red", "blue"]
}
```

To include that document, here is the query criteria you could use:

```
{"favoriteColors": "green"}
```

Array searches and projection capabilities in MongoDB are very powerful. If you take the time, you can learn how to match on things like an element in a specific index, or do something like return the first numeric element that is larger than some value. You will have to learn that yourself, as it is tricky to explain all the nuances for these. See the MongoDB documentation. For example, look at the `$elemMatch` operator documentation.

# Data type mismatch problem

Equality comparisons can end up producing an undefined outcome if the property data type specified does not match up with the test value data type. For example, you cannot test for a number value with a property that is a string. The test statement syntax of MongoDB does not work the same as it does in the JavaScript language. The following query will not work because of the data type mismatch:

```
// The selection will not work, as the _id property is a string
// in the document, and you are comparing it with a number
{
    "_id": {
      "$eq": 77
    }
}
```

With the following JavaScript code sample, you can see that data type coercion happens. A boolean test between a string and a number does work in JavaScript.

```
// JavaScript uses "==" for equality testing.
// Coercion rules apply and both equality tests evaluate to true
var v = "77";
v == "77"; // true result
v == 77;   // true result as coercion happens
```

# 3.2 Projection criteria

Just because you have your query criteria returning the proper result set of documents does not mean that you are done. You may also want to set up projection criteria to just return the properties that you need. You have seen this demonstrated already, but now you can look at this in more detail.

There may be cases where documents with all of their properties are what you actually want to have returned. This may be the case with a very sparse document, making it reasonable to return the whole document every time. With larger, more complex documents, you can benefit from restricting the properties being returned. Limiting what properties are returned saves on the amount of data transferred over the network.

# Inclusion and exclusion

You have already been using projection criteria, so you really know most of what you need to know already. Just to review, if you don't provide projection criteria, then the complete document is returned. If you do provide projection criteria, then you can specify the inclusion or exclusion of whichever properties you would like. Exclusion means to return all properties except the ones you list. The inclusion and exclusion syntax is:

```
<name>: <1 or true or 0 or false>
```

`True` means to include and `false` means to exclude. You cannot mix both inclusion and exclusion in the same projection criteria. The only exception to this is if you are using inclusion criteria, you can also specify one single exclusion if it is to exclude the `_id` property.

Here are some examples of different projection criteria with a comment added to state whether they are valid or invalid:

```
{"address.state": 1}      // Valid
{"address.state": 0}      // Valid
{"name": 1, "age": 1}     // Valid
{"name": 1, "age": 0}     // Invalid
{"age": 0}                // Valid
{"name": 1, "_id": 0}     // Valid
```

As I mentioned, this is extremely handy. Let's say you want to create a list of people with their addresses. You could use the following projection criteria:

```
{"name":1,"address":1,"_id":0}
```

The following is the result set returned:

```
{
   "name": "Joe Schmoe",
   "address": {
      "street": "21 Main Street",
      "city": "Emerald City",
      "state": "KS",
      "postalCode": "10021-3100"
   }
}
{
   "name": "Jane Doe",
   "address": {
      "street": "100 S Bridger Blvd",
      "city": "Paradise",
      "state": "UT",
      "postalCode": "84328"
   }
}
```

# Arrays

There is a special operator named $slice that allows you to return just specific portions of array properties. Examine the following document that has a property containing an array of colors:

```
{
   "favoriteColors": ["green", "red", "blue"]
}
```

Here are a few examples of the use of different operators like $slice, $, and $elemMatch to pull out different elements from the array property shown above:

```
// Return first two elements
{ favoriteColors: { $slice: 2 } }

// Return first element
{ favoriteColors.$: 1 }

// Return first element that matches
{ favoriteColors: { $elemMatch: { $eq:  "red"} } }
```

For more information on these operators, see MongoDB's documentation.

# Missing properties

Since MongoDB is schema-less, it is possible that any number of documents in a collection that you are querying might not even contain the given property that you have specified in your selection criteria. For example, it is possible that booksPurchased is a missing property in some of your documents, by your own design. This is important to consider when you are constructing your query criteria and projection criteria.

The example query below will return two documents, but the second document will not have the booksPurchased property. This is because the second customer has not bought any books yet.

```
// Projection criteria
{ "name":1,"booksPurchased":1}

// Results
{
   "_id": "77",
   "name": "Joe Schmoe",
   "booksPurchased": [
      {
         "id": "1098",
         "title": "Agile Project Management with Kanban"
```

```
    },
    {
        "id": "1099",
        "title": "The Merriam-Webster Dictionary"
    }
  ]
}
{
  "_id": "78",
  "name": "Jane Doe"
}
```

If you really want this second document left out completely if the property does not exist, use a query selector to only get those with a non-null value as shown here:

```
// Query criteria
{
    "booksPurchased": {
        "$ne": null
    }
}
```

Of course, the property could still exist and just be a zero-length array and it would be returned in that case.

# 3.3 Querying Polymorphic Documents in a Single Collection

In the section on data modeling, I mentioned that you may decide to normalize some of your data. You might like to store data in completely different document types in the same collection. To do this, your query must always include a way to pick out just the documents of a particular type that you want to have returned. Using the bookstore example, if you had the customer and the book documents in the same collection, you could add a `type` property to each. The following is an abbreviated example showing this approach:

```
// Customer documents
{
    "_id": "77",
    "type": "CUSTOMER_TYPE",
    "name": "Joe Schmoe",
    ...
}
{
    "_id": "78",
    "type": "CUSTOMER_TYPE",
```

```
    "name": "Jane Doe",
    ...
}

// Book Documents
{
    "_id": "1098",
    "type": "BOOK_TYPE",
    "title": "Agile Project Management with Kanban",
    ...
}
{
    "_id": "1099",
    "type": "BOOK_TYPE",
    "title": "The Merriam-Webster Dictionary",
    ...
}
```

In every query, you would need to include query criteria that was specific for the type of document you needed. Here is an example of that query criteria:

```
// Query criteria
{"type": "BOOK_TYPE"}
```

# Chapter 4: Updating Documents

The previous chapter covered the topic of querying or the 'R' for Read in the CRUD acronym. This chapter covers the 'U' for the Update operation. I will give an overview here of how the syntax works.

When updating a document, you can certainly provide the complete document for uploading. As an enhancement, MongoDB allows you to do things like specify a single property to be updated. There are many update operators you can choose from and they can be combined in a single atomic update submission.

To use the update capability of MongoDB, you first need to provide the query criteria to identify the document or documents to be updated. That criteria uses the same syntax as already covered for the query criteria. What is new here is the update criteria that you need to provide as a second parameter. Here is the update criteria syntax:

```
{
    <operator1>: { <name1>: <value1>, ... },
    <operator2>: { <name2>: <value2>, ... },
    ...
}
```

*Note: Create and Delete operations are being skipped. Creation is really just providing the JSON document to create and a deletion operation uses the same query criteria syntax that a read does. All MongoDB CRUD operations will be covered in the service layer discussion.*

# 4.1 Update operators

The following are the currently supported operators for update operations on single value properties:
- $currentDate
- $inc
- $max
- $min
- $mul
- $rename
- $set
- $setOnInsert
- $unset

Here are some examples to illustrate some of these update operators. I will only show examples that update a single property at a time. You can certainly combine multiple operators on different properties in one update submission. These will all be committed at the same time and will result in an atomic operation at the document level.

There are many operators you can use and I will give examples of a few of them. For every update call, you need as the first parameter the query criteria to identify the document(s). The second parameter specifies the property to update. If the query criteria identifies more than one document, the update happens on all of those documents identified.

*Note: The mLab management portal does not allow the use of the update syntax right now, only query searches work. That is why I am showing the examples with code.*

# $set

The `$set` operator is the standard way to replace a value of a property. The following example sets the `rewardsPoints` property to a new value for the queried person:

```
db.collection.update({_id: "77"}, {$set: {rewardsPoints: 1000}});
```

If the property did not exist before, it is created. This operator can be used to do a complete replacement of any value, even doing a replacement of a complete array or an embedded document. It also works to replace a specific property of an embedded property.

`$rename` can be used to give a property a new name. `$unset` will delete a property.

# $inc

The `$inc` operator is used to change the integer value of a property by a specified amount. You can add or subtract from any value. Using the bookstore example, you could add rewards points to a customer. Here is an example of what that would look like:

```
db.collection.update({_id: "77"}, {$inc: {rewardsPoints: 10}});
```

# $min and $max

The `$min` and `$max` operators are used to test a given value and only replace it if the value is less or greater than the test value, depending on the operator. Here is an example using `$max`:

```
db.collection.update({_id: "77"}, {$max: {rewardsPoints: 2000}});
```

In this example, if the `rewardsPoints` property had a value of 1000 to start with, it has a value of 2000 after this update.

# 4.2 Array Update Operators

The following operators are for use with array properties to perform updates:
- $
- $addToSet
- $pop
- $pull
- $pullAll
- $push
- $pushAll

## $push

The $push operator is used to add another element to an array property. Here is an example that adds a new book review to a book document:

```
db.collection.update({_id: "1098"},
    { $push: { bookReviews: {
       reviewer: "Skylar",
       date: "20150923",
       comments: "It was really profound!",
       rating: 5
    }}});
```

The $addToSet operator is similar to $push except it checks to see if an identical entry exists already and only adds the new element if it is not already present in the array. You can use the additional operator of $each to add multiple elements at once. The $sort operator can be combined with the $push and $each operators to keep the array sorted. Combine the $position operator with $push to specify the point of insertion.

## $

The $ operator is used to specify that the update is to happen for only the first element of an array that is found to match the query criteria. The part of the $set that uses bookReviews.$.rating uses the .$ to signify that the replace should take place on just the first element match that is found. This example does a search for any document that has a bookReviews element that has a rating of 4 and then updates the first matched element:

```
db.collection.update({_id: "1098", bookReviews.rating: 4},
    { $set: { "bookReviews.$.rating" : 5 } }
)
```

## $pop

The $pop operator is used to remove elements from an array property. This example removes the first book review:

```
db.collection.update({_id: "1098"}, {$pop: {bookReviews: -1}});
```

You can use $pull to remove all entries from an array that match what you specify. You can use $pullAll to specify more than one match for the removal criteria.

# 4.3 Transactions

In the previous examples of update operations, I only showed examples of single property updates. These are atomic transactions happening on each single document identified. You can replace one or more properties on all matching documents at once as well.

If you have a requirement to change two documents simultaneously in different ways, then you need to work this out on your own. For example, if you wanted to take rewards points from one document and add them to a different document, this would require what is termed a multi-document atomic transaction. This is not currently built into MongoDB.

You would need to build that capability yourself in your own code to ensure that all document transactions are successful, or cause a rollback if one fails. Refer to information on how to implement a two-phase commit in MongoDB's documentation.

You can imagine how important this would be to get right in an application that manages financial transactions across accounts.

# Chapter 5: Managing Availability and Performance

In an ideal world, you could store an infinite amount of data, access it from anywhere, access it in near-zero time and never have any data lost or corrupted. Reality is that it takes a lot of work to approach these ideals. As you design your data model and subsequently try it out, you need to tune your DBMS for consistency, availability, and performance. You can now consider what mechanisms are at your disposal to approach these ideals.

It really takes a fair amount of time to fine-tune each aspect of the management of your MongoDB database. Many times you will be faced with tradeoffs that have to be made. This chapter will look at some of the aspects that can be "fine-tuned" for specific access scenarios.

In a PaaS environment, some of this work should be less than has been traditionally required in the past with a DBMS. MongoDB has certainly done a great job of making some things automatically happen that used to require a lot of manual configuration.

# 5.1 Indexing

Imagine you had a problem finding items such as your car keys, the TV remote, your favorite pair of socks, your wallet or purse, etc. Perhaps you would be trying to head out the door and found yourself frantically searching for your car keys.

One approach to solving this would be to keep a whiteboard right next to your front door that had two columns. One column would list the item and the other column would list the known location of that item. The whiteboard might look like this:

| Car keys | Left side pocket of jacket hanging in entry way closet |
| TV remote | In the pile of toys in the room of your two-year-old toddler |
| Purple socks | Laundry room floor under the pile of towels |
| Wallet | Under the couch cushion in the TV room |

Imagine the huge time savings this could provide. I saw one study that stated that, on average, a person spends a whole year of accumulated time looking for lost items during their lifetime.

A database index uses the same concept and outcome as the look up table whiteboard, with the goal of helping database records be located faster. A database index works by creating a separate lookup list that allows for faster querying. This alleviates the need to search through all documents in order to find the one(s) you are looking for. For example, let's say you had a lastName property in every document in a collection. If you created a query that was looking for a particular person with the last name of "Smith" then how would a query find it as quickly as possible? The slowest way to search would be to start looking at all of the documents one by one, until a document was found with "Smith" in the lastName property. That type of search has no choice but to search each and every document in an unsorted storage system. In a huge collection, this would be a major performance problem.

Indexing can speed up your search by creating a separate, sorted list of last names to match against, with each entry pointing to the corresponding complete document. A query for the last name of Smith quickly finds those entries with something like a binary search.

As an example, here is a representation of random documents. There is one row per document that exists in a MongoDB collection. This is only an abstract representation. To search for "Tuttle," you would start a sequential search from document to document until you found a match on the lastName. Unfortunately, in this case it would be the last one found.

## Customer Documents

| lastName | zipCode | rewards | age |
|----------|---------|---------|-----|
| Smith | 27896 | 77 | 32 |
| Williams | 43890 | 3 | 18 |
| Adams | 99054 | 654 | 55 |
| Tuttle | 12345 | 567 | 21 |

*Figure 16: Customer documents unsorted and with no index*

If you add a separate list that contains the `lastName` property and along with each, a link to the customer document that has that last name, then this can be sorted and your searching will be much faster. A quick binary search of the index will find the `lastName` match and then use the link to get the document from there.

Implementing a good index can be a critical part of your work to maximize the efficiency of your queries. It is well worth your time to measure and analyze the performance of your database and to fine-tune it.

The following example illustrates the concept of linking through an index:

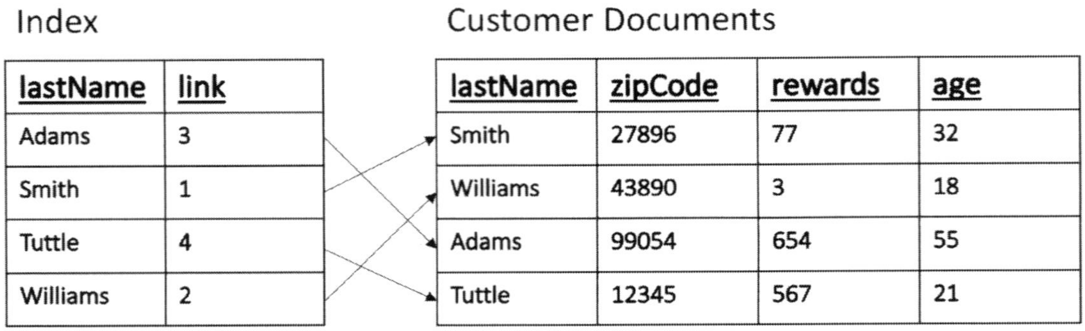

Index

Customer Documents

| lastName | link |
|----------|------|
| Adams | 3 |
| Smith | 1 |
| Tuttle | 4 |
| Williams | 2 |

| lastName | zipCode | rewards | age |
|----------|---------|---------|-----|
| Smith | 27896 | 77 | 32 |
| Williams | 43890 | 3 | 18 |
| Adams | 99054 | 654 | 55 |
| Tuttle | 12345 | 567 | 21 |

*Figure 17: Index for Customer Document linking*

You will be creating all of your indexes through the mLab management portal. There are ways to do this programmatically, but for areas of the application that only need to be set up once, I always prefer to do this through the portal. There are reports in mLab you can bring up that help you look at index performance.

***Note:*** *Index configuration can get rather complex and I can only cover the basic common scenarios pertaining to the sample application. You will have to go to the online documentation to get all the details on what is possible.*

# Single-property index

The simplest way to learn about indexes is to learn how to set up an index on a single property. This section goes over how this works for a single value or object property. The next topic explains the subtleties for what happens if the property is an array data type.

Let's go back to the example of the online bookstore. If you look at the requirements for your querying, you can see that you need to be able to search for customers by name. If you had hundreds of thousands of customers, it is certainly going to improve the performance of this query if you create an index on the name property.

The syntax used to create an index is similar to the syntax used to set up your other criteria. This example shows how to specify an index on `name`:

```
{"name": 1}
```

That is how simple it is. You can also add an index on a property of an embedded document. For example, what if you wanted to look up all customers that resided in a certain postal code? To make this query run faster, you would want to place an index on the sub-property as follows:

```
{"address.postalCode": 1}
```

You could place an index on the address property as a whole, but then you would have to put in a complete address for the query criteria, including having the properties in the same order for the match to succeed.

*Note: The _id property that has to exist on every document is automatically indexed, so you never need to add one for that.*

# Array property index

If a property is an array, you set up an index on it in the same way as for a single value property. There are just a few restrictions. One restriction is that you cannot have more than one array property index at a time. For example, if your documents have multiple array properties, you can only set up an index on one of the array properties.

The index would then be used to match on anything found in the array. The index can only be used for individual element matching and not for matching on the array as a whole. As an example, let's say you had the following documents:

```
{"name": "Kiara", "favoriteColors": ["blue", "yellow", "cyan"]}
{"name": "Tristan", "favoriteColors": ["green", "red", "blue"]}
{"name": "Halli", "favoriteColors": ["juju", "nana", "mango"]}
```

You can set up an index similar to the previous example:

```
{"favoriteColors": 1}
```

Now you can set up a query with query criteria to match a color that might be found in the array. If you search for "red," then the document for Tristan will be included in the results set. What is happening internally is that the index contains all array element entries across all documents. There would be three entries in the index for Kiara, alphabetically sorted by the color name. Each of those three would point back to the one document. Similarly, there will be three entries for Tristan and Halli.

You can also set up an index even if the array contains elements that are objects, as with the following example:

```
{"name": "Skylar", "clothes": [
  {"type": "school dress", "color": "tan", "size": 5},
  {"type": "school pants", "color": "tan", "size": 6},
  {"type": "church shoes", "color": "white", "size": 3}]
{"name": "Korver", "clothes": [
  {"type": "pajamas", "color": "green", "size": 3},
  {"type": "tennis shoes", "color": "brown", "size": 2},
  {"type": "winter coat", "color": "blue", "size": 3}]
```

The following example will set up an index just for one property for the element object:

```
{"clothes.type": 1}
```

# Multiple-property index

Many times you will have queries that specify more than one property to match on. This is used when you want to narrow down your search. Perhaps you want to run bookstore specials to encourage people to use rewards points. For example, what if you were looking for all people less than 20 years old that had no rewards points so you could give them some points as a free bonus offer to try out. The following example creates an index on `age` and `rewardsPoints` so you can search for customers that way:

```
{"age": 1, "rewardsPoints": 1}
```

This is called a compound index. Be sure to understand how this really works. The underlying index first has sorted entries for age and then, has sub-sorted entries by `rewardsPoints`. This means that you cannot use this index for a query for just rewards points, such as finding all people with over 1000. You can, however, use this index to query just by age. The order of properties listed for the index is important.

You could create two separate indexes if you need to be able to query by both age and rewards points separately as well as combined in either order. MongoDB will use something called an index intersection for you, if it can. For example, you could create the following two indexes:

```
{"age": 1}
{"rewardsPoints": 1}
```

Now you can still query by the combination of age and rewards points. But you can also query just by age, or just by rewards points. You can also reverse the combination and query by rewards points and then age, in that order. The only downside is that each index you set up means more storage you take up as overhead.

# Index sort order

Up to this point, I have always been using the numeric value of 1 in all of the index examples. What that is actually doing is instructing MongoDB to create the index in ascending sort order. You can alternatively specify -1 and get a descending sort order. For example, you could create the following index:

```
{"age": -1}
```

For single-property indexes, this does not matter. It really only matters if you want to return multiple documents of more than one property through a corresponding multi-property index and you want the result returned in a specific sort order. For example, querying for all people with the last name of "Smith" and returning the documents in descending order by age.

With the API usage, there is a `sort()` function that can follow the `find()` function that can process the sort order for you, but it will be done outside the index and be slower.

## Other types of indexes

The index examples used so far would be used with exact value and range type queries. Just so you are aware, there are a few other types of indexes that you can investigate and utilize, if they suit your needs. Other index types supported by MongoDB are geospatial, hashed and text indexes.

For example, let's say you were keeping a database of restaurants along with their menus, reviews, and location coordinates. With a geospatial index you could then perform queries to take a person's current location and find all of the restaurants within a certain radius of them.

If you have large amounts of text in a property, you can use what is called a text index. For example, if you were storing news stories and you wanted to have an index on the story content, you could find a text index very performant.

There is an index called a hash index. It can be used on properties that are single value or that have an embedded document, but it cannot be used with array properties. The hashed index is populated with the hashed values. A hash index by itself is not ideal for range-based queries, so you might want another separate single-property index for that.

For embedded documents, the index gives a hash of the complete embedded document. This then would potentially be a faster lookup as the search is just comparing a hash value to find the document. A hash index might make more sense when combined with sharding. This will be covered at that time.

## Index creation options

One of the options you can use with the creation of an index is to specify that the values for a given property are unique. For example, in the bookstore example, each customer has an `email` property. You could make the index require that all emails must be unique across all documents. Here is example that creates an index with the `unique` option:

```
{"email": 1}, {unique: true}
```

You should probably create an index like this before any data is populated. Index creation will fail if multiple documents exist that have the same value for their email property. Once an index is created with the unique option, any document creation will fail unless it has a unique value on the indexed field with this option set.

The `sparse` option can be used to create an index that only has entries for documents that contain that property. In the following example, if a document did not have the `email` property, then it would not be included in the index. Any subsequent query for values to match on using the `email` field would ignore those documents, but that is probably what you wanted. If an index exists for a property, then MongoDB will use it, so that is why the rest of the documents would not be searched that don't have that property.

```
{"email": 1}, {sparse: true}
```

## Index creation options

That about wraps up the topic of indexes. As I stated at the start of this chapter, there are no perfect solutions in the world of databases. This is true with indexing. What you need to do is to completely understand your query needs in order to understand how best to create your indexes.

For example, you might even consider not having any index created under certain circumstances. If you had a database with 95% of the operations being writes and 5% were reads, you might not want to create an index. This is because an index will slow down your write operations. There are configuration settings you can still make to speed up writes however.

If you have the opposite situation, and read performance needs to be fast, and writes are a small percentage of the load, then definitely create indexes. You can always measure your performance before and after, to make sure that your indexing decisions are valid.

*Note: Once your database is up and running and you are running code queries against it, you can get a diagnostic report on an individual database. This will tell you how well your index is performing. This is done by either using the* explain *option or the* explain() *method, depending on the API call you are making.*

# 5.2 Availability through Replication

A single point of failure is never good, no matter what service you are using. For example, in the days of the telegraph there might have only been a single telegraph line connecting two cities. That configuration creates a service that has a single point of failure. Cut the single line and communication is severed. Having two telegraph lines, would give you redundancy. It would also give you greater throughput if you put both into use at the same time.

The same redundancy is necessary with data stored on hard drives. Perhaps all of the family photos are on a hard drive. What if the hard drive fails? Doing backups to make copies is necessary. Any application data must never be at risk of being lost or being unreachable. Therefore, some form of data redundancy is necessary.

# MongoDB replica set

You can choose a single-node plan through mLab. If you have a single machine for your MongoDB database then when that goes down, you cannot access your database until it comes up again. This would be fine for occasional usage scenarios or for development experimentation.

MongoDB has the ability to configure what is called a replica set. This gives you multiple parallel, redundant copies of all data. This ensures that your data will be safe and available. This can be automatically configured as an option through the mLab portal.

In a replica set, you have multiple duplicated databases. Only one is designated as the primary one at any given time. If the primary database server goes offline, a secondary server will take over. The following diagram gives you a general idea of what this looks like:

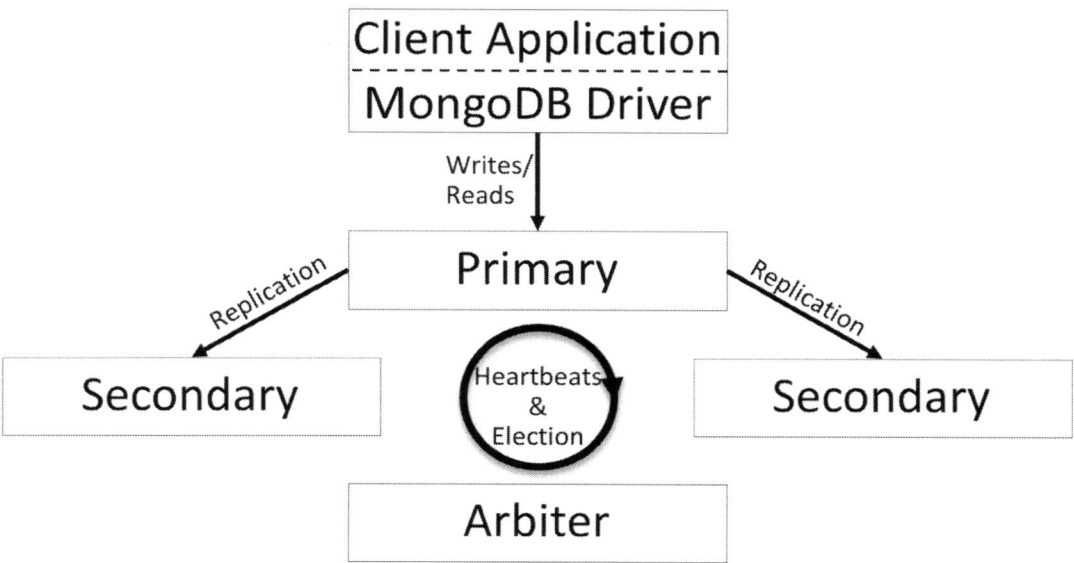

*Figure 18: MongoDB replica set*

The configuration will look slightly different based on which plan you select from mLab. The basic idea is that the primary database server receives and fulfills all read and write requests. All the while, the secondary database servers are kept up to date with all changes. The dedicated cluster plans from mLab on AWS will put each database server on its own dedicated EC2 virtual machine in different availability zones (if the region supports it).

Each server is constantly being checked with a heartbeat signal. If the primary database goes down, the two secondary servers and the arbiter would detect that, and one of the secondary servers would be switched over to become the primary database server. The arbiter is really just there to break any tie votes if needed.

*Note: With a PaaS solution, you do not have control over the replica set configuration unless you work with the provider to get something customized. There are pre-determined configurations you select when you purchase a plan. Nothing is preventing you from implementing an IaaS solution and setting up your own virtual machines and replica set configuration if that would work better for you.*

A replica set allows for faster reading of data because multiple copies exist and data can be fetched in parallel from each replica copy, if that is what you want. You can also designate reads to be fulfilled by secondary servers. Just be aware that you could get stale data that has not yet been updated by a replication process.

## Secondary consistency

There is a complication to be aware of in having replications available. Any write to the primary storage collection must eventually make it to all of the copies. Therefore, you have to make a choice as to how that replication is accomplished.

MongoDB has a setting called "write concern" that allows you to specify if you want a majority of replicas to report that the write has taken place before it is acknowledged or failed. You don't have to require this. If you don't, then all writes eventually make their way asynchronously to all replica database servers.

# 5.3 Sharding

The replication previously discussed stores the same data on multiple machines to provide emergency backup to ensure availability. Sharding also spreads data out across machines, but in the case of sharding, a given document appears in only one replica set of a cluster.

The purpose of sharding is really to allow you to grow the amount of data you can store and also increase the performance of operations. Both concepts of replication and sharding can actually be applied at the same time in an architecture. Sharding actually is just the increasing of the number of replica sets that you have as individual units.

The multiple replica sets in a cluster act as if they were one single collection. The sharding technology knows where to go for any given read or update to make it easy for you to use.

Sharding helps when you have really large data sets and are wanting to maintain high throughput. For example, you might have a lot of data constantly being accessed. This can become a bottleneck with a single SSD. If you distribute the load across multiple SSDs, then the CRUD operations would not conflict as much.

MongoDB can actually be set up to take care of everything for you. You can select a plan from mLab that has it all set up for you.

mLab has two categories of plans, one category called Single-Node and the other called Cluster. With the Single-Node plan, there is a hard limit with one single SSD block storage for your database, so you can only go up to a certain size and then you can't grow beyond that.

With the Cluster plan of mLab, sharding spreads the data across multiple replica sets. mLab cluster plans go up to a certain amount of storage once again. However, working with mLab support people, you can keep increasing the horizontal scaling of the sharding by adding more storage. Additional replica sets can in theory be added to accommodate your largest data storage needs.

# Reasons for sharding

The concept of data sharding (also called partitioning) was invented to help approach the ideal of being able to store an infinite amount of data and retrieve any part of it in a minimal amount of time. Let's dig a little deeper in into the scenarios that will cause you to implement a strategy for sharding. Here are some reasons to implement data sharding:

- **Running out of room:** With a limit to storage for a single database SSD, you might simply outgrow that capacity.

- **Machine performance:** There are utilization limits for RAM, CPU and SSD access loading that might be reached.

*Note: Using PaaS, you have the ability to choose a configuration with sharding already configured for you. In the case of mLab, you can pick a preconfigured machine architecture and then set up how your sharding will act. If you want to go the IaaS route, then you can configure this yourself.*

# How it works

Here is how sharding works. Imagine that you start out with a single MongoDB database server and on that server, you have a single collection. Each document you create could have a property that has a random capital letter chosen from A through Z. You might also set up an index on this letter property. A JSON document you might want to insert might look as follows:

```
{
    "letter": "G"
}
```

At this point, no matter what the letter property value is, all documents will be created in the same database collection. This example shows what this would look like:

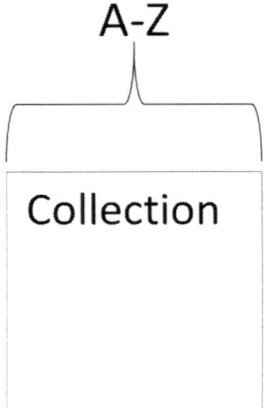

*Figure 19: Singe collection model*

Then, at some point, you realize that you need to add a whole lot more documents and want to achieve a higher level of throughput on your read and write access. The above single-node configuration can then be made into what is called a multi-node shared cluster.

MongoDB will start balancing documents between the available shards (replica sets) in the cluster to create a more evenly distributed storage. It actually does this in chunks. Even with additions and deletions of documents happening, MongoDB keeps it balanced. You can choose either a hash or a range strategy for you sharding.

Over time, your documents might end up being distributed over a three shard cluster if you chose a range strategy. See the following figure:

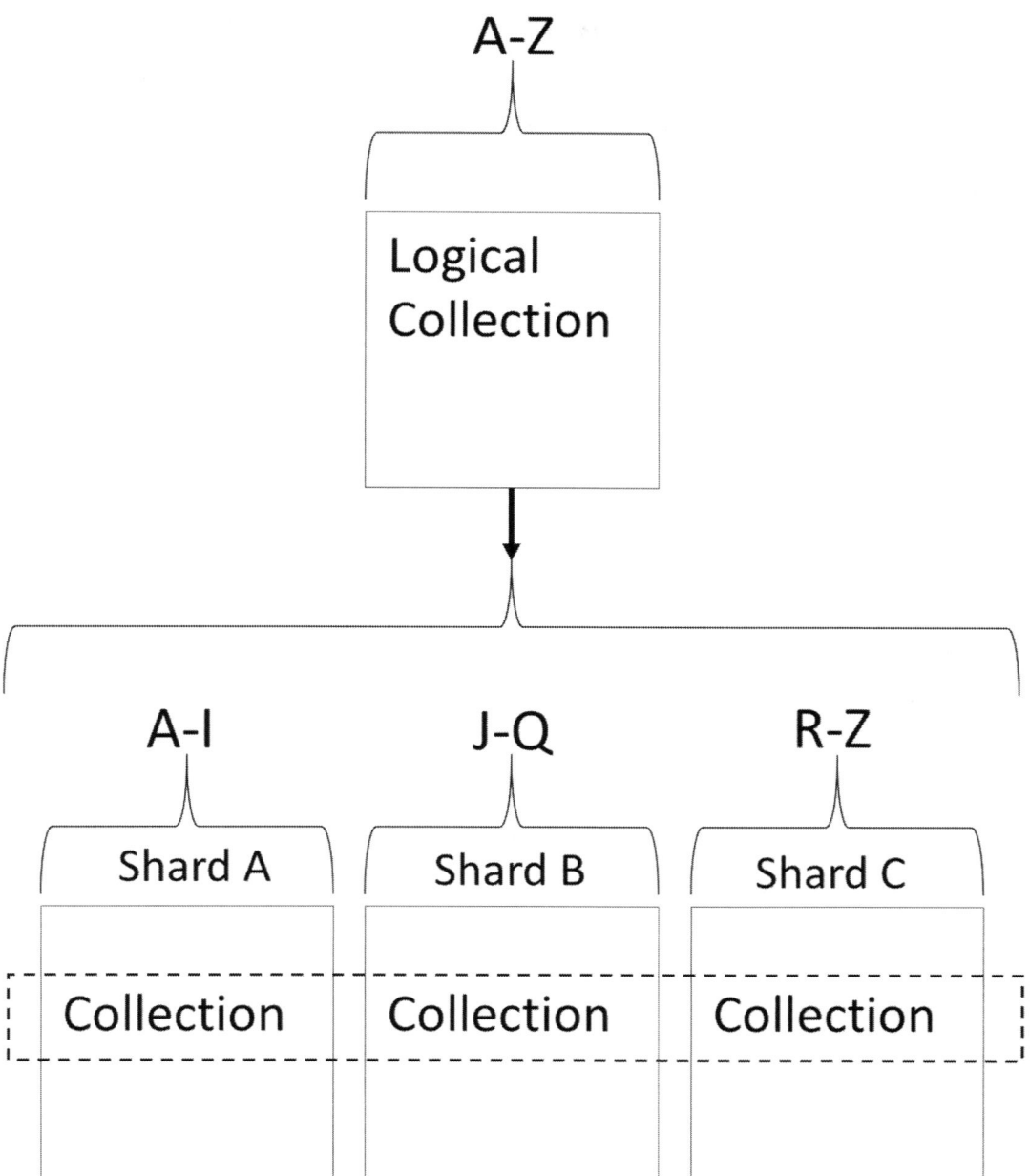

*Figure 20: Collection distributed over three shards*

As it turns out, each shard is a replica set. When a database request comes in to the cluster, MongoDB does all the work to route the request to the proper replica set shard. Your code is shielded from the fact that this is going on. This concept of having a logical collection really does all of the work for you to coordinate across the actual shards that have the real collections.

I won't go into the architectural diagram showing the components to set this up, but you can look it up online if you really want to implement an IaaS configuration on your own instead of using the PaaS solution. When you use the mLab PaaS solution, you would most likely enlist a support engineer to help you if you wanted to customize your sharded cluster.

There is also a way take shards away from your cluster. There is a mechanism to let MongoDB know that this is your intention. Once you do so, MongoDB begins migrating data off of the soon to be decommissioned shard. Once that is done, that shard can be freed up.

# Sharding key

Your shard must be set up with what is called a sharding key. A sharding key is similar to how an index is set up. With an index, you specify a property that you want to be used for a speedy lookup, using some determined algorithm, such as a range or a hash search.

Look at figure 20, and you will see three shards. The sharding key in this case, is the property that MongoDB will use to determine what shard each document exists in. For this example, it would have been the letter property.

Each document can only exist in one single shard. A shard key is thus used as a sorting property. So, if I created a document with the letter property set to 'M', it could be stored on the middle cluster because of the range strategy that was chosen.

There is a fair amount of work needed to select the proper sharding strategy and select a property to key off of. Just remember that you must know what your queries are going to look like. Don't forget that you might even have queries that cross shards, like those using range criteria. Imagine if you want documents from the prior example that had a letter greater than D and less than L? The shard service would actually know it needs to send the query to both the first and second shards and then your code would process all of the result set for what you want.

Indexes still exist on each shard, because they are just replica sets. The query lookup would first go to a shard and then the shard replica set would use the index there to find the document(s). You can have multiple indexes, but only one sharding key. The sharding key is always the same as one of the indexes. In our example, there was an index for the letter property, and that was also the property used for the sharding key.

If you had documents representing customers you could look people up by their last name. You could then use a hashed sharding key. That way, queries can narrow the location to one single shard and then quickly retrieve from that shard using the index. A hash shard key is

74

nice because it gives you uniform distribution of documents across shards. This is great for locating documents with a specific query that can zero in on the document. Range queries are not as performant with sharding. If you know you have good distribution of range values, then perhaps a range strategy would be best.

You also have to consider what your queries will look like and also what your document composition will look like. For example, a range type of query with a hash strategy causes all of the shards to be searched.

Also, if you used a range type of sharding strategy as in our example and all the documents had the values of "A" through "I" for the letter property, then all documents would end up in the same shard and you eventually run out of room. A given replica set still has a set amount of storage.

A hash strategy would of course try and spread those documents out. In either strategy, you still need to be careful and consider what the distribution will end up being.

If your query to the shared cluster does not actually utilize the shard key property, then the service has no choice but to send the query on to all shards in the cluster and then collect all of the results.

Like an index, a shard key can consist of multiple property names. You could thus use a compound key such as: last name, first name, and city. Shard keys cannot be created for a property that is an array.

# Chapter 6: NewsWatcher App Development

This chapter takes some of the concepts that you have learned and applies them in a project using the AWS hosted mLab PaaS offering to create a data layer. You will learn how to get the data layer up and running and learn some best practices along the way.

In this chapter, you will go to the mLab portal and create the MongoDB database and collection resources for the NewsWatcher sample application. To get started you must first have an active mLab account.

*Note: MongoDB is an open-source project and you could download it for free and run it on any machine you like. This is not the approach taken in this book. You can certainly investigate that option if it better meets your needs. There are also other MongoDB PaaS hosting options out there besides mLab, so do your research.*

You will be setting up the following resources:

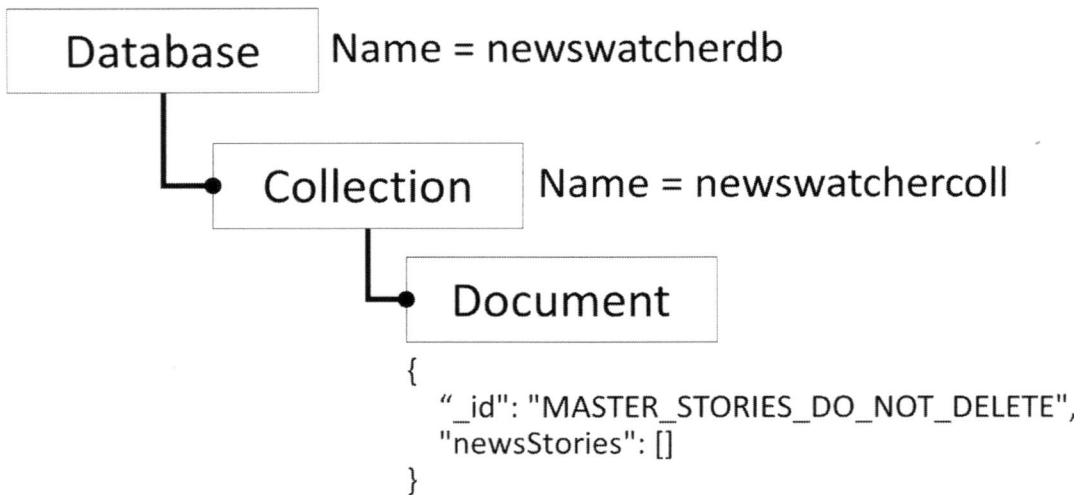

*Figure 21: NewsWatcher MongoDB resources*

The only document you will add to the collection right now is the one you should add manually. It is required for the functionality of the NewsWatcher. You could also manually add a few other documents just for testing purposes to try out queries. Later, you will see how documents will be added through code in your Node.js process.

*Note: Don't forget that you can access all of the code for the sample project at https://github.com/eljamaki01/NewsWatcherAWS.*

# 6.1 Create the Database and Collection

The first task will be to create the database. There are a few selections to make here. For the sample application, you can select the option that will give you free hosting. This will be fine for your development and testing purposes until such time that you need to scale for greater storage and performance.

You can also study the other configuration offerings available through mLab. You can even try them out, as you are only charged for the time you have them available, and you can easily delete them when you no longer want the charge.

It is certainly worth the cost to try out some of the other configurations that allow for other capabilities such as sharding. You might want to take some time to look through the plans and pricing pages on the mLab site to familiarize yourself with what is possible.

To create a database for the NewsWatcher app:
1. Open the mLab management portal website (https://mlab.com/home) and log into your account.
2. On your mLab management portal home page, click **Create new** to open the database creation page.
3. For **Cloud provider,** select **Amazon Web Services**.
4. Under **Location**, select the hosting location that will be nearest you, or in which you eventually want to host your Node.js services in.
5. Under **Plan**, click **Single-node**.
6. Under **Standard Line**, click **Sandbox**.
7. In the **Database name** box, enter "newswatcherdb" as the name of the database to create.
8. Click **Create new MongoDB deployment**.

Figure 22 shows you what the mLab console looks like at the time you choose to create a database.

# PART I: The Data Layer (MongoDB)

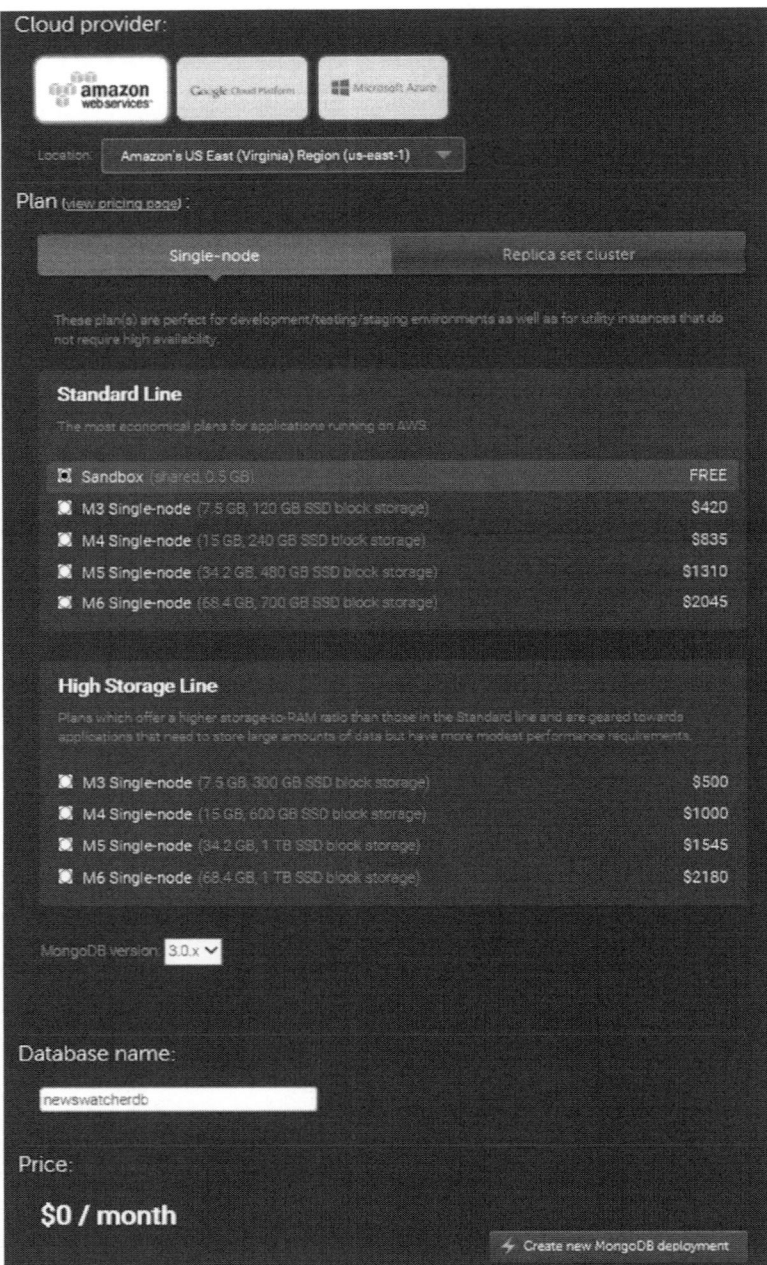

*Figure 22: Create database page, mLab management portal*

In a few moments you will be all set up and ready to start using your free MongoDB database from mLab hosted on an AWS EC2 machine.

The new database now shows up in your **MongoDB Deployments** list on the home page of mLab.

# Add a collection

Next, you need to create a collection inside of the newswatcherdb database as follows:

1. On your mLab management portal home page, click the newswatchedb database in the database list.
2. On the database page, click **Add Collection.**
3. In the **Collection Name** box, enter "newswatcher" as the name of the collection to create.
4. On the collection page, click **Create.**

The new collection will now show up in the collections list for the newswatcherdb database. You can click the collection and be taken to the following page:

*Figure 23: Create a document*

Now you can create the one required document that must be manually created. You will see later how this document fits into your data model. To create the document do the following:

1. Go to the newswatcher collection.
2. Click + **Add document**.
3. Type in the document content as follows, then click **Create and go back**:

```
{
    "_id": "MASTER_STORIES_DO_NOT_DELETE",
    "newsStories": []
}
```

You will see the document on the collection page after you click to create it.

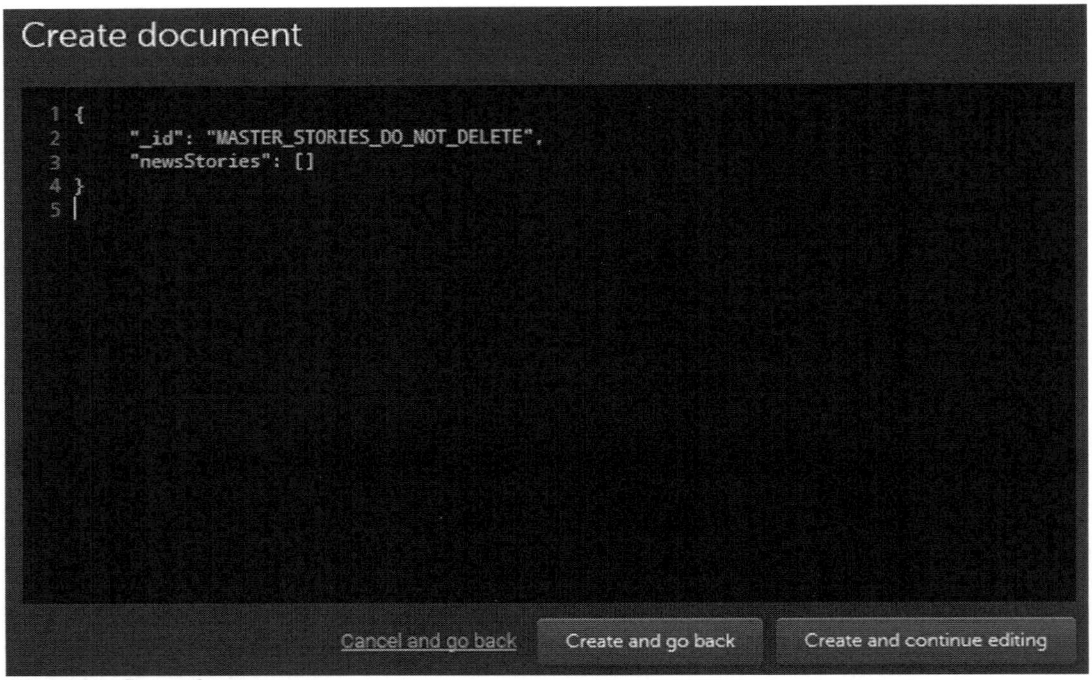

```
Create document

1 {
2     "_id": "MASTER_STORIES_DO_NOT_DELETE",
3     "newsStories": []
4 }
5 |

        Cancel and go back    Create and go back    Create and continue editing
```

*Figure 24: Create document*

That is it. Isn't PaaS wonderful?

# 6.2 Data Model Document Design

It is time to diagram out the structure and relationships of the document types that you will need for the NewsWatcher application. This is definitely an iterative process where refinements are made over and over until it is correct. Even after you have implemented a data model, you may find that it does not give you the performance you expected and you might end up altering the design.

Think again about what the requirements are for the NewsWatcher application and you can understand what is needed. You know NewsWatcher will have users that log in. Thus you have identified that there is a need for a user document.

There is also a single document that holds the master list of news stories. There will be some code that is run every few hours to collect news stories and store them there.

The third document type is for the news stories that users share and comment on. There would be multiple User and SharedStory documents, but only one MajorStories document. This model is completely denormalized, so there are no keys to link any documents together and there will not be a need for any type of join operations. The following diagram shows the needed documents:

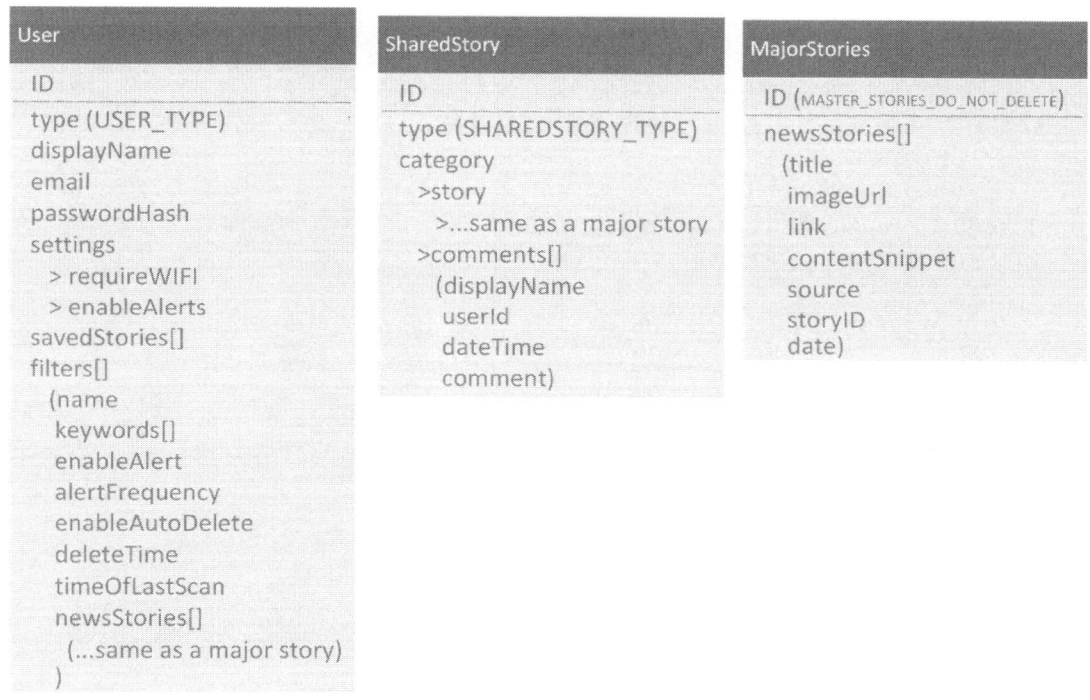

*Figure 25: NewsWatcher documents*

Let's look at what the User document contains. In there, you will want to include an email address for each user. This acts to uniquely identify your users and allows them to sign in. Users must also enter a password. You can safely store a hashed value of the password (you should never store a password in plain text). Then you can let users pick a display name that other users will see when a user comments on a shared story. You should never reveal their email to anyone else.

Next, there should be certain global values that can be used for user preference settings. You can put that in a sub-hierarchy called `settings`. For example, you will want to give users the option of not using any cellphone data plan and restrict the app to using Wi-Fi only.

You can assume that there will be some users that would like an alert feature for when news stories come in to be immediately notified. You can create a Boolean value for that.

The really compelling feature of NewsWatcher is the ability to have the app scan for the news a user cares about. NewsWatcher users are not the type that want to go to some general overall curated news page, but are interested in customizing their own specific filtered view of their news. This is done by filtering news stories with key words.

Users can set up as many filters as they like, so you can conclude that your design requires an array of filters. Each filter will need to contain a title for the filter, key words, time of the last news scan and a list of stories and their time of capture. The list of stories for a filter is populated by scanning the master story document newsStories array to see if there are any matches with the key words.

NewsWatcher has the ability to save off interesting stories so they appear separately. This is what the savedStories property is used for.

The other properties shown in the user document are for other features as outlined in the requirements.

This will give you a good start at a Minimum Viable Product to go out with. If you do a bit of advanced thinking, you can model all of this in your diagram now and just not implement everything yet. You can feel confident that your data model can accommodate your future needs.

# Entering some test data
At this point, you can open the page for the newswatcher collection and in that UI, add another document to the collection for testing things out:
1. On your mLab management portal home page, click the newswatchedb database in the database list.
2. On the database page, click **Collections.**
3. Click newswatcher in the collection list.
4. Click **Documents**, then click + **Add document**.
5. Type in the document content as follows, then click **Create and go back**:

```
{
  "type": "USER_TYPE",
  "displayName": "Bushman",
  "email": "nb@hotmail.com",
  "passwordHash": "XXXX",
  "date": 1449027434557,
  "settings": {
    "requireWIFI": true,
    "enableAlerts": false
  },
  "savedStories": [],
```

```
"filters": [
  {
    "name": "Technology Companies",
    "keyWords": [
      "Apple",
      "Microsoft",
      "IBM",
      "Amazon",
      "Google",
      "Intel"
    ],
    "enableAlert": false,
    "alertFrequency": 0,
    "enableAutoDelete": false,
    "deleteTime": 0,
    "timeOfLastScan": 0,
    "newsStories": []
  }
]
}
```

You will see the document and its automatically assigned _id show up.

For now, you can go ahead and experiment by creating a few more User documents in this same collection. Later, documents will only be added through code. At this point, all you are interested in is being able to test out some queries before developing the next layer of the application. You can get a feel for how the portal UI is used and also learn about how queries are constructed before you put those into code.

On the database page, if you click the **Tools** tab, you can see that there are ways to do bulk importing or exporting of documents.

# 6.3 Trying Out Some Queries

You might have entered a few documents by hand in the collection. You can now try out some queries against that data through the mLab management portal. At this point, you just want to get a feel for what the tool looks like and to also be ready to learn about how queries are constructed before you put those into the service layer code.

You will use the same **[new search]** UI shown in earlier chapters to run queries against your MongoDB collection. That is where you utilize the criteria syntax to query and project what you desire.

Try some queries like the following:

```
{"type": "USER_TYPE"}
{"type": "USER_TYPE", "email": "nb@hotmail.com"}
```

Now set the **Subset of fields** in the UI to be `{"displayName": 1}` and try the query again.

If your query syntax is incorrect, you will be notified of the error. However, if you mistype the name of a property you want to project or query for, you will not get an error but will get an empty result instead. For example, try the projection criteria property name as `{"blah": 1}`. If you do this, you will not get an error but will get an empty result set.

Keep in mind that MongoDB is a schema-less database and it assumes the blah property could be there in the future, but isn't there now. Properties can come and go in a schema-less document-based database.

# 6.4 Indexing Policy

You could write code to create your indexes. My approach is to not put things in code that are really one-time configurations, so I like to use the mLab management portal UI to create indexes.

For the NewsWatcher application, you can conclude that you will have a query in the service layer that will look up users by email. You need to add a specific index for that by doing the following:

1. On your mLab management portal home page, click the newswatchedb database in the database list.
2. On the database page, click **Collections.**
3. Click newswatcher in the collection list.
4. Click **Indexs**, then click **Add index**.
5. On the **Add new index** page, in the text box, type the following text:
   `{ "email" : 1 }`
6. Select the **Unique** check box.
7. Select the **Sparse** check box.
8. Click **Create in background**.

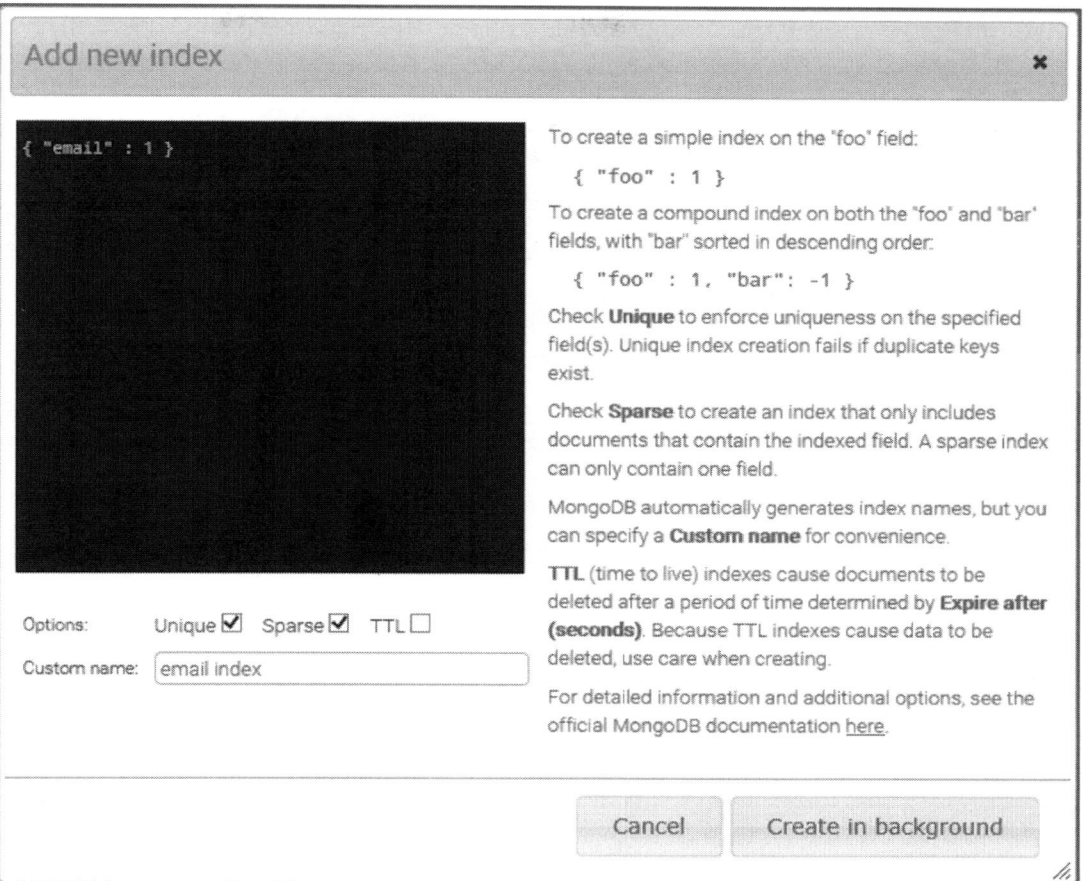

*Figure 26: Create new index page*

You have placed a check in the **Unique** check box as you don't want email addresses duplicated across users. This is a way to uniquely identify an account for a person. You have also checked **Sparse**, as documents that don't have this property will not ever be needed when you query by email, so they can be left out.

# 6.5 Moving On

That completes the work to get the data layer up and running. You can see that it was all about setting up your configuration through the mLab management portal. You did not need to write any code yet. This means that you are postponing the writing of any Node.js JavaScript server-side functionality until you work on the service layer.

# Testing

It is always a desirable practice to have tests in place for all the code you develop. In the case of the data layer, it could be reassuring to create a suite of tests that validate that your data model can support all the CRUD operations you could possibly think you might need.

For the NewsWatcher application, the service layer is the proving ground for the data layer. The service layer will connect directly to the MongoDB collection and perform CRUD operations. There will be functional tests put in place to really prove that your data model works. You will also be able to take care of the nuances that go along with your data layer, such as performance tuning and concurrency issues.

In reality, the best way to develop software is to work on it in terms of vertical slices of functionality. This means that for any features you have thought up, you would implement it in all three architectural layers at once.

# Chapter 7: DevOps for MongoDB

In this chapter, I will go over some of the data center operation responsibilities for managing a MongoDB database. For example, with NewsWatcher, you know that the data layer stores user accounts and news stories. You can think about what concerns you would have with that.

Daily DevOps work will involve the monitoring of the database. You can take a look at what the mLab management portal will let you monitor.

You will want to make sure that data access is secure and performant. You can set up replication, sharding, and indexes. Once those are set, you should leave them alone until some change comes along that causes you to tweak them for a specific reason.

# 7.1 Monitoring through the mLab Management Portal

One view you can look at is the view of machines in your database replica set. Here is a screen shot that shows all of the machines in a replica set:

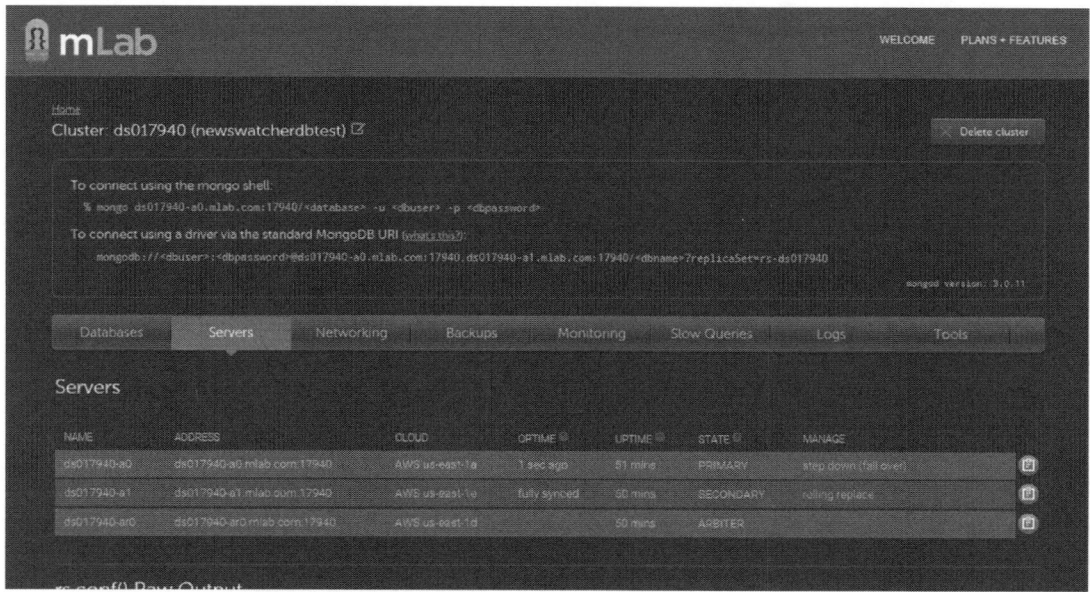

*Figure 27: mLab management portal server view*

# Telemetry charts

You can drill down further into the performance metrics of each of these machines by clicking on them. There are charts provided in the mLab management portal to show you the server utilization numbers and performance metrics. The real-time telemetry values will let you know things like how much storage you have used up. Be aware, though, that the mLab management portal's monitoring page is not available with the free sandbox plan.

You can create custom charts in the mLab management portal to view the overall performance metrics. Metrics can be multi-selected from a list so you can add the metrics that are important to you. There is a control you can press, labeled **NOW,** that lets you see immediate telemetry values that update every second.

If you prefer, you can also hook up the offering from New Relic to your mLab account so it can consume your telemetry data and utilize all of the New Relic capabilities to visualize it. Here is an image showing the mLab management portal monitoring page with the telemetry that is shown by default. In a replica set, you will have more than one machine, so you have a drop-down that lets you pick the primary or one of the secondary machines.

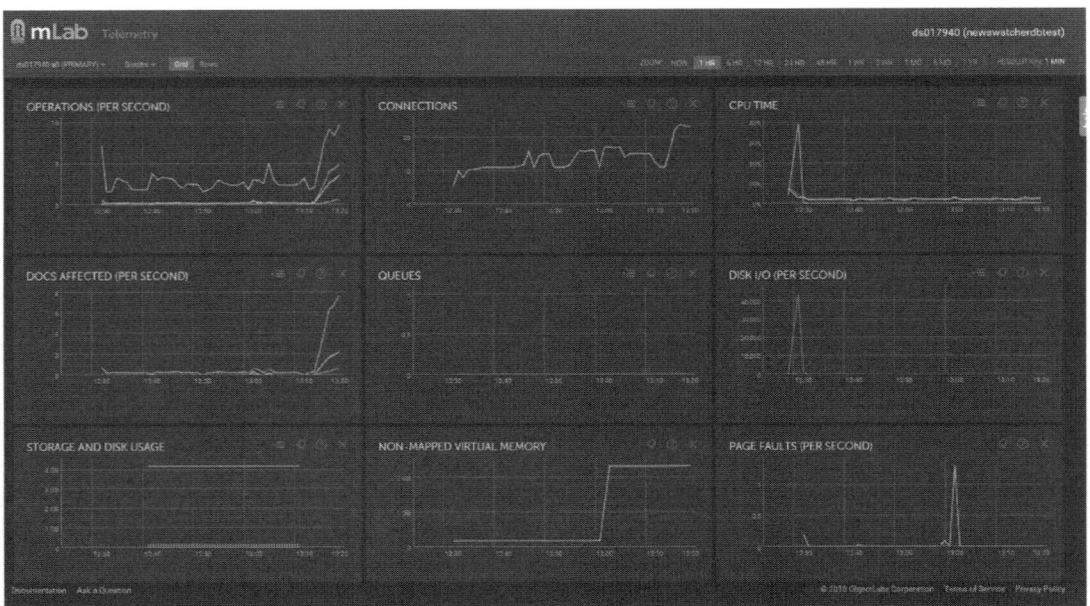

*Figure 28: mLab management portal telemetry page*

# Telemetry alerting

You probably want to be aware of how much storage is left for your database. You could set up an alert to notify you when you are reaching this limit. You might also be concerned about machine performance and set up some alerts around specific performance measurements. If you see your machine performance degrading, then you can shift to a higher tier of service with the PaaS plans offered by mLab.

For each metric in the telemetry chart page, you can click the little bell icon and create an alert based on that metric. If you go into your mLab account page and select the **Monitoring** tab, you can create additional selectable alert channels so that alerts don't always go through the same mechanism or to the same person. You can set up email, pager, and HipChat mechanisms. As of the writing of this book, mLab has announced that Webhook will soon be available as an alert mechanism.

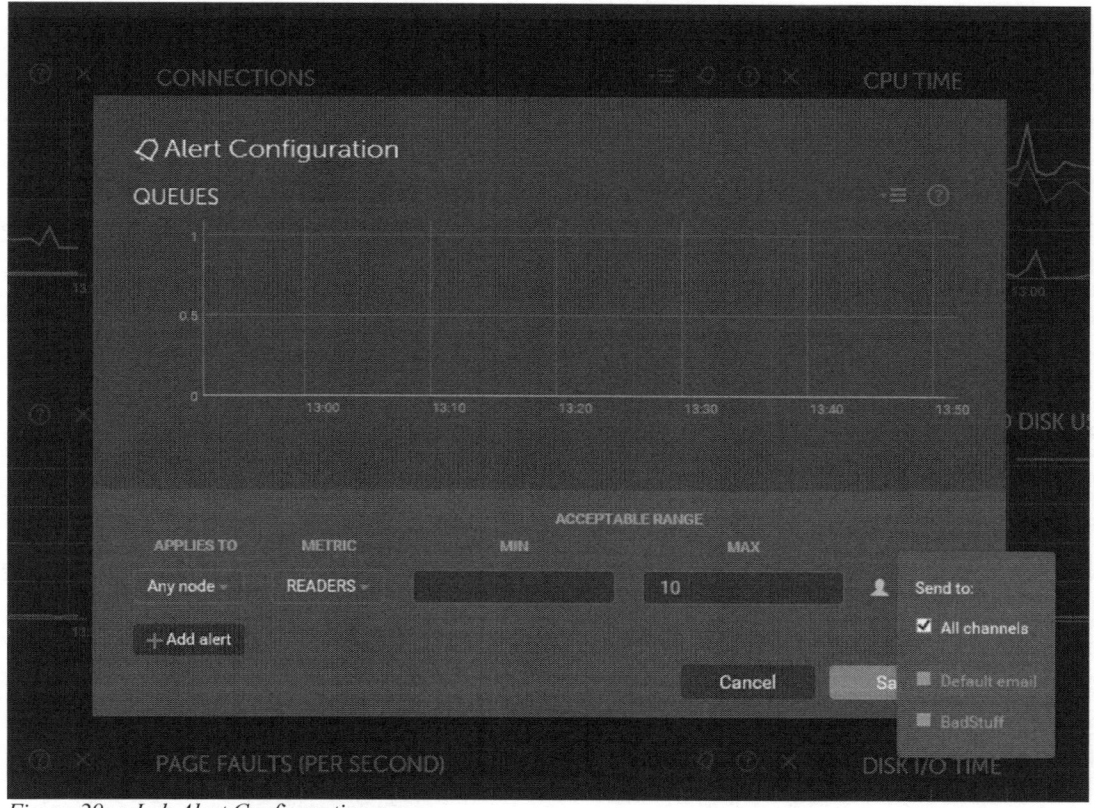

*Figure 29: mLab Alert Configuration page*

# Other tools

You can view the database server logs through the mLab management portal. There is also an overall status page you can open for an overview that might give you some idea of how healthy your database is in terms of data. Here is an example of that page:

89

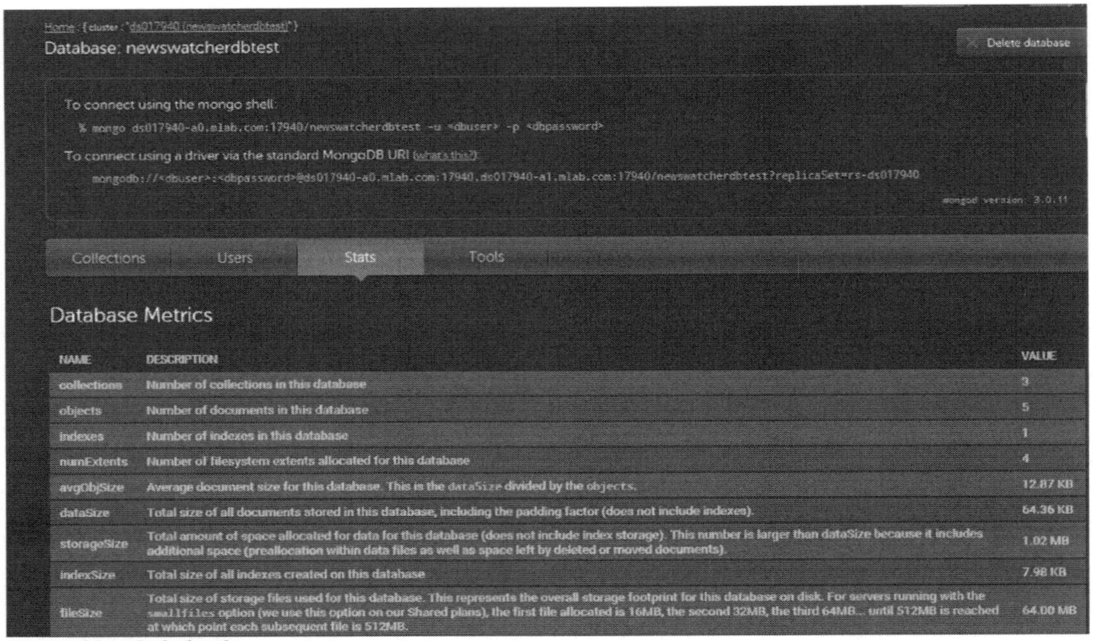

*Figure 30: mLab database statistics page*

mLab does some analysis on your queries and will give you suggestions for what you can do to improve your performance. Go to the **Slow Queries** tab to see the issues with the suggested solutions mLab is providing. In this example, you can see a suggestion to create an index in response to a slow query. There is even a link to click to create the suggested index.

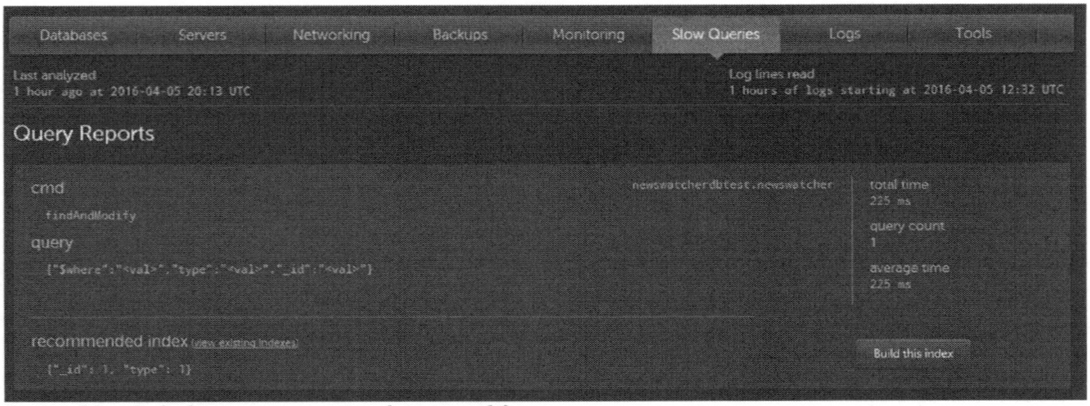

*Figure 31: mLab slow query report and suggested fix*

If you want a more detailed analysis, you can enable the database profiler for a period of time and see what information it gathers. Make sure to turn it off when you are done, as it slows everything down.

# 7.2 The Blame Game

Once your data is secure and has been tuned for the best performance, you really don't need much in the way of day-to-day care anymore. Believe me though when I say this – your potential troubles are not over by any means. From my experience, you will be spending your time caring for the integrity of the data as much as anything else. This is especially true if there are a lot of other systems integrating in with yours that touch the data at some point.

Unfortunately, every time someone sees a data corruption problem, they come to blame whoever is in charge of the DBMS. You will hopefully have confidence that most of the time the accusations are unwarranted and you will be able to track the problem down to some supporting system. For example, some external system that is feeding you data may suddenly have missing or corrupt data. It is a good idea to put data validation measures into place at all the points of integration.

You would also be wise to put some handy scripts into place to allow you to diagnose issues and fix them. For example, you might need to recover data from a backup snapshot, or reimport data in bulk from a dependent system.

# 7.3 Backup and Recovery

The good news is that you don't have to worry about disaster recovery. The bad news is that you have to worry about disaster recovery. It all depends on what your definition of "disaster" is.

With a replica set in place, MongoDB stores multiple copies of your data that are always in sync with the primary server. This means that, within a region, you have redundancy in case of network or drive failures. This is the case with the different AWS availability zones that each EC2 server is in for your replica set. You have this set up for you through the PaaS plan you select and don't necessarily have to deal with it directly yourself.

This replication means that your data is safe from drive failures, machine reboots, power outages, network outages, and such. If the drive that the primary copy of your MongoDB database is on goes bad, you are covered. MongoDB and AWS will take care of rotating this drive out and moving you to a new primary drive and adding a new replacement backup.

## You still need backups

Data replication is not the same as performing a data backup. Just because you have replication does not mean you are protected from somehow loosing or mangling your own data by mistake. It is a good idea to institute a backup process to periodically store a snapshot of all your data. That way you are able to recover from inadvertent corruption or loss of your data.

Backups are useful in many scenarios. For example, you might have some bug that was introduced in your code that causes all of your data to get corrupted. You then need to roll back to the database copy you had before the data was corrupted.

You could, for example, write some code to copy data from one MongoDB region into another region and keep that as a backup.

You could also save a collection as a file for safe-keeping on some local machine you have, or place it in EBS storage. Then you can do a restore programmatically or use a tool to import everything from your snapshot. You can export a JSON file and store it yourself if you don't want to spend the money on database collections or other online storage being used for backups.

The mLab management portal has a **Backups** tab that lets you create an immediate backup, or to schedule a time each day for one to automatically happen. The core MongoDB project has backup utilities you could also use. With a dedicated plan though mLab, you get the ability to do a file system (block-level) backup. These types of snapshot backups are much faster to create and to do a restore with.

# PART II: The Service Layer (Node.js)

Part two of this book will teach you what a service layer is. You will create an HTTP/Rest API to hook up to the data layer and then be prepared for when you will have the presentation layer client to connect up to it.

Node.js/Express.js and JavaScript are the technologies of choice for the service layer.

There are many decisions that go into creating a service layer. The very first part is to plan for what type of interface is needed over the data. This involves separating out the different types of data that your REST interface will expose, along with the JSON payloads that get transferred back and forth for each request.

You will use Amazon Web Services (AWS) to host your Node.js application and will be able to make use of a Node module to call into the MongoDB data layer you developed in the first part of this book. At the end of this part, the application will be fully functional and ready to integrate with the presentation layer.

The extremely important topic of testing will be covered and you will learn how to use the Mocha test framework to run your tests with. You will learn about functional as well as performance load testing.

In order to give full coverage to the topic, I will also discuss what it means to set up all aspects of the day-to-day operations of Node.js for actual data center operations management. You will learn how to manage and also do some debugging. Security will be an important topic that is covered.

*Note*: *Many people refer to Node.js simply as Node, and I often do the same.*

# Chapter 8: Fundamentals

This chapter presents the fundamental concepts of the middle-tier of the three-tier application architecture that is being outlined for you in this book. I will teach you what the middle-tier is typically composed of and what capabilities are essential. I can then get into the specifics and show you how Node.js can host a middle-tier service layer.

# 8.1 Definition of the Service Layer

The service layer provides the core capabilities of a three-tier architecture. The whole idea of a service layer is to build an abstraction layer over business logic and data access.

If you really simplify down the concepts of a three-tier architecture, you can say this about the lower and upper layers - the lower data layer just stores data and the upper presentation layer just shows stuff. That leaves the middle-tier service layer to do all of the real work. For the NewsWatcher application, you will certainly find more code in the service layer than in the other layers. The following diagram shows this simple view:

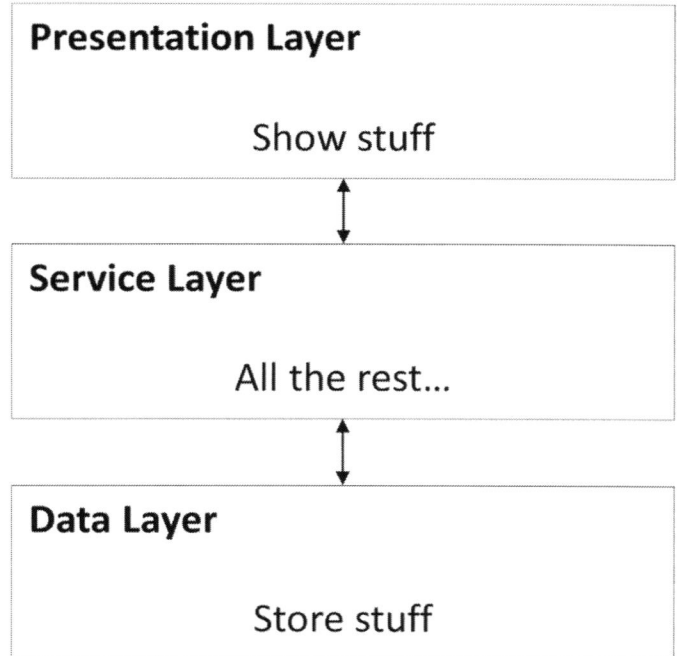

*Figure 32: Simplified three-tier architecture diagram*

It would not be reasonable to have the presentation layer handle the business workflow logic. You also do not want to expose business workflows in the data layer either. The data layer should be kept as simple as possible and should only handle the CRUD operations. This is why you will find the more complex business services code in the services layer.

*Note: Some architectures split the middle-tier out into a services and a business layer. These two concepts are combined in this book. You will find that all the needed functionality can be accomplished within the single technology framework of Node.js.*

# A contract of interaction

A service layer can actually be created with no particular UI in mind. For example, there are major companies that expose their APIs so that anyone can interface with their backend and write their own UI. Companies like eBay, Twitter, and Facebook have been successful at this. For example, you can interact with the eBay API to bid on items.

In the case of the NewsWatcher sample application, there is just one single UI that I wrote, but anyone else could actually write a different UI on top of the exposed Rest API.

Regardless of whether you are tied to one single front-end UI, or if your service layer is more open to allow many applications to connect, you need to think in terms of a strict contract of interaction. This means you must define the connection routes up front and the JSON messages that are required.

I will not be using any specific connection standard like you see with standards such as SOAP. You should explore things like Swagger on your own if you are interested in making your API generally available for people in an easy to consume and formal way. AWS has an offering known as API Gateway that can surface a formal API contract and sit in front of your Node.js service layer.

# An abstraction layer

The service layer should be built in a way that abstracts away the complexity that goes on in the back end. This will shield the presentation layer client-side code from any tight coupling. The client is also protected from any backend rework. In many cases the client doesn't even need to make any changes, when backend code is rewritten.

It may be, that a single call to the service layer results in a series of backend calls that are each processed in what can be called a workflow. This coordination falls squarely in the service layer to hide most complexities. The multiple backend services comprise your overall architecture and can be unified through a single Node.js entry point.

For example, you might have one service that does all of the storage and retrieval for user account information. Another service might contain billing account information, and yet another might deal with order information. You should never build one huge monolithic enterprise service that does everything. Do the work to split up your platforms into discreet services that each serve a role, are self-contained, and operate independently. Research what is called a microservices architecture.

This does not mean that external clients need to authenticate and connect to each of the microservices individually. The presentation layer should have only one single service layer entry point that coordinates calls to other independent microservices that each exist as autonomous services. You will actually be grateful you have done this, as you can make rather significant changes in the lower layers and minimize the code that has to change in the client.

You backend might already consist of "legacy" systems that were not written with Node. These backend systems might be written in different languages and be running on your own proprietary, on-premise platforms. In this case you can decide to write a gateway service layer with Node and have Node hook up to your backend systems. Node is great at routing and orchestration. It can parallelize work to process requests asynchronously.

All or part of your systems can have their own Node.js interfaces. It is up to you to decide what is worth your time and investment to do. The following diagram illustrates the gateway layering that could exist in the services layer:

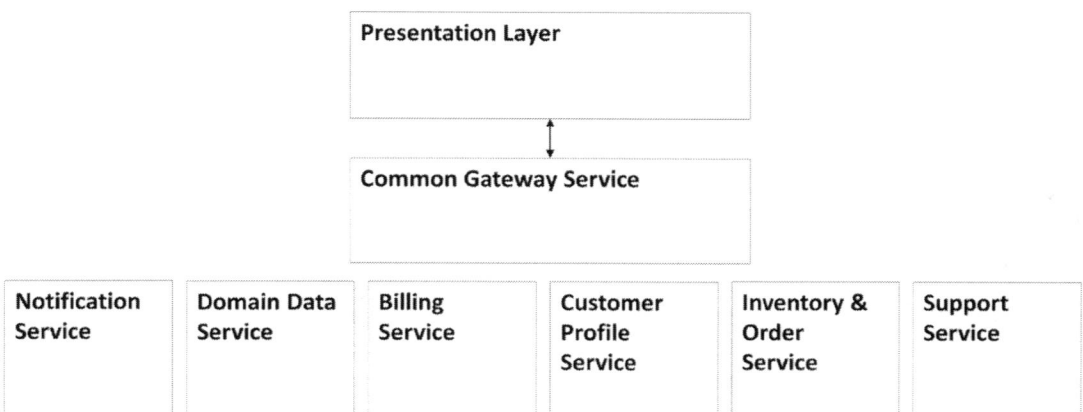

*Figure 33: Service layer gateway concept*

Now, if you have to replace the billing system, the gateway service provides the abstraction and protects the client from any changes.

## Service layer planning

Knowing what operations and workflows are needed is the first step in creating a service layer. The following questions are useful to help you determine the design of a service layer:

- What operations and workflows are needed?
- What are your security and privacy requirements?
- How are people authorized and tracked from one call to another?
- Is there a need for a pub/sub notification system to deliver push notifications?
- Is there any type of domain-specific configuration required?
- Is programmatic resource management required? Scripting or templates?
- Are all data interactions encrypted?
- Are multiple systems going to call into this? Would a message contract schema be appropriate?
- What validation can be made at the interface to not let anything invalid in?
- What meaningful errors need to be returned?
- Do you need user roles and access control?
- Is there any periodic processing of the data? Is it periodic in the background or real-time? In batches?
- What are the SLA requirements for all operations?
- What is the access volume and the rates per time period?
- Will there be bursts of activity or is access evenly distributed?

The answers to these questions should be carefully considered. Consult experts along the way before you roll anything out into a full production environment.

# 8.2 Introducing Node.js

The simplest way to describe Node.js is to say that it is a runtime that executes JavaScript code that you provide it. You might think I just described a browser environment for you. After all, this is what the Chrome browser can do. The Chrome browser has a JavaScript engine called V8 that is used for executing client side JavaScript code.

Node.js however is running on the server. To accomplish this, someone actually took the same V8 engine mentioned and made use of it in a server-side process and then added additional functionality that would only make sense to have running in server code.

You can think of Node as an abstraction layer on top of your operating system so as to make your code run and be platform independent and still get at many of the capabilities that an operating system has. Node.js provides the overall runtime execution environment.

# Platform independence

Let me put it this way - you could go and write an application in C++ for Windows that implements a web service to listen to and respond to requests and interact with the file system on the machine it is running on. But what would you have to do to take that application and make it run on Linux? You would have to port it of course.

To get that to run on a Linux OS, you would port your code to use those system calls. This image shows that you would be writing your code over and over for each platform.

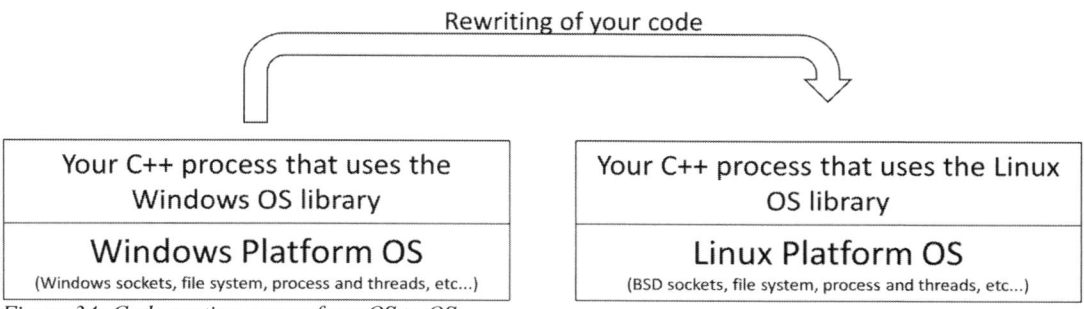

*Figure 34: Code porting across from OS to OS*

Node lets you write your application code once and then Node handles the lower level porting of Operating System level calls for you. Node.js acts to abstract away the platform OS capabilities. Not only that, but Node allows you to write all of your code in JavaScript!

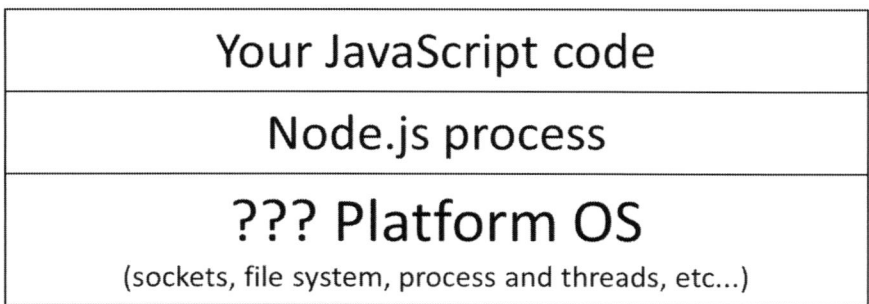

*Figure 35: Writing code once*

Node.js is an open-source project and has been ported to run on many different operating systems. Much of the core code of Node.js is written in C/C++ to enable native integration with underlying operating systems and achieve the fastest possible performance. It also utilizes the Google V8 engine to execute JavaScript. V8 actually compiles client JavaScript to native machine code, such as for x86 machine architectures, for faster execution.

Node.js is well-suited for network based I/O applications. Using Node, it is extremely simple to piece together a web server similar to IIS or Apache. You can easily set up a web service to expose an HTTP/Rest API that works with JSON payloads. Node really fulfills a lot of purposes that allow it to satisfy all of the requirements of a middle-tier service layer.

# Extensibility of Node

Ultimately, the real power of Node comes through its extensibility. Node was written to provide the core runtime of execution, scheduling and notification capabilities. Its functionality is then greatly increased through the many extension modules written for it. For example, there are modules for functionality such as WebSockets, data caching, database accessing, asynchronous processing, authentication, and many others.

Node is being widely adopted and people are constantly improving upon it and creating new modules. There is a large community of developers that has generated many extremely useful modules to give rich functionality to your application. Since the patterns of using these modules are all the same, it is extremely easy to consume them without a huge learning curve.

# JavaScript bliss

Since Node.js executes JavaScript, there is a consistency throughout the application stack that you are building. JavaScript design patterns are utilized in the construction of modules that become the self-contained components that are available to consume. You can download and integrate those offered by others as well as create your own.

There are also unit-testing frameworks that work with the JavaScript language that you will use to test your Node.js service layer.

JavaScript can now be recognized as more than just a client-side scripting language. It is now a formidable server-side language, as implemented with Node.js.

*Note: Lest I get a slew of emails accusing me of living in a fairytale, I will make a brief comment on the sensibility of using JavaScript in enterprise applications. It is true that JavaScript can be a challenge in respect to delivering on quality. Perhaps a lot of this will be addressed in the coming years as the JavaScript language evolves. Today, however, with proper design patterns and testing, you can create large enterprises services of superb quality with Node.js and JavaScript.*

# 8.3 Basic Concepts of Programming Node

A simple Node program that you can write would be one that outputs text to the terminal process window. The following is an example of what this would look like:

```
console.log("Hello World");
```

You can type this into a file, save it to disk, and then have the Node process execute it. If you had Node installed, you could open a command prompt and type the following, substituting the name of your file for *<filename>*.

```
node <filename>.js
```

If you haven't already, you should go ahead and install Node on your machine at this time. Go to https://nodejs.org/. You should see a download labeled "LTS" and another labeled "Current". You want the LTS version as that is the stable one. The other one is from the latest code and has not been sufficiently proven. These downloads are being updated from time to time.

Go ahead and create a file named server.js, place the `console.log("Hello World");` line in it and run node as shown with this file as an argument. You need to be in the same directory as your file.

You will also notice that the process does not stay running. In this case, once your code in your file has been executed, the process exits. This does not have to be the case, and I will soon explain what would cause a Node application to keep running and be able to continually perform server side processing such as web requests.

## The REPL

Node has several different options to control how it runs. If you were to leave off the JavaScript file, Node would default to what is called REPL mode. REPL is the mode where you get a prompt and can enter JavaScript to be executed as you type it in. REPL stands for Read Evaluate Print Loop and is a common thing for execution frameworks to provide. For example, MongoDB provides something similar with what is called the Mongo Shell.

In this book, you will only need to be concerned with the main means of invoking Node as shown already with your JavaScript file as an argument.

# Node executes your standard JavaScript

Here is another file to try. This one illustrates a bit more code that you could have Node execute. Running this will result in "HI THERE 343" being displayed:

```
var x = 7;
var s = "Hi there";

function blah(num, str) {
    if (num == 0) {
        return "Can't do that";
    }
    return str.toUpperCase() + " " + Math.pow(num,3);
}

var result = blah(x, s);

console.log(result);
```

This illustrates the basic JavaScript language capabilities that you can execute. If you look at the JavaScript specification, you would see all that is possible. You have datatypes, operators, structured programming logic control, built-in objects and much more.

Be careful though on what you assume is available in JavaScript just because you have programmed browser scripts before. For example, there is a function named `setTimeout()` that you might assume is a part of the core language of JavaScript. This is not the case. This is where browser implementations have added functionality to JavaScript.

The `setTimeout()` function is indeed provided, but it is actually implemented through the Node.js layers and not the JavaScript language itself. This is also true for the `console.log()` function.

As was mentioned, the Node process will run and exit upon execution of your lines of code. This is because Node.js will only run while it knows it has code to execute. Try running the following code:

```
while(true){
  console.log("Hello World");
}
```

You will have to press **<Ctrl> C** on your keyboard, or close the window to stop the Node.js process. Later, you will see code that requires Node.js to run forever because it has been set up to respond to events that could perpetually happen.

# Using built in modules

As was explained, Node extends the basic capabilities of JavaScript by providing a set of built-in modules. There are quite a few of them, and you can review them if you go to https://nodejs.org/en/docs/. Click on an API version on the left to see the list of modules. You will see things in the list such as HTTP, Net, OS, Crypto, File System, Console and Timers.

You can now see how to use the Node.js provided `console.log()` and `setTimeout()` functions. Here is some sample code that takes advantage of these added capabilities:

```
setTimeout(function () {
  console.log('World!');
}, 1000)

console.log('Hello');
```

If you are not familiar with how `setTimeout()` works, you have to be aware that this schedules your callback function to run some number of milliseconds in the future. Thus, the string `Hello` prints first and then one second later you see `World!`.

Let's now look at how simple it is to create an HTTP Web server with code that Node would execute. The following example is all the code that it takes if you use the built in HTTP module:

```
var http = require('http');

var server = http.createServer(function (request, response) {
  response.writeHead(200, {"Content-Type": "text/plain"});
  response.end("Hello World\n");
});

server.listen(3000);
```

If you were to execute this with Node on your local machine, you could then open a browser and navigate to http://localhost:3000/ and see your `Hello World` message appear.

The only non-obvious line of code is the very first one. This is a function defined in Node.js that you call to load the http module that provides the web server capability.

Node uses the concept of modules as its extensibility mechanism and the `require()` function simply returns an object with functions and properties placed on it that are specific to that module for you to use. In this case, you call `require('http')` and get an object, and then use the `createServer()` function from that object.

Some things like the `setTimeout()` function are made available globally without you needing a `require()` statement.

# Using external modules

In some programming languages and runtimes, you mostly rely on what comes built in. For example, this is the case with the combination of C# and .Net. In Node, however, you will constantly be looking for external modules to add to your application to give you all of your capabilities. As a matter of fact, since there are so many of these external modules provided online, you will need to become good and how to best search for something and then determine what the best option is.

There is a package manager site you can go to for searching and downloading modules. Go to https://www.npmjs.com/ to take a look. Be aware that some of what is found in NPM are actually the code modules you can use, while others are actually tools you can download and run, such as the testing tool called mocha.

When the NPM modules are utilized, the layers of code now looks as follows:

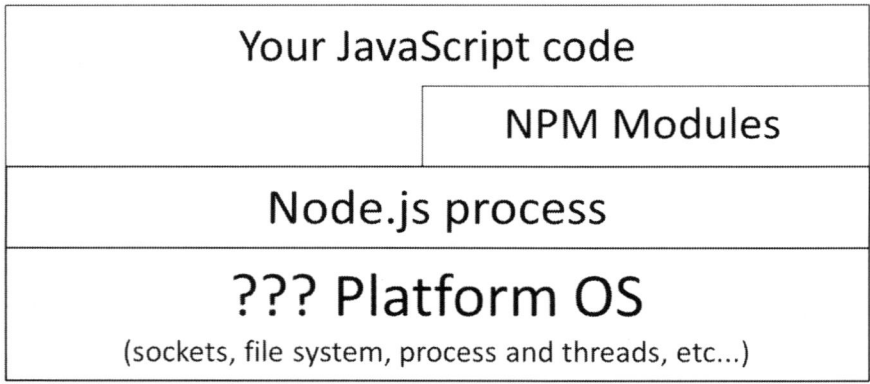

*Figure 36: Adding NPM modules to the architecture*

This gives you the highest level view of the different blocks of code.

In order to use additional external modules from NPM, you need to have them installed alongside your JavaScript file. There are two steps needed to accomplish the usage of an NPM code module:

1.  Create a file named package.json.
2.  Run the command "`npm install <module> --save`" for each module you want to use.

Running the npm install command will actually add a line in your package.json file. The very first time you run it in a directory, a folder named node_modules is created. If you look in that folder, you will see all of the module code. When you run Node with code that requires one of these modules, Node will be able to find them.

You can try the steps now by creating the package.json file with the following lines in it:

```
{
  "name": "test",
  "dependencies": {
  }
}
```

Now run the following command:

```
npm install async --save
```

After running this, your package.json file will look as follows:

```
{
  "name": "test",
  "dependencies": {
    "async": "^1.5.2"
  }
}
```

Look at the new folder created named node_modules. You will see the async module files installed there.

There is a convention in the package.json file for listing modules. The name is listed followed by the version you desire. You can specify an exact version, or you can specify just the major number and have NPM get the latest minor version. The versioning required is flexible.

If you actually add dependency modules in your package.json file by hand and specified the exact version, you could then run the install command. NPM will install the latest version for what version numbering you specify. This is what you run if you edit package.json first and then want to install the modules you edited in:

```
npm install
```

It is typical for developers to stick with a known good working version for all of their versions of modules and not update to any new major versions even when they become available. When you feel you need some new capability of a newer major version, then do an update and do extensive testing of everything again.

Here is another code sample you can run. It makes use of the async module. Put this code in your server.js file:

```
var async = require('async');
var fs = require('fs');

async.eachSeries(['package.json','server.js'], function(file, callback) {
  console.log('Reading file ' + file);
  fs.readFile(file, 'utf8', function read(err, data) {
    console.log(data);
    callback();
  });
}, function(err){
    if( err ) {
      console.log('A file failed to load');
    } else {
      console.log('All files have been successfully read');
    }
});
```

You will learn more about the async module at a later time. This is basically using async to sequence through an array of values and do what processing you want on each entry in sequence.

Note that you are using the fs module. You don't need to run an install or list the fs module in the package.json file. This is because this module is part of Node.js, but you still need the require statement. Now, if you run node server.js, you will see the contents of your files printed out.

*Note: Deployment of your Node.js application is easy. You can just copy everything, including the node_modules directory, to some cloud machine. I will later go over the usage of a PaaS hosted environment. When you use a PaaS environment install, such as with AWS Elastic Beanstalk, you will see that you don't need to copy the node_modules directory. AWS will run an npm install for you and have that created.*

# Callbacks and concurrent processing

You have seen Node code that uses the callback style of coding. This style is prevalent with everything you do in Node. The Node.js library provides for these non-blocking asynchronous callbacks. Your code never blocks, but returns immediately and then at some later time, the callback function is executed. This gives you the concurrent execution speed that Node is famous for.

To start with you need to understand that there is just one main thread of execution in your program. This is the thread that starts up your application and begins execution of your

JavaScript. From there, Node.js sends all of your code to the V8 JavaScript VM engine, or OS ported calls to begin its execution.

Everything at the highest level of your JavaScript takes up processing time on a single thread. Only one thing can happen there at a time, so you need to be sure that it is not compute intensive.

**Note:** *VM stands for Virtual Machine and is a concept that V8 uses to isolate JavaScript execution. Don't confuse this definition of a VM with a VM that you find hosted in AWS or Microsoft Azure.*

# Code execution flow

Code execution is interesting to trace through. I will now explain a bit of how this all works. Look at the following code that will be used to help understand the execution flow for your JavaScript code:

```
var x = 7;
var s = "Hi there";
var fs = require('fs');

function blah(n, s) {
   if (n == 0) {
      return "No";
   }
   return s.toUpperCase() + " " + Math.pow(n,3);
}

console.log(blah(x, s));

fs.readFile('package.json', 'utf8', function(err, data) {
   console.log(data);
});
```

If this code is in your server.js file and you execute it on the command line as `node server.js` your execution looks as shown in figure 37. You can see the code boundary crossing. You can also see that almost everything is non-blocking. At a lower level, there is a thread in Node that does end up being blocked, but this thread does not affect you at all. Your code still has the callback that is asynchronously called, but you are not blocked on it.

In the illustration the execution time moves left to right. I have illustrated the boundary between your main JavaScript thread and the Node.js framework with Libuv. The upper part is your code being executed in the V8 VM.

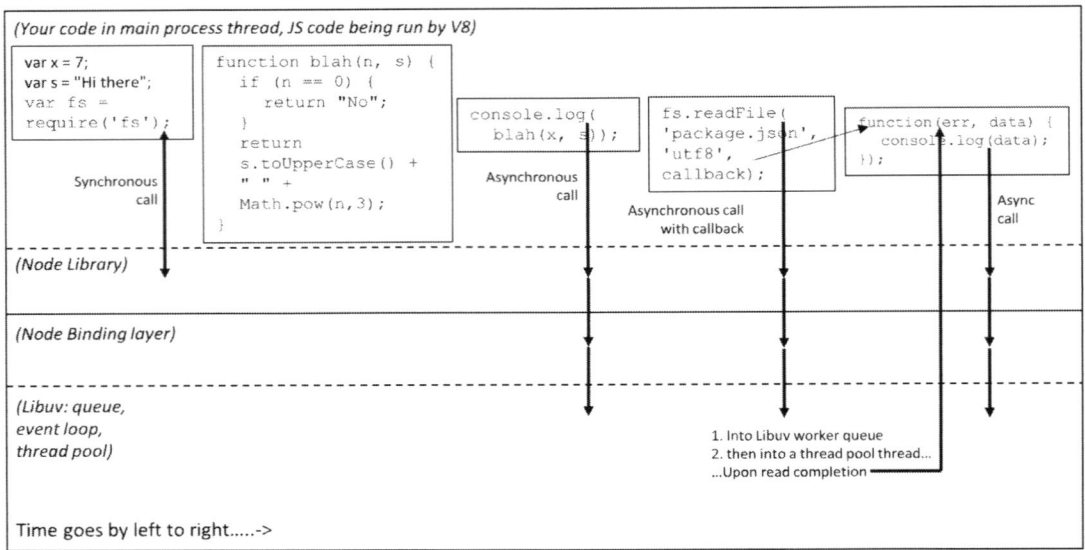

*Figure 37: Code execution flow*

Follow left to right and you see how each bit of code is run. The require() function blocks. The console.log() call does not block your code and does not process a callback, so the main thread continues on. The lower layer will asynchronously print out the value. The JavaScript Math.pow() object function executes in V8 and not in the Libuv layer.

The fs.readFile() call uses an asynchronous callback to keep your upper layer code non-blocking. You can see the third parameter to the readFile() function is a function callback. The Node.js framework starts executing readFile() for the first bit of code, but the Node.js code is just calling into Libuv to hand off the request to be executed on its thread pool. This then immediately frees up your call.

The Libuv execution thread for the file I/O eventually returns and then the anonymous function eventually gets called and runs on the main thread. You cannot get access to the thread pool processing directly from your JavaScript code.

Filesystem calls go to the thread pool of Libuv. Network calls don't as will be explained later. Libuv does all of the work for you to make things work across platforms and in a non-blocking way. You can see that the main processing thread is not blocked and your callback will execute in an asynchronous concurrent manner.

# Continuous processing with Node

Another concept that you need to be introduced to is that of how Node might be running in a continuous processing loop. As shown, the previous code sample runs to completion and then the Node process exits. This is because Node knows if there is any more work to execute and if there isn't any it just exits.

You can understand that there are certain modules you can use that will basically keep the Node process running forever. If this is the case, you can stop the process as you would normally do on your OS.

You saw code earlier that had a while loop that never had any way to exit. That example would be a little odd, since it runs all of the time, and completely blocks the single processing thread. A more reasonable piece of code would be something that uses an interval timer to do some periodic computation. Here is some simple code that keeps Node running:

```
setInterval(function () {
  console.log('Hello again!');
}, 5000)

console.log('Hello World!');
```

There is actually something similar to what the NewsWatcher code does. NewsWatcher will need to run some processing work on a periodic basis.

Another thing that will keep your process running forever would be the use of modules such as HTTP, Net or Express. When you set up code to listen for TCP connections and listen on a socket, you set up code that will run in the lower level of Libuv. Take the following example that was used once before:

```
var http = require('http');

var server = http.createServer(function (request, response) {
  response.writeHead(200, {"Content-Type": "text/plain"});
  response.end("Hello World\n");
});
server.listen(3000);
```

What happens here is that Libuv is set up to use the low level OS socket capabilities to listen and respond to incoming connections and requests. Libuv then has a loop to respond to any of these events. When they happen, your code callbacks can run, such as the one above.

The main Node.js process loop actually checks with Libuv to see if it needs to be in the mode of running because of work it has in its queue, or is listening for. If so, then the process is kept alive.

*Note:* *the Libuv thread pool is not involved with the socket listening, because the low level OS capabilities are set up to handle the async non-blocking processing and notify of events being generated.*

# 8.4 Node.js Module Design

Node itself is composed of various modules that run as part of the core service. Modules are what enable all functionality in Node besides what is provided with the JavaScript language. The simple "Hello World" example demonstrated this. That example made use of the **console** module. Other modules that I will soon show you, such as the **express** module, are third-party modules you install to bring in additional functionality. As mentioned, you use the Node Package Manager (NPM) to get all your external modules installed on your machine and then use a `require()` statement to use them in code.

If you are really ambitious, you might even want to write a module yourself that has some functionality that others would find useful and then make it available as a download from the NPM repository.

I will now show you how a module is constructed and you will see how Node exposes the functionality of a module. You don't necessarily need to know how this works, but I include this information for those that are curious.

## A module is just a JavaScript object

Modules contain JavaScript code that is typically set up as an object. The object is then exposed in a special way so that a client can make use of it through the `require()` function as shown in a previous example. Node.js does the work to take your module code and surface it through its internal exposure for other code to call. Node keeps track of all the loaded modules and manages loading, configuring, running, and caching of the modules.

All you really need to know is that module code is exposed through a special Node object named `exports`. The `exports` object is created for you by Node in each and every module file. Then, when code calls the `require()` function, Node returns the `exports` object with whatever functionality was placed in it, such as a function. The following example shows a simple module you could write that exposes a single function:

```
// mymodule.js that holds your module code
module.exports.welcome = function(name) {
  console.log("Hi " + name);
}
```

As I mentioned, you provide functions and properties in a module file. These are then exposed outside of that file. You can add properties to the exports object such as the `welcome()` function in the previous example. What Node did for you in the above code was to create the exports object when it ingested your file.

Node takes your code and does something analogous to the following by wrapping it in the `require()` function:

```
function require(file) {
  module.exports = {};

  // Node parses your file and inserts the code such as...
  module.exports.welcome = function(name) {
    console.log("Hi" + name);
  }
  // End of your code

  return module.exports;
}
```

An empty object is created in the first line of the function. Then the object has add any properties to it you like, such as the function you see. Then, the object is returned so other code can call this and reference the function off of the object.

For code to use the function in the module, it needs to use the `require()` function. The `require()` function takes the name of the file that has your module code in it. You reference mymodule.js as follows, and call the function you have exposed.

```
// file server.js that uses the sample module
var w = require('./mymodule.js');
w.welcome("Bob");
```

Node actually has an internal `module` object that it creates for each module exposed. There is a lot more that is going on behind the scenes than that, but you don't need to really know any more of the details. You can certainly learn more of the internals if you are curious by reading through the actual source code, since it is an open-source project.

# A more complicated module

You can hang multiple properties off of the exports object, such as objects, strings, numbers, arrays, etc. In one of the previous samples, I showed you the use of the HTTP module. It had a `createServer()` function attached to it. This is a design pattern known as the factory design pattern. You don't use the function directly, as was done with the `welcome()` function in the previous example, but call it to get an object that you can then use.

You can also expose a class through a constructor function that clients take and construct themselves, or you can go further and provide a function that does the creation for them like the factory pattern I just mentioned. If you have multiple classes to expose, then you would want to use the factory pattern. If you only have one class, then you can expose that with a constructor function.

A constructor function being provided in a module would look as follows:

```
// mymodule.js
var a = require('http');

function Welcome(nameIn) {
  this.name = nameIn;
}

Welcome.prototype = {
  this.name = null,

  showName: function () {
    console.log("Hi " + name);
  },

  updateName: function (nameIn) {
    this.name = nameIn;
  }
};

module.exports = Welcome;
```

The following example shows how this module can be used:

```
var Welcome = require('./mymodule.js');
var w = new Welcome("John");
w.updateName("blah");
w.showName();
```

The `welcome()` function acts as the constructor in this example. The `prototype` keyword in JavaScript allows you to set properties that exist for all instances and are thus not created again for every instance.

Note how I included the usage of the http module to be used by the sample module above. Modules can require other modules for their own functionality and do so with the standard `require()` function. These included modules are not visible outside of that module code. So the code using the module can't actually get access to the http module, unless it also had a `require('http')` statement as well.

# 8.5 Useful Node Modules

If you go to https://nodejs.org/api/, you will find all of the official documentation on the core Node.js modules. Glance through what is there so you can keep it in mind if you need to reference it in the future.

Besides the modules that come with Node, there are plenty of other installable packages from NPM. https://www.npmjs.com/browse/star is a site that lists the most popular ones.

Remember that some of these NPM downloads are for code modules you use inside an application and others are tools that you download and run. Some code modules are also for use as express middleware. I won't explain any of those in this chapter but will cover some of them later.

Here is a very small list of some code modules you might find useful. Some of these come with Node and others you download from NPM.

| Module: | Purpose: |
|---|---|
| async | Used to force your code to run in a particular workflow. Instead of doing things like nesting callbacks, you can use async to set up sequential calls. Also used to run parallel functions with the ability to know when all have finished. |
| child_process | For child process spawning and management. |
| cluster | For setting up a cluster of Node.js processes to distribute the load across. |
| events | A primitive module that many others are actually built on, to emit or listen to events. |
| express | Web server functionality for configuring routes, serving up static files and providing template databinding functionality. |
| fs | Standard OS filesystem functionality. |
| helmet | For mitigating different types of HTTP security vulnerabilities. |
| http | This module actually serves a dual purpose. You can use it to set up a listening service for incoming HTTP requests. You can also use it to make outgoing HTTP requests. |
| joi | For performing validation on HTTP request JSON body properties. |
| mongodb | Used to interact with a MongoDB database. |
| net | Standard low-level networking functionality for servers and clients. |
| os | Basic utility functions for accessing OS information. |
| process | Standard type of functionality for working with processes on an operating system. |
| response-time | Displays the response time for HTTP requests. |
| socket.io | A higher level way to build bi-directional communications between clients and servers. |
| stream | A primitive module that many others are actually built on to provide readable and writable streams on top of data. |
| url | Utility functions for working with URLs. |
| util | Internal utility functions that Node itself takes advantage of that are exposed for you to use. |
| zlib | For compression and decompression. |

# 8.6 Scaling of Node

Could the Node.js process ever get overloaded? For example, let's say 1,000 HTTP Get requests come to your Node.js server all at once? Maybe this in turn requires 1,000 requests to read files from disk? Node is set up to be able to manage a sizable workload, so it may do just fine. You would need to do some profiling for your particular work load to know.

Node.js always makes your requests non-blocking and handles things differently depending on the type of OS call you are making. For file system interactions, the requests are shuttled off to threads in the Libuv thread pool to run in parallel. Each of those do their work and return back to the event loop for callback execution scheduling. Thread pool threads get freed up and are given more work. Eventually, all of the 1,000 file read requests are fulfilled. This happens in the least amount of time possible and also with the least amount of resources, like memory. All of this can be handled quite efficiently by one single node process.

You can visualize this queue handoff as shown in the following diagram. Note that the event loop of the Node process simply sequences through everything in its queue if more than four requests were stacked up. You could configure through code to have more than four threads if you like and you could experiment to see what performance improvements you might have.

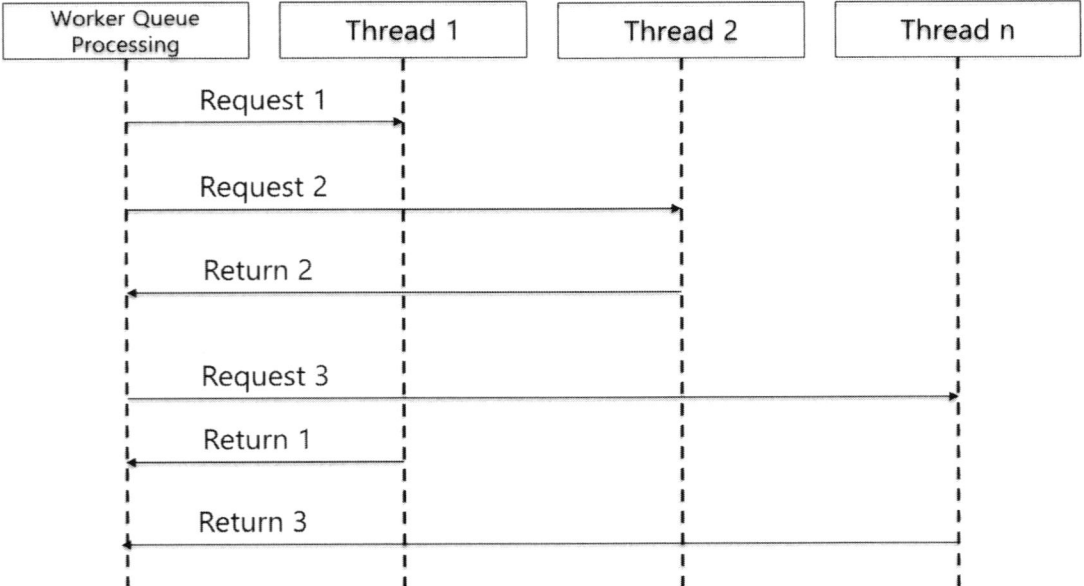

*Figure 38: Node thread pool handoff for file system requests*

Results are always interleaved and processed one by one on your one single main thread. As always, the performance is affected by your JavaScript code for results processing. That is where the bottlenecks almost always happen.

The NewsWatcher sample application will be connecting up to the MongoDB database in the data layer. This module is written to use low level TCP calls to the MongoDB service. The module you go through to make those calls uses the Net module of Node which eventually calls the library code of Libuv to be making platform network calls for whatever machine your application is running on.

This network I/O is handled differently than file system calls, and does not use the Libuv thread pool queue as was discussed for file system usage.

There is obviously a limit to how many operations you can achieve per second before performance degrades. Perhaps you have network I/O requests going off to some slow-returning database call. The requests could grow out of control if they are not handled fast enough as they come in. Of course, you also need to provide scalability in your data layer, or that will become the bottleneck.

*Note: At some point, Node has to rely on the OS and hardware, like disks and network cards to do their job. Remember, that you also have other system contentions to be aware of such as disk controller contentions.*

# Multiple Node processes per machine
Eventually you can move to other architectural variations to handle your load. To scale to a greater capacity, you can start up multiple Node.js processes on the same machine and distribute the load across those. If you have lots of cores on a machine, you can make use of all of them with a Node process for each core.

To do this scaling of Node across the cores of a single machine you can use the cluster module of Node.js itself to do the load balancing. There is also a process manager named PM2 that you can download from NPM to do the load balancing. PM2 has other capabilities such as monitoring, restarting of a Node process, and running deployments.

If you deploy your Node.js application through an AWS service such as Elastic Beanstalk you can utilize the power of PaaS to scale everything for you by scaling up the number of cores and the number of EC2 instances.

# Scaling horizontally
You can decide to scale horizontally across multiple machines for even greater scalability. Perhaps you have two or four cores per machine and already have your main Node process

on one core. You can count on the OS making use of other cores for you for the thread pool threads that do file system operations. Perhaps you are also forking some processes from the main Node process to offload some heavier computations and to do periodic batch processing. If you are doing this, then you don't have the spare cores to use with cluster or PM2 anyway. The better approach is to spread out horizontally across machines. You have to do this anyway for really high scale needs.

Scaling across machines is easy to configure in AWS. Elastic Beanstalk will uses the Nginx load balancer for your Node.js application. You can learn about how to build out your scale units from there that are run with EC2 instances.

With horizontal scaling you can perform rolling upgrades for application updates, or OS patches. For example, if you had three machines, you can drain off traffic, one machine at a time, and use the PaaS capabilities to do so and have each rotated out and then put back all fresh and ready to go.

Each EC2 machine would also be in a different availability zone to give you redundant failover if needed. This is in addition to the load balancing benefit. Here is what that looks like with two EC2 VM instances.

*Figure 39: Elastic Beanstalk load balancing*

You can also set up Elastic Beanstalk to use an auto-scaling group instead of individual EC2 instances. This will give you even greater scaling ability.

Be aware that with any of these scaling mechanisms, you must ensure that you are running in a completely stateless way and avoid any affinity settings to truly be able to distribute calls across all Node processes. To manage a connection requiring state, you can insert the use of something like Redis to fetch state if needed, or keep state only on the client.

## Misuse of Node.js

The main event thread should only be used to do fast, inexpensive processing for inbound or outbound results. Take the following example:

```
var http = require('http');
var bcrypt = require('bcryptjs');
var count = 0;

var server = http.createServer(function (request, response) {
  for (i = 0; i <= 10; i++) {
    bcrypt.hashSync("hjkl5678jhg", 10);
  }

  response.writeHead(200, { "Content-Type": "text/plain" });
  response.end("Hello World\n" + count++);
});

server.listen(3000);
```

Every web request that comes in will cause this compute-intensive code to run. This would basically devour all of the compute time if requests keep coming in. Your event loop would certainly not have any time to process any incoming requests.

The point here is that you should never do CPU intensive calculations in your main thread Node callback code. If you do, it will prevent the entire system from working correctly.

You can, however, solve this problem in a simple way with Node. There are built-in capabilities to send expensive processing to separate forked processes that do not affect your main Node.js process. Processing can be forked to child processes or even to an executable running on your computer that you have written in another language. You might even consider some remote service calls if you have capabilities accessible that way. There are many creative things you can do to solve this problem.

# 8.7 Node.js Internals

You actually know enough to use Node without knowing any more about its internal working mechanisms. You are thus free to skip this section if you like. You may however want to come back to this section later as it might help clear up some advanced questions that might arise.

*Note: This section was written after I had the chance to read through the actual source code for Node.js that is found on GitHub. Go to https://github.com/nodejs/node if you are interested in the internal workings of Node.js like I was.*

# The layers of Node.js

You can see from the block diagram in figure 40 that there exists a main Node.js codebase with dependencies below that. The top two layers of code are what make up the Node.js framework. The bottom two layers are dependencies that Node.js relies on.

The very top layer is the JavaScript library that you will be using directly from your code. Any time your code does something that is outside of the standard JavaScript calls, you will end up using something that is found in this layer. For example, all of the following code is made possible by the library layer:

```
var http = require('http');

var server = http.createServer(function (request, response) {
  response.writeHead(200, {"Content-Type": "text/plain"});
  response.end("Hello World\n");
});

server.listen(3000);
```

This top layer is what is documented on the Node.js official site https://nodejs.org/en/docs/ as its API. To really get started and use node, that is the only layer you are really required to know anything about. All core Node modules are exposed through this library layer.

Here are the four layers that comprise the operation of Node as a framework runtime:

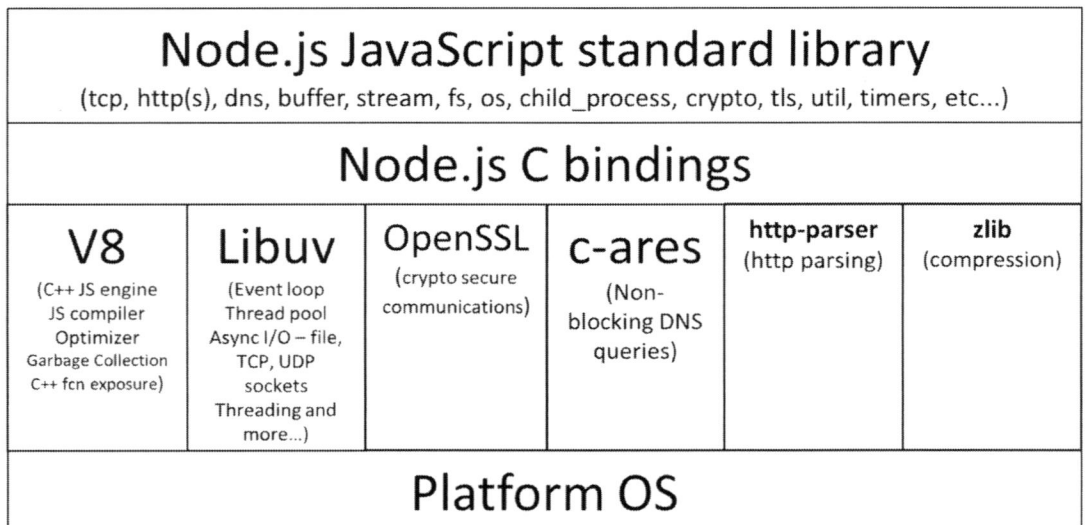

*Figure 40: Node.js platform*

Chapter 8: Fundamentals

It would be great if the OS itself could understand JavaScript, but it does not have the libraries exposed like it does for C/C++. Thus, there needs to be some translation from your code to code that the operating system can understand. This is why the bindings layer is needed.

The Node.js C bindings layer is made up of C++ code. This is what takes your code that is in JavaScript and allows it to call down into code libraries like Libuv that are written in C.

Node uses V8 as a dependency. It does so for two main purposes. V8 makes it possible for your JavaScript code to call through to C++ code running in the Node.js process. Take the following example of some Node.js JavaScript application code you might have. This code displays the size in bytes of your package.json file:

```
var fs = require('fs');

fs.stat("package.json", function(error, stats) {
  console.log(stats.size);
});
```

The way it works is that Node has exposed the fs module in the library layer that is being used here. Node uses some capabilities of V8 to actually take the fs.stat() call and have that make a call to a C++ function in the bindings layer called Stat(). This C++ function in the binding layer then makes a call to Libuv, which in turn call OS appropriate low level code. Eventually it makes its way to a Unix flavor OS library call of stat() or on a Windows system, the call made is NtQueryInformationFile() that is exposed in ntdll.dll. The callback makes its way back to your JavaScript where the asynchronous operation completes.

V8 acts as a Virtual Machine in the sense that it can isolate and execute some code and be hosted many times on one machine independently. It provides all of the aspects necessary for a language runtime. You can read an introduction to V8 JavaScript engine by going to https://developers.google.com/v8/intro#about-v8. Here is some text from the google site:

*"V8 is Google's open source, high performance JavaScript engine. It is written in C++ and is used in Google Chrome, Google's open source browser...V8 compiles and executes JavaScript source code, handles memory allocation for objects, and garbage collects objects it no longer needs...V8 does however provide all the data types, operators, objects and functions specified in the ECMA standard. V8 enables any C++ application to expose its own objects and functions to JavaScript code."*

Besides Libuv and V8, there are a few other dependencies that Node uses for operations as noted in the diagram. To actually look at what the dependencies are of Node.js, you can go to the GitHub project and look in the deps folder. Node.js is very portable as its dependencies have been ported to many platforms.

# Operation of Node

You have now seen how all of the layers fit together. You see that JavaScript code can be executed and that function calls can make their way through Node modules. Some of those modules invoke code through the binding layer in C++ down into Libuv.

The next thing to understand, is how the processing loop comes into play. I left out explaining this thus far, but it is important to understand. Understanding the processing loop helps you to be aware of where the processing takes place and how important it is for you to keep your async callback code as performant as possible so as to keep the main processing thread free.

Do not believe everything you read about Node.js. Some people are under the misconception that Node.js only has a single thread. This is obviously not true. I will dispel that misconception and teach you exactly how Node.js executes.

You have seen the layers of code that your application sits on top of. You are now ready to see how these layers actually operate to orchestrate the execution flow of a Node application. The main operation of Node is illustrated in the following diagram. Not every dependency component has been included, just the main ones concerning processing flow:

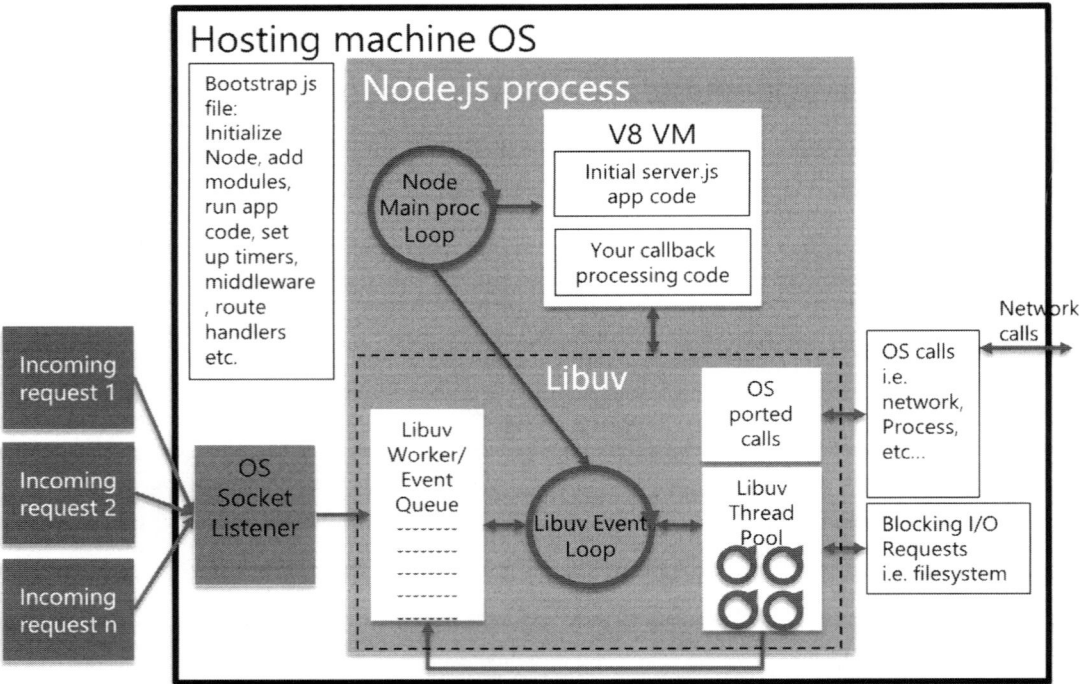

*Figure 41: Node.js conceptual architecture*

# Chapter 8: Fundamentals

Node.js has a single-threaded architecture for its main JavaScript processing. When you develop a Node application, mostly what you do is provide JavaScript functions for Node to execute in response to events. These are in the form of callbacks. Almost everything that happens in Node is asynchronous. This gives you concurrent processing.

Internally, Node may use multiple threads to shuttle work off to. Node.js utilizes a callback code pattern which frees up the developer from having to manage the threading and polling themselves. For example, you make your call for retrieving data from a backend database and, as part of that call, you provide a callback function. Your code immediately returns and then Node.js takes care of knowing when the data is returned and schedules your callback to run at a later time. Your callback is thus run asynchronously.

Node.js does not have any sleep, mutex lock, or any similar functions that you might see in other runtimes.

If you go back and consider the code sample that used the fs module, you saw that it eventually made it all the way down to the lowest level OS `stat()` function call. That call is obviously a blocking call! This is where Libuv does the work for you to queue up that request to take it off your thread and return immediately. Libuv will then run the `stat()` call on a thread pool thread it owns. When the call finishes, Libuv knows the callback to call and sends it back up to execute in V8.

The thread pool threads of Libuv are being used over and over. There are four of them by default, but you can change that to be more if you find a need. The NewsWatcher sample does not use the filesystem directly, so it does not alter that. The net module ends up being used by the NewsWatcher database interactions and that does not use the Libuv thread pool.

If you look back at figure 41 you can see the upper left part has what is termed the bootstrapping of Node. This is something that Node sequences through to get up and running. Here is the general sequence and explanation of the diagram, including the bootstrapping:

1. The Node process is run from a command line and has a main() function that is called as its process entry point.
    a. The main function creates the environment and then loads it.
    b. An object called "process" is created that has properties and functions on it. This object is very important and is used throughout the code.
    c. A node provided JavaScript file is now run with the V8 VM that bootstraps the whole process. It was at one point named node.js, but has since been renamed to bootstrap_node.js.
        i. Some internal Node modules are read in and made available.
        ii. The file argument (i.e. server.js) that node was started with is read in and run in the V8 VM.

2. Your server.js file runs and at this point can use the full capabilities of node and do things like use JavaScript, set up timers, set up HTTP listeners, make HTTP requests, set up middleware etc.
3. After your server.js code is finished being processed, the Node process enters its perpetual processing loop. At this point, the process keeps running as previously stated as long as there is work to process.
   a. Libuv processes work on its queue with its process loop and threads.
   b. Callbacks make it back to the main thread to be run by the V8 VM. V8 would queue calls that come in and process them.

For those of you that are still skeptical about my stating that there are two processing loops, here is the proof. Here is the code from node.cc that the main() function eventually enters and keeps executing. This is really what can be called the main processing loop of Node:

```
bool more;
do {
  v8::platform::PumpMessageLoop(default_platform, isolate);

  more = uv_run(env->event_loop(), UV_RUN_ONCE);
  if (more == false) {
    v8::platform::PumpMessageLoop(default_platform, isolate);
    EmitBeforeExit(env);

    // Emit `beforeExit` if the loop became alive either after emitting
    // event, or after running some callbacks.
    more = uv_loop_alive(env->event_loop());

    if (uv_run(env->event_loop(), UV_RUN_NOWAIT) != 0)
      more = true;
  }
} while (more == true);
```

Note how the Libuv processing loop is not allowed to continually run, but is called and is under the control of the main loop of the node process. It is the main Node process loop that calls libuv to let it run with the UV_RUN_NOWAIT flag. The main loop thus is continually calling to have the Libuv loop run over and over. Here is the Unix ported version of the Libuv processing loop being called:

```
int uv_run(uv_loop_t* loop, uv_run_mode mode) {
  int timeout;
  int r;
  int ran_pending;

  r = uv__loop_alive(loop);
  if (!r)
    uv__update_time(loop);
```

```
while (r != 0 && loop->stop_flag == 0) {
  uv__update_time(loop);
  uv__run_timers(loop);
  ran_pending = uv__run_pending(loop);
  uv__run_idle(loop);
  uv__run_prepare(loop);

  timeout = 0;
  if ((mode == UV_RUN_ONCE && !ran_pending) || mode == UV_RUN_DEFAULT)
    timeout = uv_backend_timeout(loop);

  uv__io_poll(loop, timeout);
  uv__run_check(loop);
  uv__run_closing_handles(loop);

  if (mode == UV_RUN_ONCE) {
    uv__update_time(loop);
    uv__run_timers(loop);
  }

  r = uv__loop_alive(loop);
  if (mode == UV_RUN_ONCE || mode == UV_RUN_NOWAIT)
    break;
}

/* The if statement lets gcc compile it to a conditional store. Avoids
 * dirtying a cache line.
 */
if (loop->stop_flag != 0)
  loop->stop_flag = 0;

return r;
}
```

You can see that the while loop has code to cause a break statement to happen in the case of Node calling it.

Callback functions in your JavaScript usage of modules such as with fs.reafFile() are kept by Node in a structure and then later, when the low level Libuv call returns, the callback happens on the C++ main thread of Node.js. If you look at the diagram again, you can see there is a two way arrow from Libuv to the V8 VM.

The call coming down from JavaScript through the C++ bindings uses the V8 FunctionTemplate class to accomplish this. The callback going up from Libuv makes it back to the C++ bindings layer code and uses the V8 Function::Call() function to have the V8 VM execute the actual JavaScript callback you had provided. This callback is not executed on the Node process thread that is orchestrating all of this, but is executing in the VM. Node is in no way managing any queue, event or processing loop for the JavaScript execution. This is all done by V8.

# Chapter 9: Express Fundamentals

The E in the MEAN acronym stands for Express. The Express module is not a part of the Node.js install, but can be downloaded and installed separately and integrated into your application. Express is consistently one of the most downloaded Node.js modules on NPM. The Express module allows you to implement the functionality of a web server. For example, it provides a simple way to specify the routes for incoming requests and also simplifies the response generation.

One of the things Express does for your project, is to remove the need for the HTTP module that comes with Node. The HTTP module that is built into Node.js requires you to write lots of code in order to set up the routing and responses. Express makes all of that easier.

The following are the key capabilities of Express:
- Specify the route handling of incoming HTTP requests.
- Mechanism to inject middleware into a request to modify it as it gets passed along.
- Easy integration of third-party middleware to provide extended capabilities for request processing.
- Provides a `request` object with properties and methods to look at everything connected with the incoming request.
- Provides a `response` object to use to set everything up for a response.
- Configuration for JSON payload serving.
- Configuration to serve up static files.
- Pairs up with server-side template engines to set context and return filled-in HTML through data binding.

# 9.1 The Express Basics

As with any external Node module, you have to state in your code that you are requiring Express. You can do this at the top of a file such as your server.js file. You can then make the Express listener active. Here is some simple code to set up and use Express:

```
var express = require('express');
var app = express();
app.listen(3000);
```

This requires that you first install Express using the NPM command. I will walk you through the construction of the NewsWatcher sample application and show you how to set everything up later in this book.

# Express configuration settings

As part of using the Express module, you will need to configure some settings in your code. You use the Express object `set()` function to do this. The `app.set(name, value)` syntax is for setting a value for predefined names that Express uses as configuration. The `set()` method will configure things such as what port to listen on. Here is an example:

```
var express = require('express');
var app = express();
app.set('port', 3000);
```

To disable a setting, you can call `app.set(name, false)`. You use the `app.get(name)` method to retrieve any set value. There are `enable` and `disable` functions, but they are the same thing as calling set with a true or false. The following settings are used by Express for determining its mode of operation:

**Settings with Value options:**

| | |
|---|---|
| case sensitive routing | A Boolean to determine route interpretation as to case sensitivity. For example, if set to false, then "/News" and "/news" are treated the same. |
| env | A string value that sets the environment mode such as "development". This is purely for your use to set and read. For example, you would have logic to determine which URL endpoints, database connections, etc. depending on if you are running the code to try out new development code, or if the code is running in production. |
| etag | Used to set the ETag response header for all responses. Set it to `strong`, `weak`, or `false` if you want to disable it. You can also pass in a custom function. The default value is `weak`. |
| jsonp callback name | A string to specify the default JSONP callback name such as `?callback=`, which is the default. |
| json replacer | A string to specify the JSON replacer callback. This is a function you define to decide on a property-by-property basis if they are returned on a JSON route response. |
| json spaces | Specifies the number of spaces to use for JSON indenting for readability. |
| port | The port to listen on. |
| query parser | You can set this to `simple` or `extended`. `simple` is based on the query parser from Node and `extended` is implemented by the qs module and is the default. |
| strict routing | A Boolean to set to `true` is you want routes like "/News" and "/News/" treated as different paths. The default setting is `false`. |
| subdomain offset | A number that defaults to 2 for how many dot-separated parts to remove to access the subdomain. |

| trust proxy | To be used if you have a front-facing proxy. You will need to set this up to be trusted. This is `false` by default. |
|---|---|
| views | The directory(s) to use for template lookups. |
| view cache | A Boolean that enables template caching. If the `env` setting is set to `production`, then this value defaults to `true`, otherwise it defaults to `false`. |
| view engine | A string to specify the template engine to use with your provided templates. |
| x-powered-by | A Boolean that defaults to true to enable the "X-Powered-By: Express" HTTP header to be returned. You would set it to `false` so as not to return it to prevent any hackers from knowing too much about your implementation. |

The Express object also has a property named `locals` on which you can place your own custom properties that you might want to associate with your Express application. You use the `app.locals` object as shown in the following example:

```
app.locals.emailForOps = 'Help@myapp.com';
```

# Listening

With all of the code in place to manage your settings, all you need to do next is make a function call to allow the Node.js runtime to actually run its platform-specific code and set up a socket connection for the given port on the server machine to listen on. Any incoming connections to the IP address of the machine at that specified port number will be bound through to your code for it to respond to. Here is the code to do that:

```
var server = app.listen(3000, function() {
  debug('Express server listening on port ' + server.address().port);
});
```

With some understanding of the initialization and settings, you can look at implementing a fully functional web service with some request route handling.

# 9.2 Express Request Routing

When an HTTP request comes into Node, the request will make its way to the Express module code you have written to service it. Your Node.js instance will be running on a given machine that is hosted and exposed on the Internet. Node will be executing in a process on that server, and through the Express code, it would be listening on a port socket for incoming connections.

HTTP requests that come to your server browser page or requests from a native mobile app each make REST web service API requests and deal with JSON payloads. The URL request could be something like the following:

```
http://newswatcherscale-env.us-west-2.elasticbeanstalk.com/news?region=USA
```

With express, you have the ability to set up request handlers for specific REST paths and get at query strings. The following diagram shows how this Express routing conceptually works:

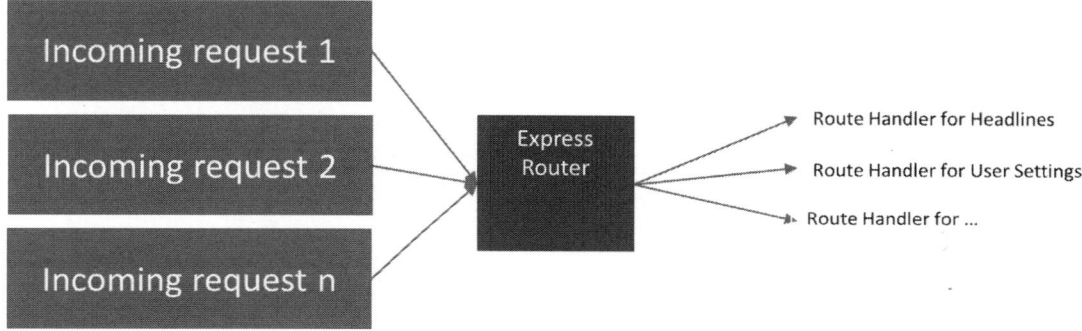

*Figure 42: Express routing*

You could actually set up code to service lower level TCP or UDP types of connections or service the HTTP protocol requests. This chapter will only be concerned with servicing HTTP requests with Express.

# Routes

Once you have the Express JavaScript object through the require statement, you can use methods that set up the servicing of HTTP requests. Express will then listen for connections on the specified port and can understand the various HTTP verbs and break down what is being passed in as part of the URL, query string, and the HTTP headers and body.

The Express object gives you functions to use for handling the various HTTP verbs (get, put etc.). Here are the standard verbs that would be used for CRUD type operations to expose an API in your service layer.

```
app.get(path, callback);    // Read item(s)
app.post(...);              // Create a new item
app.put(...);               // Replace an item
app.patch(...);             // Update an item
app.delete(...);            // Delete an item

function callback(req, res) {
   res.send("Send something back");
};
```

Express supports the following HTTP methods:
- checkout
- connect
- copy
- delete
- get
- head
- lock
- m-search
- merge
- mkactivity
- mkcol
- move
- notify
- options
- patch
- post
- propfind
- proppatch
- purge
- put
- report
- search
- subscribe
- trace
- unlock
- unsubscribe

For m-search, you will have to code it as `app['m-search'](...)`. Please see Express's documentation for the complete list of supported methods. The general signature looks as follows:

```
app.<METHOD>(path, callback [, callback ...])
```

`<METHOD>` would be replaced by one of the methods such as `get`. The first parameter is the URL path. This is not the complete URL, but the portion of it after the domain name.

The second parameter is the callback function that gets called for that request. You can actually provide multiple callbacks and they will each get called sequentially. I will cover more about this later.

Route paths can be strings, string patterns, or regular expressions. They can also be an array that combines any of the mentioned formats. As a string, a route path can be things like "/books". The query string portion is not considered part of the path.

You can use "/" to specify that all paths should be picked up. If you omit the path parameter completely, all paths would be picked up.

The callback function you provide has at least two parameters in its standard form. The first parameter is the request object, which contains information about the incoming request. The second parameter is the response object, and is used to send back a response, such as serving up an HTML file.

This example shows the use of a pure REST style URL. You just need to provide the routing path that occurs after the domain portion of the URL. Here is the URL and the way you would specify the path.

```
// http://mysite.com/news/categories/sports
app.get("/news/categories/sports", callback);
```

For each verb, such as get, you might have different routes for different resources that are being retrieved. Here is some code that sets up multiple paths for the get HTTP verb, each returning something unique:

```
app.get('/about', function(req, res) {
   res.send("About page");
});

app.get('/news', function(req, res) {
   res.send("News page");
});
```

Be aware that the ordering of your route handling code is very important. Any incoming request is basically consumed by the first path that is found to handle it.

# A single path for multiple verbs

If you find you have several verbs that all respond to the same path, you can specify them together by using the route() method. This might help you alleviate typing in the path multiple times. An example of this is:

```
app.route('/customer')
   .get(function(req, res) {res.send('Get a customer');})
   .post(function(req, res) {res.send('Add a customer');})
   .put(function(req, res) {res.send('Update a customer');});
```

# All verbs at once

Besides the standard verbs, there are also the methods `all` or `use` to respond to all verbs of the incoming requests. The first route handler below is for all verbs that are for the path `/test`. Then the second is set up for everything else and returns a 404 - Not Found code. The `use` function here is not using a path, so it is for all verbs and all paths not serviced yet.

```
app.all('/test', function(req, res) {
   resp.type('text/plain');
   resp.send('This is a test.');
});

app.use(function(req, res) {
   res.type('text/plain');
   res.status(404);
   res.send('404 - Not found');
});
```

# Advanced path specification

So far, you have seen the simplest of cases with route handling paths. There is a technique that can give you more advanced parsing capability for a URL path. Below is one of the URLs from a previous example:

```
// http://mysite.com/news/categories/sports
app.get("/news/categories/sports", callback);
```

The problem with this example is that you might need to service 20 different categories of news stories. For example, what about the paths `/news/categories/science` or `/news/categories/politics`? It could get very monotonous to set up routes for each and every one. To make this easier, Express allows you to set up placeholder parameters in the path that you can then get at later in the callback code.

To be able to retrieve parts of a path, you use special syntax in the `path` parameter by placing a colon character in the string. This then sets up a JavaScript property you can later access in the handling function as part of the request object. The code below sets the path up as you see with a colon. A property will then be available on the request object as shown.

```
// http://mysite.com/news/categories/sports
app.get("/news/categories/:category', function(req, res) {
   console.log('Your category was ' + req.params.category');
});
```

With this code, you just have the one route that can service all requests for news stories and can just feed that category into the backend retrieval mechanism.

130

The `req.params` property can be used as an array. In JavaScript, that means you can also access it as shown below. The following example shows this, and also shows that you can have more than one of these parameters set up to use:

```
app.get('/products/:category/:id', function(req, res) {
  console.log(req.params[0] + req.params[1]);
});
```

You can also construct your URLs so that they contain query strings. For a query string that you want to process such as `/news?category=sports`, you don't need any special syntax in the path string parameter. Just specify the path up to the start of the query string and stop there. The name-value pairs of the query string will automatically be parsed out and made available to you as part of the `query` property of the request object. For this example, there would be a property named `category`, with a value of `sports`:

```
// http://mysite.com/news?category=sports
app.get('/news', function(req, res) {
  console.log(req.query.category);
});
```

# 9.3 Express Middleware

At this point I have shown you how to set up callback functions that get executed for a given incoming request. Now I'll introduce the concept of middleware as a means of inserting route processing code that will happen before your ending route handler runs. Some middleware code will be provided by Express, others can be handled by downloaded NPM modules, and others can be handled by what you write.

The concept of middleware is that you can have code run as an inserted step that is placed before your route callback gets run. This middleware code gets chained together in a series of calls that you specify. Middleware can then act upon and modify the request object that is being passed along the way. You can do this as a way to reuse code across multiple routes.

Some inserted middleware terminates the request, as it takes care of everything and the requests never go to any of your route handling. An example of this is the Express static file serving middleware. You might also have some middleware that intercepts calls to verify a user's authorization and does not continue if the request is determined to be invalid.

Another example of middleware might be something that caches content for you. Another example would be a function that logs all operations.

Many available middleware modules are really simple to add, yet very powerful in what they provide. I'll show you several of them in this chapter. Conceptually, you can take the Express routing diagram shown previously and modify it as follows to show middleware being injected that pass functionality down the chain:

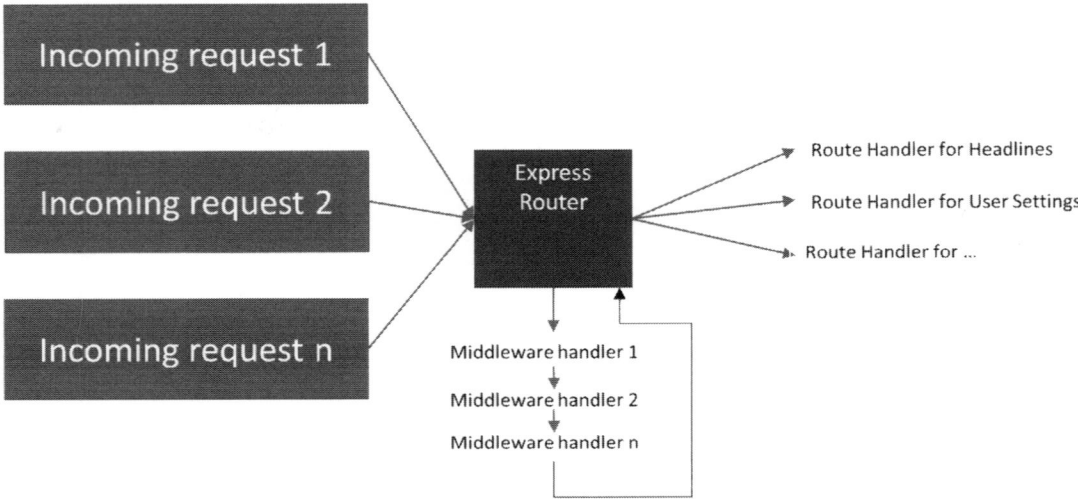

*Figure 43: Express routing with middleware*

Middleware functions look almost identical to what you have seen already as callbacks. They are really just callback functions with the same signature you have seen and thus have access to the request and response objects. This means that the request object can be modified before being passed along. For example, the request body in the response object could be modified to have additional data added to it before it gets to its final destination-handling callback.

Many modules that act as middleware are available from the NPM repository. This middleware can accomplish things like authentication, caching, logging, session state, cookies, etc. These act as shared pieces of code that you can use across all or just certain routes.

Middleware extends the capabilities of Node.js beyond its core functionality. For example, let's say you are writing a web server that will serve up static files, such as image files. Node.js allows you to do that, if you write the code. However, there is a module that acts as middleware in Express that makes it incredibly easy to implement. The module that does this is the `static` module and it comes as part of the Express install. It can be hooked up to serve up static files with very little code.

*Note: Don't confuse the concept of a middleware module with the general concept of a module in Node.js. They are still provided though the* `requires` *function, but are used differently than regular Node modules.*

# Hooking up your own custom middleware

Route processing stops at the first match that is found for a path and a callback is run. However, if you make one minor modification to your code, you can actually string together multiple callbacks for the same route. Notice the one modification made below:

```
// First handler
app.get('/test', function(req, res, next) {
  ...
  console.log("Got here first");
  next();
});

// Second handler
app.get('/test', function(req, res) {
  ...
  console.log("Got here second");
});
```

The difference is that the first route callback function has a third parameter named `next`. This function usage tells Express that you want the callback to act as middleware code to be injected before the actual end route is called. Order is important as stated before.

`next()` is a function that is passed in that you call when your middleware code is done. You must call `next()` or the request will be abandoned and not make it to your end handler. In the example, the first handler runs and then, because of the `next()` function being called, execution continues in the second handler.

The previous example code could also be structured so that the callbacks are not separated out. You then just list out callbacks one after another. You need to have the code in the cb1 function that calls `next()` or cb2 will not be run.

```
app.get('/test', cb1, cb2);

function cb1(req, res, next) {
  console.log("Got here first");
  next();
});

function cb2(req, res) {
  console.log("Got here second")
});
```

# Universal middleware

You can hook up some middleware that will get inserted into every single route and for every single verb. To do this, you simply use `app.use()`. This sets up Express to use this function across all incoming requests. You can leave off the path in this case as "/" is the default path if you don't provide one. Of course, you may want to provide a path so that the middleware only gets run for a certain path.

```
app.use('/', function(req, res next) {
  ...
  next();
});
```

You can insert as much middleware as you need for your routes. The order in which you list them in your code will be the order in which they are sequenced through. Be aware that certain third-party middleware from NPM are required to be placed before others. Refer to the middleware's documentation for more information.

Now I'll show you a practical example of some custom middleware you might want to implement. Let's say that you have a special path that you only want administrators to have access to. You can create a function that does validation before giving access to the request for further processing. Here is how you do that:

```
// Middleware injection
app.all('/admin/*', doAuthentication);
app.get('/admin/stats', returnStats);
app.get('/admin/approval', approval);
```

With the `app.all()`, the authentication happens for all verbs and acts as middleware. Inside the `doAuthentication()` would be code to determine the authenticity of the request. If it was detected to be invalid, then you would not call next() and the other two route handlers would never be called. You will see something similar to this in the NewsWatcher application.

If you call `next()` with an error object parameter, then that route terminates from being handled normally. Error handling middleware then gets invoked. This error handling will soon be explained.

# Parameter middleware

Express allows you to set up a middleware callback function for a given parameter property you defined in other route handlers. You do this with the `app.param()` function. This callback is called before any route handler. Here is an example:

```
// Using the global param handler
app.param('id', function(req, res, next, value) {
   console.log("someone queried id " + value);
   if (value != 99)
     next();
});

app.get('/products/:category/:id', function(req, res) {
   console.log(req.params[0] + req.params[1]);
});
```

If you don't have any routes with "id" in them, then the `param()` callback will never get called. The `param` callback will be called before any route handler in which the parameter occurs. You still need to call `next()` to continue the processing.

# Router object

If you really have a lot of routes and want to subdivide them for better organization, you can use the `router` object and keep each in their own modules. In that way, you can isolate your logic and also not have it affect the other routes you have set up.

You set the `router` objects up independently. Until you activate them with `app.use()`, they will not be functional. The following is an example of setting up some middleware and a route in a router and then activating it in the app:

```
var router = express.Router();

// Here is some middleware
router.use(function(req, res, next) {
   ...
   next();
});

// Here is an end route for /news/weather
router.get('/weather', function(req, res) {
   ...
});

// only requests to /news/* will be sent to the "router"
app.use('/news', router);
```

# Middleware error handling

Any middleware function, whether yours or one from a third party can return an error by calling the `next(err)` function. If that happens, then execution of the middleware and any subsequent routing is ended and processing of the error takes place. To process the error, Express has a default function that it calls that writes the error back to the client.

You have the option of providing your own single function or chain of functions as error handling middleware. If you provide a function or chain of functions, then the default one will not be called. In the following example, note how there are four parameters with the error handling middleware function, the first one being the error object:

```
app.get('/test/:id', function(req, res, next) {
  if (req.params.id == 0)
    next(new Error('Not Found'));

  next();
};

// A middleware error handling function
app.use(function(err, req, res, next) {
  console.error(err);
  res.status(500).send('Something bad happened');
});
```

Once execution has shifted to the error handling middleware, you can return back to regular route processing if you do a `next('route')` call. Doing that will jump you to whatever is the next defined route handler.

The diagram of Express routing can be further expanded to add in middleware error handling.

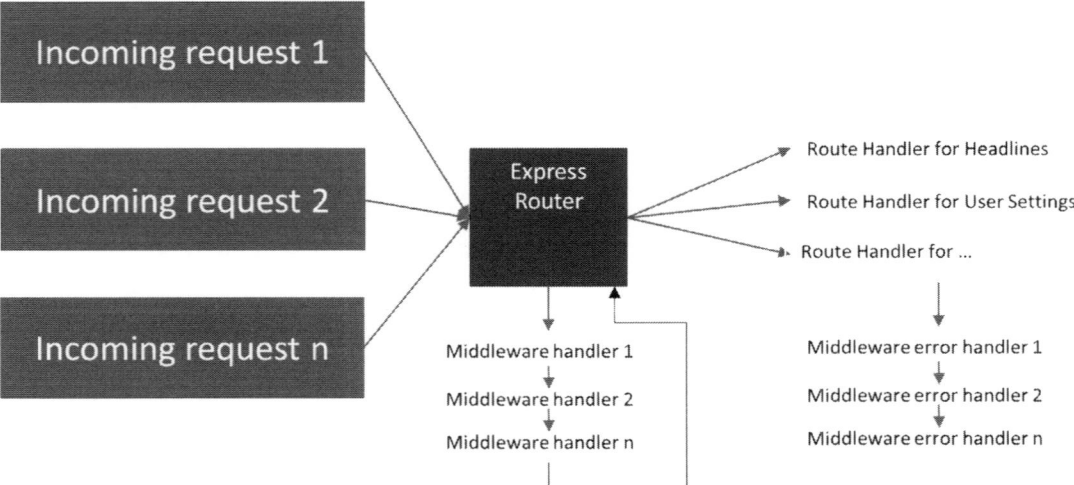

*Figure 44: Express routing with route handing and middleware error handling*

# Using next() even if your handler is not middleware

I should clear one thing up for you though. Just because you add a `next` parameter on a route handler does not mean you are actually implementing some middleware. For example, you will most likely need need `next()` as a parameter on all your end route handlers in order to do central error processing.

As an example, the following code is an end route being handled by the Express router object. As it is written, you assume nothing will go wrong and just carry out some operation:

```
var router = express.Router();

router.delete('/:id', function (req, res) {
   res.status(200).json({ msg: 'Logged out' });
});
```

What if you wanted to detect an error and use the middleware error handling explained in the previous section? This is where you will need to add the `next` parameter to be called if there happened to be an error. If there is no error, the route will complete by calling the `res.status()` function to send back a response. Nothing else gets in the way and if running normally, you don't call `next()` because there is nothing else to chain.

In order to use the error handling middleware, an end route itself must be able to pass control to the error handling chain. To do that, the code needs to be modified to add in the `next()` function to be called.

As mentioned, in the end route handling code you never call `next()` without giving it an error parameter. The following example shows the additional error handling:

```
var router = express.Router();

router.delete('/:id', authHelper.checkAuth, function (req, res, next) {
   if (req.params.id != '77')
      return next(new Error('Invalid request'));

   res.status(200).json({ msg: 'Logged out' });
});
```

# Static file serving middleware

One middleware module that comes with Express is the `static` middleware that allows interception of requests for files and returns them. This alleviates the need for you to provide an end route handler of your own. For example, if you want to serve up jpg image files, you can use the following code:

```
var express = require('express');
var app = express;

// Middleware injection
app.use('/images', express.static('images'));
app.listen(3000);
```

`app.use` is setting up the middleware route. Instead of the callback function being provided by you, you insert the call for using `express.static()`. This takes care of everything for you to send a response back. In your Node.js project code you would need to provide the folder of images. An HTML page could access an image as follows:

```
<img src="http://yousite.com/images/someimage.jpg"/>
```

As a second parameter to `express.static()`, you can pass in an options object that can have the following properties on it:

- `dotfiles`
- `etag`
- `extensions`
- `index`
- `lastModified`
- `maxAge`
- `redirect`
- `setHeaders`.

For example, `setHeaders` is a function you would use to set headers to send with the files. Another example would be setting the `lastModified` property to true and the `Last-Modified` header value is set to the date of the file being sent. For more information, refer to Express's documentation.

# Third-party middleware

There are a growing number of third-party modules that provide Express middleware for your applications. Go to the Express site (http://expressjs.com/resources/middleware.html) to find a list of modules you can download.

To use the middleware, you typically call `app.use(<middleware>)`. This means that all paths and verbs will flow through it. Most third-party middleware that intercepts routes before you get them will call the `next()` function so that processing will eventually reach your code, if you have that need.

Here are a few useful middleware components for your reference:

**Express middleware Node.js modules:**

| | |
|---|---|
| passport | Used to authenticate requests. You can set this up to log a person in using OAuth (i.e. through Facebook), or federated login using OpenID. There are more than 300 strategies available through the passport module. |
| body-parser | This middleware intercepts any HTTP Post verb requests that have body data, such as from a form submit. The middleware code runs and then by the time your handler code runs, the response object has a body property with sub-properties off of it for each of the body values.<br><br>`var bodyParser = require('body-parser')`<br>`app.use(bodyParser());`<br><br>`// In your handler, you can look at the values`<br>`app.post('/', function(req, res) {`<br>`  console.log(req.body);`<br>`}`<br><br>You can specify that JSON is to be parsed and placed in the body. Query string values can also be placed into the body object for you.<br><br>`var bodyParser = require('body-parser')`<br>`app.use(bodyParser.json());`<br>`app.use(bodyParser.urlencoded({ extended: true }));` |
| compression | This will compress requests that pass through the middleware. You would place this statement before any other middleware or routes, unless you only wanted certain routes to be compressed. If you look at the headers of a returned response, you would see the headers have an entry for Content-Encoding.<br><br>`var compression = require('compression')`<br>`var express = require('express')`<br>`var app = express()`<br>`app.use(compression())` |
| cookie-parser | This middleware does all the work to make available a cookie property on your request object.<br><br>`var cookieParser = require('cookie-parser')`<br>`app.use(cookieParser());`<br><br>`// look at all of the properties on body`<br>`app.post('/', function(req, res) {`<br>`  console.log(req.cookies);`<br>`}` |

| errorhandler | This accomplishes the sending back of stack traces to the client when an error occurs. Make sure to only use this when running in a development environment.<br><br>```<br>var errorhandler = require('errorhandler')<br>app.use(errorhandler());<br>``` |
|---|---|
| express-session | Server-side session data storage. |
| response-time | Response time tracking to add the X-Response-Time header. The value inserted is in milliseconds. You could use this to track your SLA over time and be alerted as to what needs further investigation for performance optimization. |
| morgan | This is for request logging. This frees you up from writing any of your own `console.log` statements. For example, incoming HTTP requests go through this middleware and its logs those requests to the console window. You can also specify the format of the logging and direct the output to a file.<br><br>```<br>var fs = require('fs')<br>var morgan = require('morgan')<br><br>// create a write stream (in append mode)<br>var accessLogStream = fs.createWriteStream(__dirname +<br>'/access.log', {flags: 'a'})<br><br>app.use(morgan('combined', {stream: accessLogStream}))<br>``` |
| serve-favicon | For customizing the icon in the browser. |
| express-validator | For validation of incoming data. |
| connect-redis | Session store using redis cache. |
| connect-timeout | For routes that might run into some backend processing issues and need to be limited in the amount of time they take, you can use this to cut them off and return an error. You still need to determine what the right approach is for termination and resubmission of requests.<br><br>```<br>var cto = require('connect-timeout')<br><br>app.get('/some_questionable_route', cto('5s'),<br>  function(req, res, next) {<br>    ...some possibly long running code...<br>    ...check req.timeout to see if it is ever true and<br>    ...then return false<br>    return next();  // finished processing in time, go<br>to next function<br>  },<br>  function(req, res, next) {<br>    res.send('ok');<br>  }<br>);<br>``` |

# 9.4 Express Request Object

Let's look more in-depth at the usage of the request object in Express route function handlers. The request object contains all of the information you need to digest the incoming request. For example, you have seen how the properties `req.params` and `req.query` are used. You have also seen some third-party middleware that adds more properties to the request object. Here is a reference to some of the properties that are available. You can refer to the Express documentation to find the complete list.

The request object is a parameter of your express route callback function. You can name it anything you like. "req" is a good name for it. The following example shows getting the complete URL that this request came in from.

```
app.get('/', function(req, res) {
  console.log(req.url);
});
```

Here is a reference to the properties that are available on the `request` object. Refer to the Express documentation for the complete list.

**Request object properties:**

| | |
|---|---|
| `app` | A reference to the instance of the express application object. |
| `params` | This is used to access route parameters. You need to first have set the route specification string and then you can use the `params` property of the request object.<br><br>```app.get('/user/:id', function(req, res) {   res.send('user' + req.params.id); });``` |
| `query` | Used to get the URL querystring. A property will exist on the query object for each.<br><br>```// For URL "/users/search?q=Smith", app.get('/users/search', function(req, res) {    console.log(req.query.q); });``` |
| `body` | Contains properties of key-value pairs of data submitted in the request body. You need to add the body-parser middleware for it to work.<br><br>```var bodyParser = require('body-parser'); app.use(bodyParser.json());``` <br><br>```app.post('/', function (req, res) {   console.log(req.body);})``` |

| route | This is an object that has properties of the current route such as `path`, `keys`, `regexp`, and `params`. |
|---|---|
| cookies | When using the cookie-parser middleware, this property is an object that contains cookies sent by the request. Each cookie that is attached is a property on the cookies object.<br><br>`req.cookies.someName` |
| signedCookies | Exists if the cookies have been signed and protected from tampering.<br><br>`req.signedCookies.someName` |
| ip | The remote IP address of the incoming request. |
| protocol | Such as `http`, `https`, or `trusted` if setup with a trusted proxy. |
| secure | This has a value of `true` if SSL is in effect. |
| headers | The HTTP headers you can access.<br><br>`req.headers['x-auth']` |
| url | The url of the request. |
| path | The path part of the request, without the query string. |
| route | An object that contains the matched route and lots of other properties such as the method and function that handled it. |
| hostname | The host from the HTTP header. i.e. example.com |
| subdomains | The subdomain part that is in front of the hostname. i.e. ["blah", stuff"] if from stuff.blah.example.com. |
| xhr | This is set to `true` if the request came from a client call such as from XMLHttpRequest, which had set the X-Requested-With field. |

Here is a reference to some of the methods that are available on the `request` object. Refer to Express's documentation for the complete list.

**Request object methods:**

| get(field) | To get at the request header fields.<br><br>`req.get('content-type'); // i.e. "text/plain"` |
|---|---|
| accepts(types) | To check if a certain type is available, based on the Accept header field. If what you send in as a parameter does not match one of the values, then you will receive an undefined return.<br><br>`req.accepts('html');` |
| is(type) | To find out what type the incoming request is.<br><br>`req.is('text/html'); // i.e. returns true` |

| acceptsLanguages(lang [, ...]) | Based on the Accept-Language field of the header, it returns the first language on a match, or false if none are accepted. Similar calls are acceptsCharsets and acceptsEncodings. <br><br> ```var lang = req.acceptsLanguages('fr', 'es', 'en'); if (lang) { console.log('The first accepted is: ' + lang); } else { console.log('None accepted'); }``` |
|---|---|

# 9.5 Express Response Sending

Requests are routed to your callback because of a routing path you have set up. You will eventually return a response back to the requester, so this is the object you use to do that with. You should at least send back an HTTP status code. You might also return some HTML or better yet, a JSON payload.

Methods on the response object are combined and have a cumulative effect on the return response. The example code below sets the status of 200 OK for a successful HTTP request:

```
var express = require('express');
var app = express();

app.get('/', function(req, res) {
   res.status(200);
   res.set({'Content-Type': 'text/html'});
   res.send('<html><body>Some body text</body></html>');
});

app.get('/test_json', function(req, res) {
   res.status(200);
   res.set('json spaces', 4);
   res.json({name:'me', age: 37});
});

app.listen(3000);
```

In the first route, the Content-Type is set as "text/html" and then the send() method is used to finish the returned response with some returned HTML. The second route returns some JSON.

# Response object

The response object has many useful properties and methods. Each usage of the response object is used inside a function callback. You can name it anything you like. "res" is a good name for it.

Here is a reference to the properties and methods that are available on the response object. Refer to the Express documentation for the complete list.

**Response object properties:**

| | |
|---|---|
| app | A reference to the Express application. |
| headersSent | A Boolean value that is true if HTTP headers have been sent. |
| locals | Local variables scoped to the request, might be identical to app.locals. A template can use these for its data binding. |

**Response object methods:**

| | |
|---|---|
| status(code) | Used to set the status of a return in the case of an error.<br><br>`res.status(404);` |
| accepts(types) | For content negotiation on a return.<br><br>```if (req.accepts('text/html') == 'text/html')```<br>```  res.send('<p>Hello</p>');```<br>```} else if (req.accepts('application/json') ==```<br>```'application/json')```<br>```  res.send({ message: 'Hello' });```<br>```} else {```<br>```  res.status(406).send('Not Acceptable');```<br>```}``` |
| set(field [, value]) | For setting the fields of the response header.<br><br>```res.set({'contentType': 'text/plain', 'ETag': '123'});``` |
| get(field) | Retrieves what the setting is for a header field.<br><br>`res.get('contentType');` |
| redirect([code,] URL) | Path to redirect to instead of the one it came in at. You can provide an optional status code. A 302 "Found" is the default value of the code. You can also redirect relative to the current URL of the service.<br><br>`res.redirect('http://example.com');` |
| cookie(name, value, [options]) | Sets a cookie. The name is the identifier of the cookie. The value parameter can be a string or object converted to JSON. The options parameter can set up things like |

| | |
|---|---|
| | domain, expires, httpOnly, maxAge, path, secure, and signed.<br><br>`res.cookie('rememberthis', '1', { maxAge: 900000, secure: true });` |
| json([body]) | Send a JSON body back.<br><br>`res.json({ msg: 'Hello' })` |
| jsonp([body]) | For JSONP support.<br><br>`res.jsonp({ msg: 'Hello' })` |
| attachment([path to file]) | You can set an attachment to be returned. If you pass a parameter, it is expected to be a file. The Content-Disposition and Content-Type are set for you.<br><br>`res.attachment('path/to/logo.png');`<br>`// Content-Disposition: attachment;`<br>`filename="logo.png"`<br>`// Content-Type: image/png` |
| sendFile(path [, options] [, fn]) | Transfers a file.<br><br>`res.sendFile('me.png', {maxAge:1, root:'/views/'}, function(err){});` |
| end([data][,encoding] | Use this to end the response without any data being returned.<br><br>`res.status(404);`<br>`res.end();` |
| format(object) | Use this if you are going to receive requests for content of more than one type. You can line up multiple pieces of code for each Accept HTTP header type.<br><br>`res.format({`<br>`  'text/plain': function(){`<br>`    res.send('Hi');`<br>`  },`<br>`  'text/html': function(){`<br>`    res.send('<p>Hi</p>');`<br>`  },`<br>`  'application/json': function(){`<br>`    res.send({ message: 'Hi' });`<br>`  },`<br>`  'default': function() {`<br>`    res.status(406).send('Not Acceptable');`<br>`  }`<br>`});` |

| append(field [, value]) | Adds the specified text and value to the header.<br><br>`res.append('Warning', '199 Miscellaneous warning');` |
|---|---|
| send([body]) | Sending of an HTTP response.<br><br>`res.send({ message: 'Hello' });` |
| sendStatus(code) | Sets the response code for the return.<br><br>`res.sendStatus(200);` |
| render(name, [, data][, callback]) | Template response sending. See the next section of this book for more information.<br><br>`res.render('user', { name: 'Tobi' },`<br>`function(err, html) {`<br>`   ...`<br>`});` |

# 9.6 Template Response Sending

One of the things that Express enables is sending server-side HTML generated from templates that have data bound to them. There are several popular template languages that are similar to HTML markup that are supported through Express. I will highlight just one, but you can investigate others.

Using the Express response object, you can formulate a response to send back with a function named res.render(). This function takes a file that contains the template as one parameter, referred to as the view. As a second parameter, you can provide the data object that binds to the template. The template that you have loaded through Express binds the data and produces the resulting HTML as the output to pass back on the request.

You can pass a third parameter as a callback function to get the rendered string, and process any errors that might have occurred. Here is what the code looks like that utilizes a template to send back as a response to a request:

```
app.set('views', path.join(__dirname, 'views'));
app.set('view engine', 'jade');

app.get('/test', function(req, res) {
  res.render('test.jade', {
    title: 'My News Stories ',
    stories: items
  });
});
```

146

First you need to have incorporated the NPM jade module into your project. Then you need to make calls to tell Express what directory the template files are in and also what template engine you are using. Express will then internally use the Jade module you have included in your project.

Notice the two `app.set()` calls used to configure the use of Jade. The `app.get()` sets up the request route with a handler. It is in that handler function you have the call to render the template with the given data to bind to it.

Refer to Jade's documentation to learn about the template syntax. It uses a curly brace syntax to bind to properties. Here is a Jade template that could take the passed in data context and bind those values to elements:

```
// test.jade file content for the template view
doctype html
html
  head
    title my jade template
  body
    h1 Hello #{title}
    div.newstbl
      each story in stories
        div.storyrow
          a(href=story.link)
            img.story-img(src=story.imgUrl)
            h6 #{story.title}
```

Be aware that, if you use template rendering, you are relying on server-side rendering of your HTML. If you prefer to utilize a SPA architecture on your client-side native or browser application, you would not want to do this. In part three I will describe how to return HTML that has Angular directives in it for client-side data binding and rendering. This will then give you as SPA architecture.

# Chapter 10: The MongoDB Module

This chapter is one of the most important ones in part two of this book. That is because the main purpose of your middle-tier service layer is to provide access to the data layer. To do that, you will be utilizing a Node.js module that has been created to interact with MongoDB on the back end. You will be learning how to use the "mongodb" module from the NPM repository.

It is necessary to include this module in your package.json file so that it is made available in your project. The usual `require()` statement is then used to make its functionality available in your code. I will cover that again later when you construct the NewsWatcher sample application.

I can now show you a few of the methods exposed with the "mongodb" module. The focus will be on learning the functions necessary to perform the CRUD operations.

*Note: The mongodb NPM module API is quite massive and it would take a large book to document it all. The purpose of this book is not to make you an expert in all of its usage. For example, there are functions to create and delete collections and perform other administrative duties that I have chosen to perform through the mLab management portal. You should certainly make a quick pass through the API to see what other capabilities it has that you might want to take advantage of. You can find the mongodb module on the NPM site and from there find a link to the documentation.*

## The MongoClient object

To begin with, your code needs to establish a connection to a MongoDB server. To do this, you use the `connect()` function of the mongodb module object. After establishing a connection, there are a lot of useful functions for interacting with a MongoDB collection. An example of the function signature to connect with is as follows:

```
connect(urlConnectionString, [options], [callback])
```

The first parameter of the function is the URL of the service endpoint for your MongoDB instance. The second parameter contains options that can be used for settings on the server, such as for a replica set, etc. The last parameter is your callback function, where you will receive the database object that you are connected to.

If you have an incorrect URL, you will get an error returned. You can find the URL connection string you need to use by opening the mLab management portal. Go to your home page and click on your deployment to get to your database. You will see the connection string listed at the top of the page.

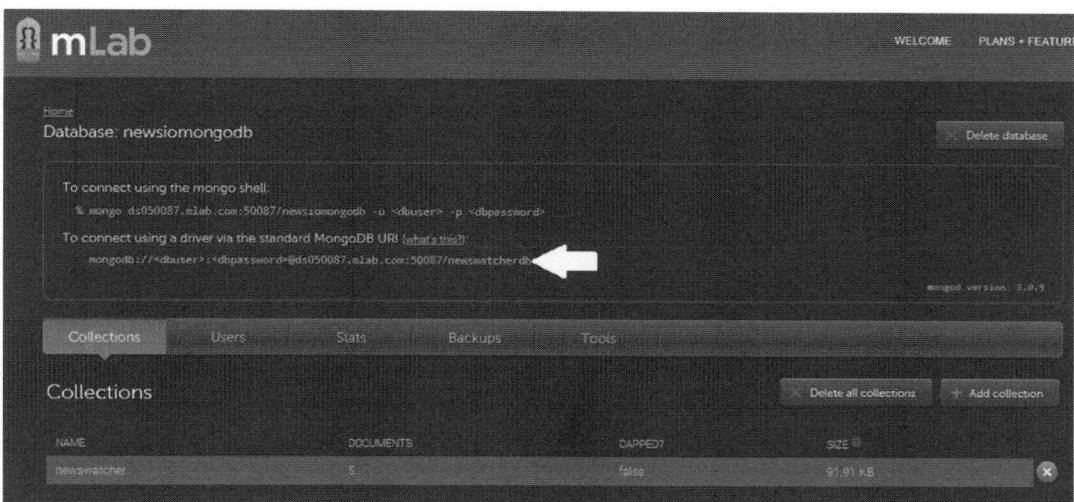

*Figure 45: mLab database page with connection url*

In more readable text, this is something like:

```
mongodb://<dbuser>:<dbpassword>@ds050087.mlab.com:50087/newswatcherdb
```

There are placeholders in there for a user and password. You need to click the **Users** tab and create a user login that you will use in your code. This is different from the account login you use with the administrative mLab portal.

Don't click the checkbox to make the user account read-only when you create the user. Here is some example code calling `connect()` to establish a connection using the URL from the above example with a made-up username and password.

```
var db = {};
var MongoClient = require('mongodb').MongoClient;

MongoClient.connect("mongodb://myUser:myPasswrd@ds050087.mongolab.com:50087
/newswatcherdb", function(err, dbConn) {
   db.dbConnection = dbConn;
   db.collection = dbConn.collection('newswatcher');
});
```

The code in the callback uses the database connection and calls the `collection()` function to get the "newswatcher" collection object that will be used to perform CRUD operations with.

149

# 10.1 Basic CRUD Operations

With the collection object now obtained, you are ready to perform the CRUD operations. You can now learn about the four fundamental CRUD operations necessary to utilize a MongoDB database. In the terminology of MongoDB (for single document interactions) CRUD translates to the following functions:

- `insertOne()`
- `findOne()`
- `findOneAndUpdate()`
- `findOneAndDelete()`

Now I'll walk you through each of the four functions and show you how to use them. Later, you will put together the NewsWatcher sample application and use them all again, plus a few others. At that time, you will make your code more robust with error handling.

*Note: There are actually variations of the CRUD functions listed above. For example, to find multiple documents, it is necessary to use the* `find()` *function. When reading any of the documentation, be careful to pay attention for any text stating that it is deprecated.*

## Create

The following is the function signature used for creating a document in a collection:

```
insertOne(doc, [options], [callback])
```

The first parameter is the JavaScript object that you want to have inserted. This then gets created as a BSON document. If you do not provide an `_id` property in your passed in JavaScript object, MongoDB will generate one for you when it stores the document.

Your callback function will have as the first parameter an error object that you can check to see if something went wrong on creation. Here is a sample that sends in an object, does not set any options, but uses the callback function to check for an error:

```
db.collection.insertOne({property1: "Hi", property2: 77}, function (err,
result) {
  if (err) console.LogError("Create error happened");
  else console.log(JSON.stringify(result.ops[0], null, 4));
});
```

The options parameter of the `insertOne()` function is an object that has a set of properties on it. This same object is used for many of the calls in the API. I will describe it here for your reference, as you will see this used again. All of the properties of this object are optional. You will not need them in the construction of the sample application. Here is a table that describes the properties of the `requests options` object:

**Request Options Object Properties:**

| Property: | Purpose: |
|---|---|
| w | The write concern. Dealing with the level of acknowledgement required, i.e. "majority". |
| wtimeout | The timeout you want for the write concern. |
| j | To specify the journal write concern. |
| serializeFunctions | Bool to serialize functions on any object. |
| forceServerObjectId | Bool for server assignment of _id values instead of driver. |
| bypassDocumentValidation | Bool for driver to bypass schema validation in MongoDB 3.2 or higher. |

The `result` parameter in the callback function has some properties you might be interested in. One of them is the `ops` property. It was used in the previous example and contained the returned document. The `result` parameters are as follows:

| Property: | Purpose: |
|---|---|
| insertedCount | The number of documents inserted. |
| ops | An array of all the documents inserted. |
| insertedId | The generated ObjectId. |
| connection | The connection object used. |
| result | The command result object returned from MongoDB |

# Read

To retrieve a single document from a collection, use the `findOne()` function. The following is the function signature for reading a document:

```
findOne(query, [options], [callback]) -> {Promise}
```

The first parameter is the query criteria. You can go back to chapter three to review what that looks like. What this function does is to simply return the very first document that matches the query criteria and then ignore the rest. The callback has an error object followed by the document return parameter. Here is an example usage of `findOne()`:

```
db.collection.findOne({ email: "nb@abc.com"}, function (err, doc) {
  if (err) console.LogError(err);
  else console.log(doc);
});
```

`Options` is an optional object with 20 optional properties you can use. Refer to the mongodb module's documentation for a complete list of properties. The following is a description of a few of them:

| Name | Type | Description |
|---|---|---|
| fields | object | The projection criteria to specify the fields to include or exclude. |
| hint | object | To tell the query what indexes to use. |
| explain | boolean | Return an object with query analysis and not the result. |
| raw | boolean | Return the BSON. |
| readPreference | ReadPreference \| string | Which machine in replica set to read from, such as the primary or secondary. |
| maxTimeMS | Number | How long to wait in milliseconds before aborting the query. |

`findOne()` returns a JavaScript promise if no callback was provided.

You can use the `explain` option to take a look at how well your indexes are working. You will see some JSON returned that gives you some interesting data about the query. Make sure to remove this option afterwards as it prevents your actual result from being returned.

# Update

The following is the function signature for updating documents in MongoDB:

```
findOneAndUpdate(filter, update, [options], [callback]) -> {Promise}
```

The first parameter is the filter parameter which is the query criteria needed to identify the document. The second parameter is for the update operators to be used. Your callback function will have as the first parameter, an error object that you can check to see if something went wrong on the update. Here is an example usage that uses an option to have the updated document returned in the callback:

```
db.collection.findOneAndUpdate(
   {email: "nb@abc.com"},
   { $set: { name: "Charles" }},
   { returnOriginal: false },
   function (err, result) {
      if (err) console.log(err);
      else if (result.ok != 1) console.log(result);
      else console.log(result.value);
});
```

The following is a description of the `options` object properties:

| Name | Type | Description |
|------|------|-------------|
| projection | object | The projection criteria to specify the fields to include or exclude in the return. |
| sort | object | Species a sorting order for multiple documents that are matched. |
| maxTimeMS | Number | How long to wait in milliseconds before aborting the query. |
| upsert | boolean | Create the document if it did not exist. |
| returnOriginal | boolean | Set this to `false` if you want the updated document returned |

`findOneAndUpdate()` returns a promise if no callback was provided.

# Delete

The following is the function signature for deleting documents in MongoDB:

```
findOneAndDelete(filter, [options], [callback]) -> {Promise}
```

The first parameter is the filter parameter query criteria needed to identify the document. Your callback function will have, as the first parameter, an error object that you can check to see if something went wrong on deletion. Here is an example usage:

```
db.collection.findOneAndDelete({email: "nb@abc.com"}, function(err, result)
{
  if (err) console.log(err);
  else if (result.ok != 1) console.log(result);
  else console.log("User Deleted");
});
```

Here is a description of the options object properties:

| Name | Type | Description |
|------|------|-------------|
| projection | object | The projection criteria to specify the fields to include or exclude in the return. |
| sort | object | Species a sorting order for multiple documents that are matched. |
| maxTimeMS | Number | How long to wait in milliseconds before aborting the query. |

`findOneAndDelete()` returns a promise if no callback was provided.

# 10.2 Aggregation Functionality

In the data layer chapters where the MongoDB capabilities for querying were covered, I omitted one specialized type of query. What I omitted was the capability of MongoDB to perform aggregation over the data. Aggregation gives you the ability to report on summarizations of data such as grouping, or finding the sum, min, or max.

This gets rather involved, so I left it until here to even mention this capability. You really need to make this a focus of some serious study in order to master all that is possible with the aggregation capability.

Here is a simple example to give you a feel for how it works. Imagine that for the example bookstore used in prior examples, you wanted to find out the number of customers living in each state. You would use the aggregate() function for this. The following example is the signature of the aggregate() function:

```
aggregate(pipeline, [options], callback)
```

The pipeline parameter is an array of MongoDB supported aggregate commands. Think of these as stages the data is being piped through from one to the next. There are quite a few aggregate operators you can string together.

Here then is an example usage that would give the resulting count of people by state:

```
db.collection.aggregate(
  [
    { $group: { "_id": "$address.state", "count": { $sum: 1 } } }
  ]).toArray(function(err, result) {
    console.log(result);
});
```

The result might be as follows:

```
[{ _id: 'UT', count: 54 },
 { _id: 'KS', count: 988 },
 { _id: 'FL', count: 1259 }]
```

The callback has an error object you can check.

There are operators like $match and $project that you can insert to help narrow down the documents and what properties are passed through.

# 10.3 What About an ODM/ORM?

This book shows how to directly connect to MongoDB with a node module created specifically for that purpose. But there is another NPM module you can use that approaches interfacing with MongoDB in a completely different way.

Those from a relational database background will understand that there are such things as Object Relational Mappings (ORMs) for connecting to a SQL Server. Perhaps you are familiar with Entity Framework for .Net, or Hibernate for Java? The equivalent in a document-based database is called an Object Data Mapping (ODM).

Look up "mongoose" on NPM or GitHub and you will find an ODM/ORM that sits on top of MongoDB. This module can be used instead of the mongodb one that we covered.

The mongoose module adds an additional abstraction. With this, you get features like schematization of the data and validation.

Here is what code would look like that uses the mongoose module to save and query a document. I will take the sample of the customer document that might exist in the online bookstore example. I will cut way back on the number of properties though, so it is a shorter example. Here is what some code would look like that uses mongoose:

```
var mongoose = require('mongoose');
mongoose.connect('<The usual connection URL>');

var Customer = mongoose.model('Customer', { name: String, age: Number,
email: String });

var c = new Customer({ name: 'Aaron', age: 32, email: 'ab@blah.com' });

c.save(function(err) {
  if (err) console.log(err);
});

mongoose.model('Customer').find(function(err, customers) {
  console.log(customers);
});
```

There are ways to put each of the ODM capabilities in on your own. For example, to add in a simple module that helps you do server-side input validation, you can use "express-validator" or "joi". But why go to all the work, if an ODM already exists? An ODM module may be the way to go to give you more robustness with your application.

# Chapter 11: Advanced Node and MongoDB Issues

There are some particularly difficult issues to be aware of that require careful coordination across Node and MongoDB technologies. There are also certain intricacies that must be handled. Done incorrectly, it can be disastrous. Done correctly, everything will hum along. This chapter will cover a few of the subtleties you might need to address.

# 11.1 Scheduling Code to Run

A timer function can be used to schedule code to run at a later time. This can be done as a one-time request, or it can be set up to happen on a recurring interval. The following code schedules a function to run in five seconds and also shows how to pass in a parameter:

```
setTimeout(myFcn, 5000, "five");

function myFcn(param1) {
    console.log("Hi %s", param1);
}
```

The callback is not going to happen exactly at 5000 milliseconds, but Node will do its best to fit it in when it is time and the callback is then given to V8 to run.

Use the function `setInterval()` to schedule a recurring function. If you want to cancel the recurring timer, you can cancel it at any time with `clearInterval()`. The following example shows how this would look:

```
var id = setInterval(myFcn, 5000, "five");
...
clearInterval(id);
```

Be aware that Node will run your function over and over, even if the previous call has been blocked and has not yet completed. If you want a callback executed only if the previous one has completed, you could write your own implementation of `setInterval()` to prevent that behavior.

Another function named `setImmediate()` is available to use that does not have a timer to go off, but places the callback to be executed after I/O, but before `setTimeout()` and `setInterval()` events are processed.

If you are interested in scheduling code to run at an even higher priority, you can use the process object `nextTick()` function. Be careful to not use this unless you are using it responsibly. This call will place your callback to be executed above all other processing in the event queue, even before I/O callbacks are executed. If you over do this too often, at some point you will completely cut out all I/O processing.

# 11.2 Being RESTful

It is up to you to design the URLs that your Node application will respond to. You can create a RESTful service and even support OData if you like. You are also free to include support for query strings, if that is your preference. If you go the RESTful route, there are a few things to keep in mind.

The first thing to remember is that RESTful web services are intended to be stateless. If you are scaling your server-side Node process and using the cluster module, or have scaling through Elastic Beanstalk, then you most likely have stateless servers. Any one of your servers can process any incoming client. If you really want state information kept around, you can store state information with the client, or have it cached for server-side retrieval in something like a redis cache.

Make sure to carefully design your REST API URLs so that they make sense. There are standard things to consider such as using nouns and not verbs in your paths. You may run into some dilemmas, but there is probably an answer for your challenge in a forum somewhere.

When you come out with a new version of your REST API, you need to make that apparent and perhaps support multiple versions for a while. You can strive to keep your API as backward compatible as possible. You can insert a version number into your path to move clients from one version to another. For example, if you had "/api/users" as a path, you could have clients start using "/api/v2/users" for new functionality. You can always tack a query string on the end to specify the versioning such as "?Version=2015-12-22". An HTTP header setting is also possible such as "x-version: 2015-12-22".

# 11.3 Concurrency Problems

Once your application starts to have multiple concurrent users, you can run into issues updating documents in MongoDB. Let's take the example where you have a single document that contains a list of high scores for an online game and you want to keep the top five scores. As users finish a game, a call is made to submit the score they achieved and insert it into the list of top scores, if it fits. High scores are best, so if a new score is added, the lowest score is then dropped off the list.

If multiple players all submit their scores at the same time, you can see that some contention might arise with updates to this single document. Here is a diagram of how this might look:

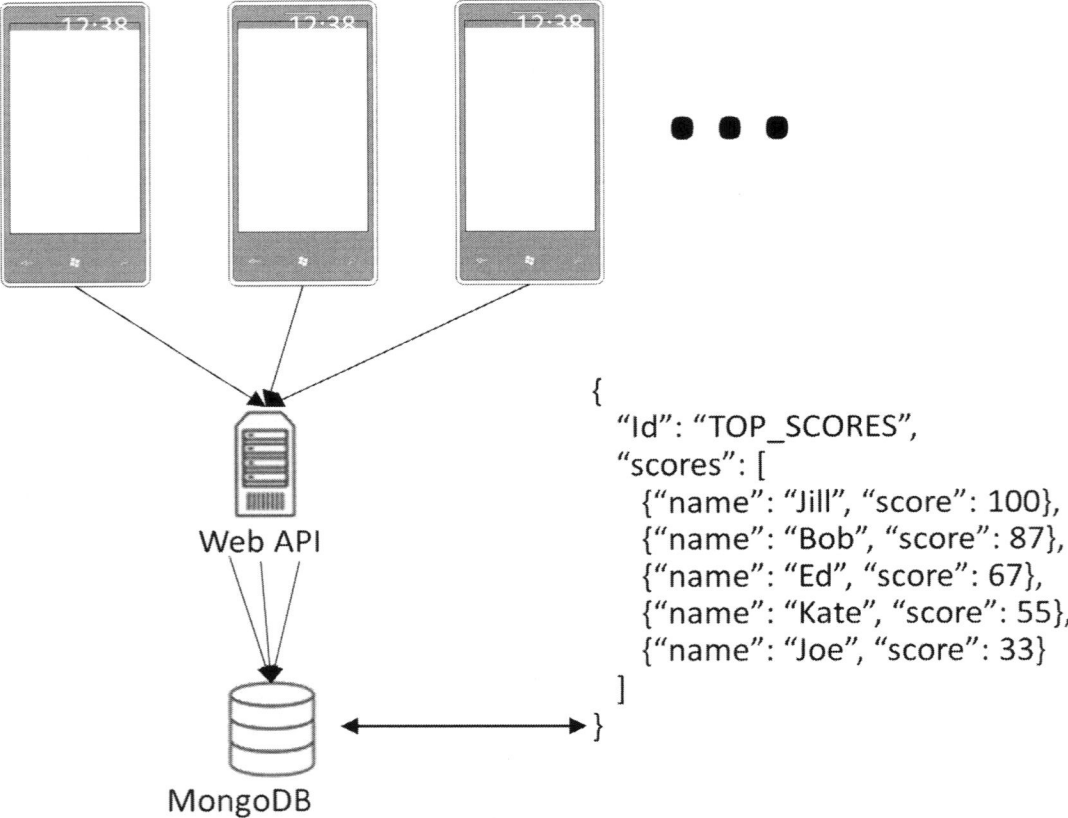

*Figure 46: Top score contention illustration*

The thing to realize is that all of these users are causing score insertion code to run in parallel. Each request gets sent to a Node.js framework call to allow multiple simultaneous calls to read and update the single document in the MongoDB DBMS.

What would happen if two scores are submitted for processing at the exact same time? Each request would first read the document and then insert a score if it is higher than the lowest number in the list. The document would then be sent back for replacement in the collection. Here is a sequence diagram that illustrates the problem with time flowing top to bottom:

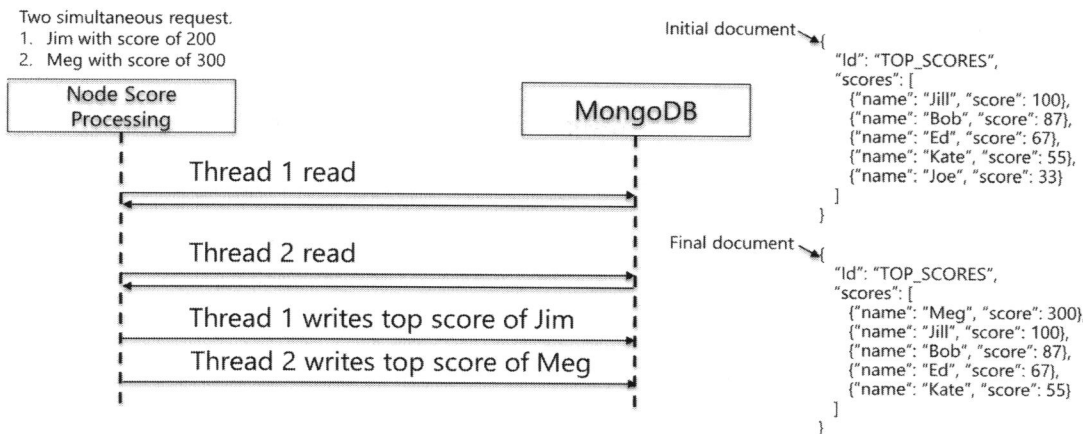

*Figure 47: Simultaneous update*

If you look carefully, you can see that the final document is not what it should be. You would want to see both Meg and Jim inserted at the top and then Kate and Joe dropped off from the bottom of the array. Instead Meg is at the top and only is Joe dropped off. Jim is really going to be disappointed when he checks the high scores and does not see his name listed.

The desired outcome does not happen. This is because neither update knew what the other was doing and so the last write "wins". This is a classic problem and not something unique to MongoDB. There have indeed been many solutions invented over the years. For example, some database technologies offer locking. The problem with this is that locking can produce deadlocks that require detection and deletion. MongoDB does not support user API code-controlled locking. It does, however, do this on its own for certain calls you make.

The solution that MongoDB and its underlying storage engine, WiredTiger, implement for you is termed optimistic concurrency at the document level. First of all, you need to use the `findOneAndUpdate()` function. If you were to use read, followed by update functions, simultaneous reads will still get the same data and one write will be preserved.

With `findOneAndUpdate()`, if two calls come in, the first one locks out the second one from doing anything until the first call has finished on that document. The second call will not even do the read until the first one has completed its write of the data. The second call keeps retrying for a time until it is successful.

Let's go back to the initial sequence diagram and draw this out one more time, this time with retries put in:

# PART II: The Service Layer (Node.js)

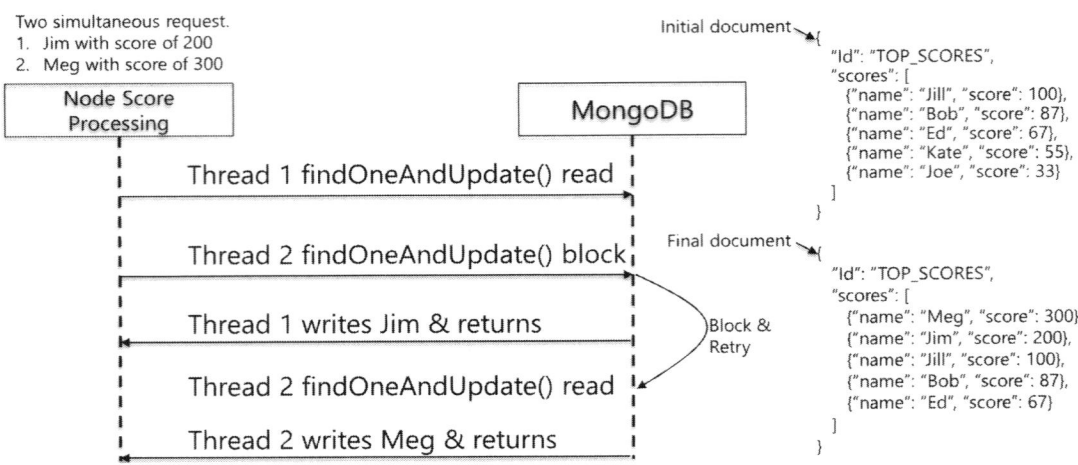

*Figure 48: Simultaneous writes with optimistic concurrency*

Optimistic concurrency retry logic can be inefficient if your database is always being locked and retries are constantly happening. Imagine if four users consistently update their scores at the same time every second over and over. If four attempts are made at the same time, only one can succeed and then the other three must try again. The second round has three attempts and one works, and so forth.

The point is that you might be wasting MongoDB compute time. This may cause your MongoDB service to perform poorly. This is one good reason to implement sharding, as data is spread out to more than one database and you have fewer write conflicts if they are all with different documents. You may still run into cases where you simply have a "hot" document with lots of simultaneous updates all of the time, as was illustrated with the game scores.

If you want to really implement the ultimate architecture to handle massive scaling and avoid the conflicts you get with optimistic concurrency, you need to create a single queue that is outside of all your node processes.

You would place your update operation requests in an external AWS SQS resource for global access across all node processes. You then need to create a single unique node process that would watch the AWS queue and process the requests. The following example shows this solution. The dots indicating multiple clients and also multiple machines with load balancing on incoming requests:

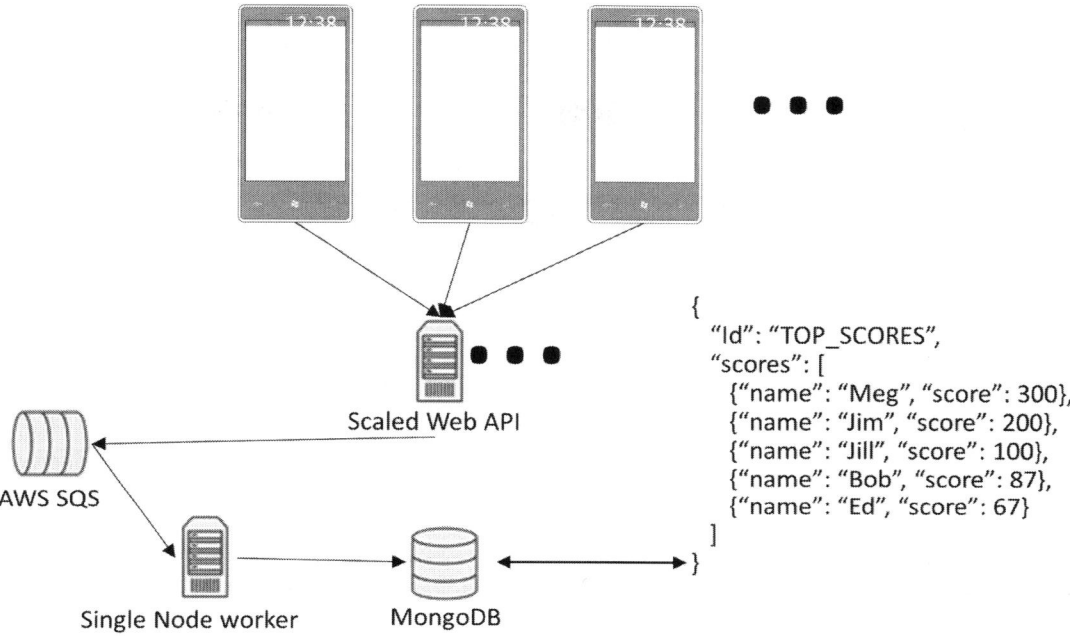

*Figure 49: Queue serialization solution*

This would also be the safest solution if you really had to ensure consistency and repeatability. There is one main drawback with this solution — you need to deal with the issue of returning back to the initial caller if the operation succeeded. This might not be important, but it could be.

You can decide to take the "fire-and-forget" approach and always return success. Perhaps, losing a top score for some reason can be considered acceptable if later the worker role fails to insert a score for some reason.

What if, however, you had a bank transaction that you want to be sure succeeded and give a notification one way or the other back to the user? You would need to implement some way to do that return indication in an asynchronous way.

Of course, you must always step back and look at the data model design that caused this contention issue in the first place. Perhaps you will need to normalize the data so that you don't have concurrent access happening.

# 11.4 Secure Access Authorization

You should conduct a review of all of your data connection points and scrutinize all data that is being transferred and stored. Make sure to take appropriate precautions with sensitive data you are safeguarding for your customers. Information such as a home addresses can be used to identify a person and should never be leaked. Financial and medical records many times have laws and regulations concerning their storage and transmission.

You are not just trying to ensure your business interests are safe, you are responsible to safeguard your customers from any harm.

One very important detail you need to work out is how users will identify themselves and be allowed to access your Web API from a client application. The other security concern you need to solve is how to prevent any eavesdropping or man-in-the-middle type of hacks as information flows back and forth from the client to the Web API service.

This section will explore these and other related topics and present a solution for each.

## Access token

Once a person is identified by their logging in, a Web Service needs to recognize them and allow them access to data associated with their account. One possible means of user interaction authorization is to have them sign in and then use a session cookie with every request coming in.

Another similar mechanism is to generate an access token and have that passed in with every client request. There is a standard way to do this with something called a JSON Web Token (JWT).

A JWT is something that can be generated on the server side in response to a client login request when they present a username and password. The JWT is basically an encoded set of information about the user that is signed to make sure it is not tampered with.

The JWT should always be transferred using HTTPS because it can easily be decrypted. It really should not contain anything that could compromise your security. Here is the sequence diagram for how a JWT is created and passed from layer to layer:

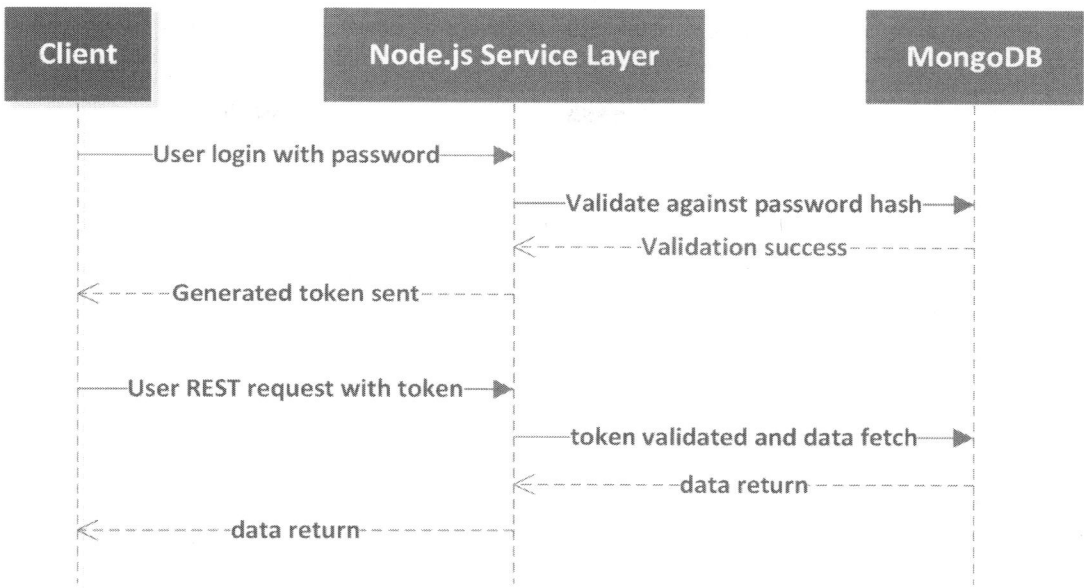

*Figure 50: JWT token passing*

You can pack into the JWT whatever you want. Put in it anything that would help you in your processing going back and forth. One nice thing would be to add in the IP address as well as the HTTP user-agent header value. This can then be validated on later calls to make sure you still have the same person using the token. You can also set an expiration time on the token so that a person is required to log in every so often.

If you want to completely offload the user authentication, you can use the Oath 2 standard. This allows you to have a person redirected to some other web presence they already trust and log in there first. Users might prefer this, as they only need to have one single sign-on credential to manage.

With the NPM passport module, you can implement Oath 2 to delegate the user authentication to an externally trusted site such as Google or Facebook, etc. The user is redirected to sign in through one of those sites and then a token of authenticity is passed back that has information about who they are.

# All data traffic should be encrypted
One of the first things to do once you have sufficient momentum on your code, is to implement certificate-based authentication and encryption using the HTTPS standard. This will enable your site to be viewed as legitimate and also ensure that data is transferred using the encrypted TLS/SSL protocol.

If you search on the internet, you will find code samples that show you how to configure Express to require HTTPS. If your Node.js service were to be hosted on a machine directly exposed on the Internet, this is what you would need to do:

```
const https = require('https');
const fs = require('fs');

const options = {
   key: fs.readFileSync('keys/agent-key.pem'),
   cert: fs.readFileSync('keys/agent-cert.pem')
};

https.createServer(options, (req, res) => {
   res.writeHead(200);
   res.end('hello world\n');
}).listen(8000);
```

However, if you choose to use a PaaS solution, the above code is not necessary. This is because your Node.js service is hidden behind the server that acts as the reverse proxy and load balancer. This means that the AWS Elastic Beanstalk service external-facing load balancer needs to be configured for HTTPS. You will see how this is set up when the sample application is put together.

# 11.5 Service Attacks

When you expose a service on the Internet, it will be vulnerable to attacks of all kinds. Some attacks might be intentionally malicious and others just annoying. All threats should be taken seriously. At a minimum, they can disrupt your service, which is unacceptable. Beyond that, attacks can steal sensitive information and do damage to your customers and to your own reputation.

Obviously, a simple native mobile phone application game of tic-tac-toe would not have as large an attack surface as a three-tier e-commerce application. The more infrastructure and code that you have, the larger your attack surface will be. Hackers will look for the vulnerability that is easiest to exploit. Your security is only as good as your weakest point of attack.

To really get an accurate look at all possible avenues of attack, you need to draw out a data flow diagram that shows all the processes, interactions, data stores, and data flows. Each process would represent those that you own, or ones that you are relying on. Some of those could be classified as completely external and possibly out of your hands, but they should still be on the diagram.

For each of the elements in the diagram you would do some analysis to determine what threats could exist. For example, if you had a SQL database in your diagram, you would determine what it is storing, how data gets in and out and what configuration and administration is happening. You would likely discover that your SQL database would be vulnerable to a SQL injection attack.

With all of your analysis done, you would mitigate each of the vulnerabilities. In some cases it might simply involve a few lines of code, in other cases you might need to re-architect parts of your system. To really address this topic, you should buy a book specifically dedicated just to this topic. I will now present a few security concerns associated with Node.js and Web API interactions.

# Never trust ANY input!

One basic strategy to remember is to never trust any input. Always do what you can to validate any data before using it. Look into using the node modules "validator" or "joi". Using a data layer ORM/ODM can give you these data validation capabilities, but you still need to sanitize your data from script injections. Here is some validation using the joi module:

```
var schema = {
    displayName: joi.string().alphanum().min(3).max(50).required(),
    email: joi.string().email().min(7).max(50).required(),
    password: joi.string().regex(/^[a-zA-Z0-9]{3,30}$/)
};

joi.validate(req.body, schema, function (err, value) {
    if (err)
        return next(err);
});
```

You can see that only alphanumeric characters are allowed for the user display name. The joi module is also making sure no extra properties exist on the body. These types of restrictions are extremely important, so don't underestimate their usefulness.

Another issue is data transmission size. What if someone started sending really large JSON packages, or ones that had extra objects or properties in them? You can set up your body-parser middleware to turn down requests that are too large. The default size is 100kb so you can make that smaller just to be safe. Here is how you set that up:

```
app.use(bodyParser.json({ limit: '10kb' }));
```

Let's now looks at some of the types of attacks that could occur on your exposed Web API. None of these are really specific to Node.js. They exist because of the fundamental way that browsers and HTTP work.

# DOS/DDOS attack

The denial-of-service (DoS) or distributed denial-of-service (DDoS) attack is where traffic is thrown at your web app to try to bring it down. It might be possible to overwhelm it so that others are prevented from using it. If successful, the attack will deny service to the actual people that are intended to use it. In some cases, it might actually lead to incorrect behavior of your application, so as to exploit it for other gains.

The distributed version just means that the attacker is employing multiple distributed machines at once. The term bot is commonly used, meaning that these machines are set up to run scripts or programs that carry out the attack and constantly enlist other machines to also participate. It acts like a virus and replicates.

A DoS attack is purely malicious and would rarely happen just by accident. Regardless, you need to be prepared for it and mitigate this risk. You can be sure that big e-commerce sites like Amazon and eBay see these kinds of attacks and take them seriously. An attack like this might even cause your scaling infrastructure to kick in unnecessarily and start costing you more money in cloud operating costs.

I must of course bring up what has already been mentioned – never do anything compute intensive on the main Node.js thread. This is because, if you have a lot of requests coming in that trigger some intensive synchronous code then you will have your process basically unable to respond. This will just make it easier for a real DoS to occur if you let your main thread get overloaded. Let's now look at ways to mitigate a DoS attack.

When you create your Elastic Beanstalk Node.js application environment in the first place, it sets up Nginx to act as the reverse proxy and load balancer. Nginx can be configured to limit the rate per IP address as well as limiting connection count per IP address.

Another approach you can take using AWS is to set up an AWS API Gateway in front of your service layer. That will give you a lot of what you need for defense, such as throttling per connection to head off a DoS attack. Besides that, you also get authorization, reporting, and API consumption of your web API contract.

You could also do some type of IP blocking on your own, such as tracking the access time per IP and then limiting each IP to once per second access. Check out the NPM module express-rate-limit. Of course, you could use a cloud-mitigation provider that would use their expertise to track patterns of attack and identify DDoS attacks and disable them.

# XSS – Cross-Site Scripting

An XSS hack is where some foreign script gets injected and run as part of your web-rendered site. A likely vulnerability would be where you are accepting input from the user and then later re-displaying that back to them and others that view the site. The browser does not bother to stop JavaScript that was maliciously put in, as it cannot tell the difference. Especially, if you consider that your application allowed the user to enter something in the first place. Normal users will not be typing in malicious scripts to be run, it is the hackers that love to do this for fun and profit.

Let's take an example of something that could affect the NewsWatcher application. In that application, people can comment on a shared news story. This is an occasion where input from the user is accepted and later displayed back to them. Let's say that as a comment on a news story, a malicious user enters the following:

```
<script>alert("Hi");</script><img src="smiley.gif">
```

Now all other users looking at the comment will be affected. In the UI, you might have some HTML that displays all of the comments and the DOM ends up looking as follows:

```
<ul>
  <li>
    <p>'<script>alert("Hi");</script><img src="smiley.gif">'</p>
  </li>
</ul>
```

Everyone will now see an alert box and also a cute little smiley face staring back at them. You never intended for this to happen, but you did nothing to stop it. The savvy hacker could even hack the client-side JavaScript code and mess with the JSON before it gets sent back to the server. Web APIs simply can never trust the data that is sent to them

Imagine though if the hacker referenced some script across the internet that really wreaked havoc? If the hacker understood what your API was on the backend, they could run any command as if they were a logged in person and really do some damage. This means they would have hijacked the user session.

This goes back to the simple statement that you should never trust user input. To mitigate this, you could take action to validate the input as you collect it. For example, in the NewsWatcher code, you validate things like the user name and don't allow anything but alpha numeric characters. Your sanitization could also scan all characters and change character like '<' into "&lt;".

Fortunately, for the NewsWatcher application, when you are using Angular and bind your data, Angular does the work to disable any scripts from running. Angular simply displays the actual text without letting the browser interpret it. In the case of the example above, you would actually see the literal string "<script>alert("Hi");</script><img src="smiley.gif">" in the list and all would be good.

# CSRF – Cross–Site Request Forgery

A CSRF hack is where a request is made to a site you are currently logged into with your browser. You would have already been authenticated and had an authorization cookie stored by the browser. The attacker would trick you into viewing a page they had set up and as that was loaded in the browser, it would run a script that would send a request to the site you had already been logged onto.

As an example, let's say you were logged on to your banking web site. Now, while still logged on, you open up an email that was from a malicious attacker that said "Click here and win a million dollars!". When you click on the link, the destination URL directs you to their malicious site that loads a page that runs a script that sends requests to your banking site and transfers money to them and changes your password at the same time. Since you are already logged on, the browser happily sends the authentication cookie along with the request and you are hacked. The banking site had no idea that this request was not valid.

Our NewsWatcher sample application does not use cookies, so it is not vulnerable to this attack. The JWT token sending is under the control of your client code, and is not automatically sent by the browser like a cookie is.

If you do end up having implemented some design that is vulnerable to a CSRF hack, you can use the "csrf" NPM module to implement a mitigation. This will create a secret token that only your site knows that is only sent from your pages.

# The NPM Helmet module

I have discussed each of the security concerns and discussed mitigations. In this section, you will take a look at the Helmet NPM module that would give you the ability to further mitigate possible attacks.

The Helmet module tweaks your HTTP headers to set things up to utilize certain best practices for security risk mitigations. The Helmet module works as Express middleware by injecting itself into the request-response chain. It does not do anything that you can't do by hand. I recommend it though, as it would take you a lot more lines of code for you to accomplish everything that is does with a single line.

I will show you some code that will be the starting point when using Helmet. This code will set up things like enforcing HTTPS, mitigating clickjack attacks, certain XSS mitigations, and attacks based on MIME-type overriding attacks.

You can take the defaults and further specify any deviations from there that you like. Refer to documentation for any of the specific HTTP headers you want to individually control on your own. The following code shows you how easy it is to use helmet:

```
var express = require('express');
var helmet = require('helmet');

var app = express();
app.use(helmet()); // Take the defaults to start with
```

The one usage you do need to control on your own is that which is used with the setting of a Content Security Policy (CSP). This basically lets the browser be aware of where resources can come from. This will then prevent resources unknown to you from being injected. The basic usage of helmet with CSP added in becomes the following:

```
var express = require('express');
var helmet = require('helmet');

var app = express();
app.use(helmet()); // Take the defaults to start with
app.use(helmet.csp({
   // Specify directives for content sources
   directives: {
      defaultSrc: ["'self'"],
      scriptSrc: ["'self'", "'unsafe-inline'", 'ajax.googleapis.com',
                  'maxcdn.bootstrapcdn.com'],
      styleSrc: ["'self'", "'unsafe-inline'", 'maxcdn.bootstrapcdn.com'],
      fontSrc: ["'self'", 'maxcdn.bootstrapcdn.com'],
      imgSrc: ['*']
      // reportUri: '/report-violation',
   }
}));
```

If you want to have violation notifications sent back to your service, you can uncomment the reportUri setting and then handle that Express route in your code. Refer to documentation for some sample code for that. Helmet cannot be your only mitigation for security threats. You need a thorough analysis of your data flow diagram to come up with every threat and start building your security plan.

# The Node Security Project initiative

There is an ongoing initiative to audit the code of some of the more popular Node modules. This of course is by no means comprehensive, but it is good that this is underway. You can download a tool to run that will scan your package.json file and tell you if there are any known vulnerabilities with the NPM modules you are using. Here is how you download it and run it:

```
npm install -g nsp
nsp check
```

Make sure to execute it in the folder where your package.json file is.

# Chapter 12: NewsWatcher App Development

It is now time to begin constructing a Node.js Service layer that integrates in with the existing MongoDB data layer set up in part one of the book. This chapter now takes the concepts you have already learned about Node and applies them in a real project. What you will be creating is a RESTful web API that your presentation layer will be able to hook up to. You will learn how to implement everything needed for a fully functional cloud web service. You will also utilize best practices for testing and DevOps in the chapters that follow.

*Note: Don't forget that you can access all of the code for the NewsWatcher sample project at https://github.com/eljamaki01/NewsWatcherAWS.*

# 12.1 Install the Necessary Tools

One of the amazing things about Node is how simple and quick it is to set up a server. Node.js runs on every major OS out there, including being hosted in AWS as a PaaS offering using Elastic Beanstalk. Using Elastic Beanstalk is a great choice because it is a proven way to set up and run a scalable production environment.

Install the following:
- ✓ A code editor such as Visual Studio Code, Sublime text, Vim, etc.
- ✓ Node.js from https://nodejs.org/. Get a stable version. This installs the node executable for you to run and also includes NPM.

*Note: Visual Studio Code is not equal to Visual Studio. VS Code is a completely new tool that offers a rich editing environment as well as integrated features for source code control and debugging. VS Code has the capability to launch tasks through the means of tools like Gulp with no need to jump out to a command line. These tools can be used to automate build and test steps that you need to run frequently. With Visual Studio Code, you will be able to create a project and run it locally on your machine and have access to IntelliSense, debugging, and web app publishing through Git/GitHub.*

# 12.2 Create an Express Application

Start by creating a folder for your application named "NewsWatcherVSCode". You can now create the minimum amount of code required for a Node.js application. To help maintain your sanity, you should start with the smallest amount of code possible and push it all the way to deployment. This will eliminate many unneeded investigations of issues unrelated to just getting the basics up and working.

Launch Visual Studio Code and click **File->Open Folder**, then select the "NewsWatcherVSCode" folder you just created. With VS Code open, you see the **EXPLORE** view open and in there find two subfolders.

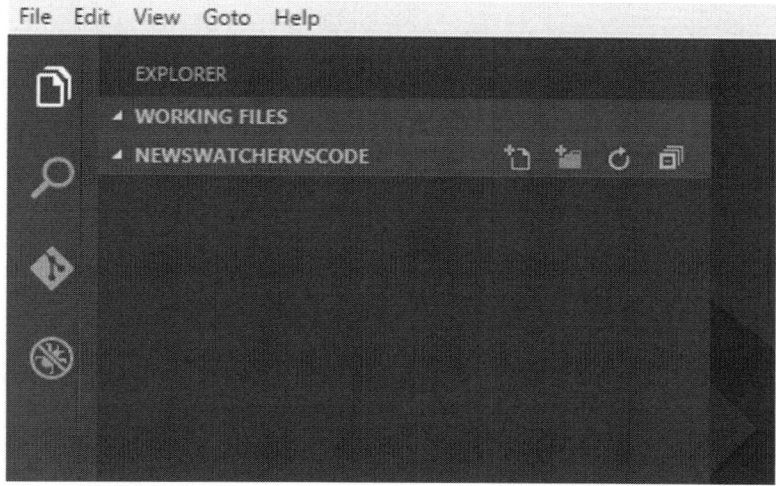

*Figure 51: VS Code UI*

The **NEWSWATCHERVSCODE** folder shows you all files and subfolders you would see with your file explorer. The **WORKING FOLDERS** subfolder shows your recently edited files, so you can keep them visible for quick access.

You can now get started and create a simple Node.js application, and then deploy it to your AWS Elastic Beanstalk web server. Once that is verified as running ok, you can add more code to it to fill out the full functionality of the REST web service.

On the NEWSWATCHER subfolder, click on the icon to create new files. Start by creating these three files:
- .gitignore
- package.json
- server.js

The .gitignore file will not be used right now, but would come into use when you make use of Git and GitHub. You place in there what files you want to exclude from Git control.

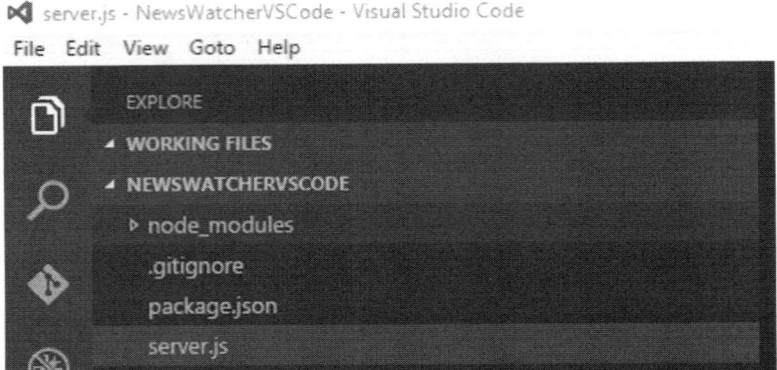

*Figure 52: VS Code's initial three files for NewsWatcher*

The node_modules folder will automatically be created when you install the node modules with the npm install command.

Add the following code to the server.js file:

```
var express = require('express');
var app = express();

app.get('/', function (req, res) {
  console.log('Send message on get request');
  res.send('Hello full-stack development!');
});

app.set('port', process.env.PORT || 3000);

var server = app.listen(app.get('port'), function () {
  console.log('Express server listening on port:' +
              server.address().port);
});
```

Add the following lines to the package.json file:

```
{
  "name": "NewsWatcher",
  "version": "0.0.0",
  "description": "NewsWatcher",
  "main": "server.js",
  "author": {
    "name": "yourname",
    "email": ""
```

```
  },
  "scripts": {
    "start": "node server.js"
  },
  "dependencies": {
    "express": "^4.13.4"
  }
}
```

Save all of the files, then open a command prompt window and navigate to your project's directory. At the command prompt, type `npm install`. This will look at your package.json file, install the standard Node modules, and also install the Express module that is listed as a dependency. A new directory will be added with the name `node_modules`.

You can now try running your Node project locally. Once it is proven to function, you will work on getting it deployed to AWS. At the command prompt, type `npm start`. You can also type `node server.js` to run. If the project runs successfully, you will see the following console output:

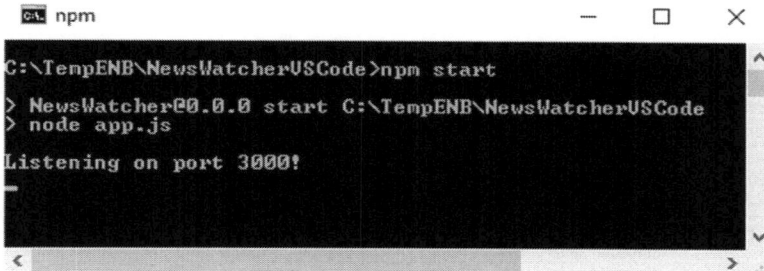

*Figure 53: local console output*

Open a web browser and navigate to http://localhost:3000/. In the browser window, you will see your message:

*Figure 54: Project message in a browser window*

173

# 12.3 Deploying to AWS

It is now time to create your Elastic Beanstalk app through the AWS Management Console. You must already have an AWS account to continue.

To create the app:
1.  Open a web browser and navigate to https://console.aws.amazon.com/console/.
2.  In the upper right corner of the web page, for **Region**, select **US East (N. Virginia)** as the region you want your services to be running in. It's important to select this region because you will later want to set up a certificate to be able to require HTTPS with your site. As of the writing of this book, you must use this region.

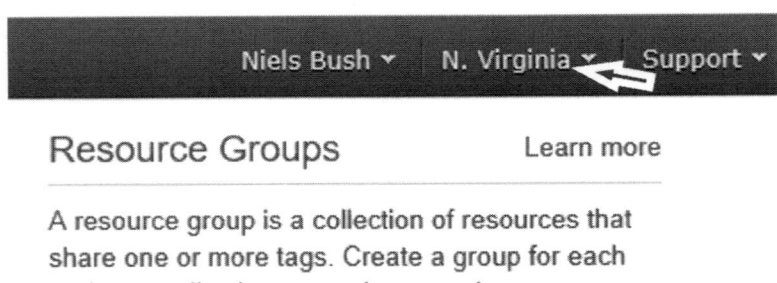

*Figure 55: Region selection*

3.  From the selection of services, click **Elastic Beanstalk**:

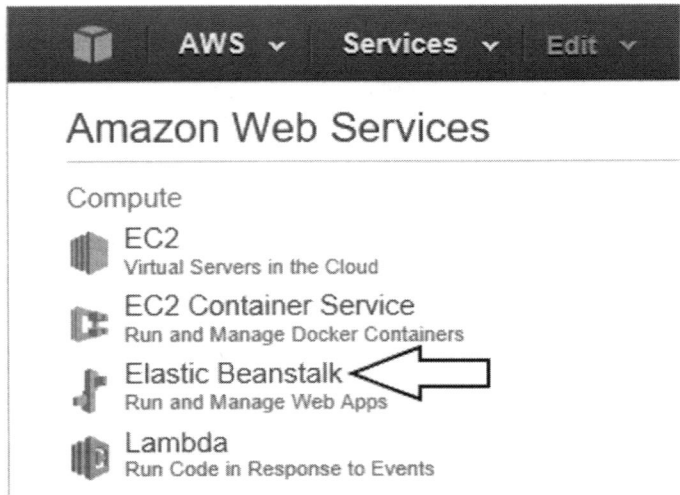

*Figure 56: Select Elastic Beanstalk*

4. Select **Node.js** as your platform.
5. Click **Launch Now**. This will give you a preconfigured machine that knows to startup and launch your Node application.

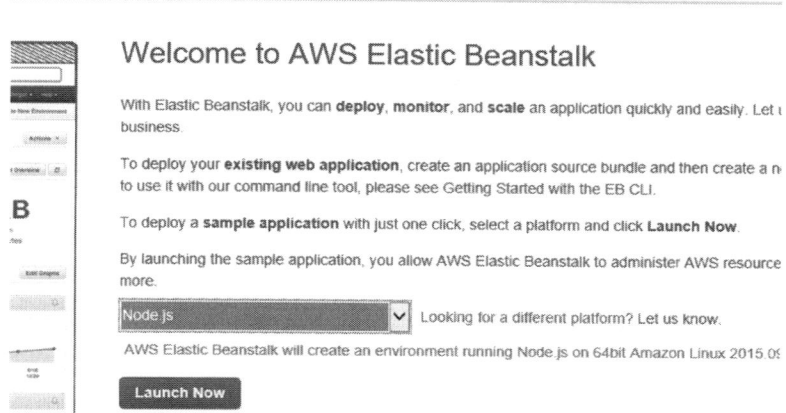

## Welcome to AWS Elastic Beanstalk

With Elastic Beanstalk, you can **deploy**, **monitor**, and **scale** an application quickly and easily. Let t business.

To deploy your **existing web application**, create an application source bundle and then create a n to use it with our command line tool, please see Getting Started with the EB CLI.

To deploy a **sample application** with just one click, select a platform and click **Launch Now**.

By launching the sample application, you allow AWS Elastic Beanstalk to administer AWS resource more.

Node.js ⌄   Looking for a different platform? Let us know.

AWS Elastic Beanstalk will create an environment running Node.js on 64bit Amazon Linux 2015.0!

**Launch Now**

*Figure 57: Platform selection*

Unfortunately, this creates something for you without letting you walk through the steps to decide things like the name. You can terminate this environment later. It is just one of those quirks with AWS when you first get started and create your first environment.

To create an application that you can control the settings for:
1. On the upper right corner of the Elastic Beanstalk console, click **Create New Application**.
2. Enter NewsWatcher as your application name.

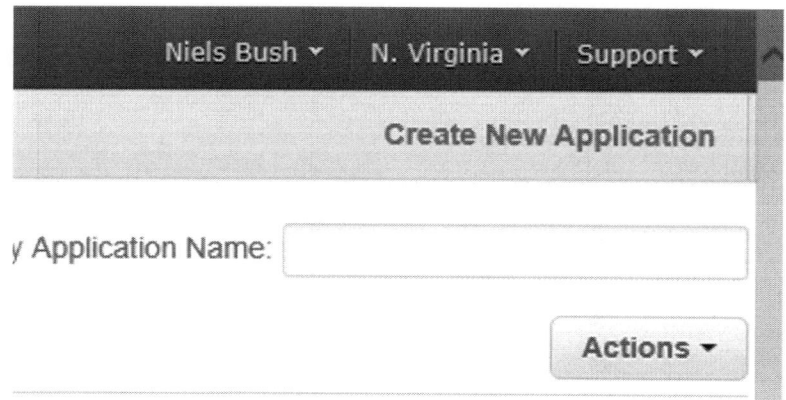

*Figure 58: Elastic Beanstalk create new application*

3. In the Elastic Beanstalk console, select the NewsWatcher environment.
4. Click **Actions** -> **Create New Environment**.
5. Click the **Create web server** button.
6. Select Node.js **Predefined configuration**.
7. Select **Load balancing, auto scaling** in Environment type and click **Next**.

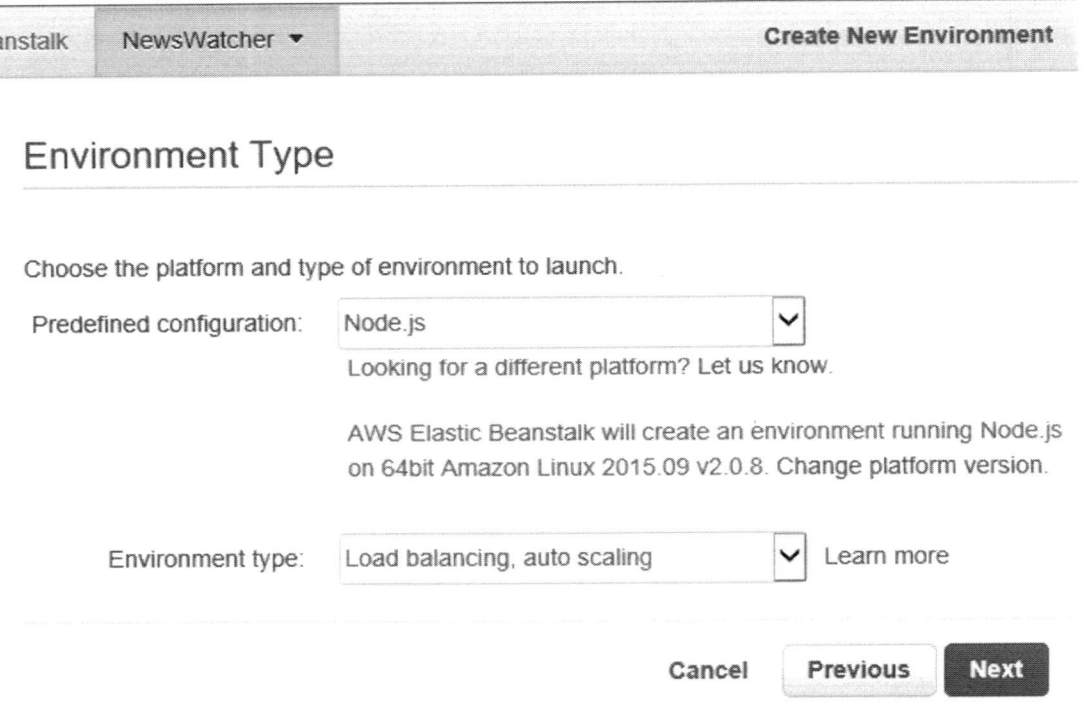

Figure 59: Elastic Beanstalk choose environment

8. Leave everything as is on the next page and click **Next**.
9. On the **Environment Information** page, type "newswatcher" as the **Environment name** to "newswatcher" and click **check availability**. If that name is not available, keep editing the name and checking availability until you have a name that is available.
10. Click **Next**.

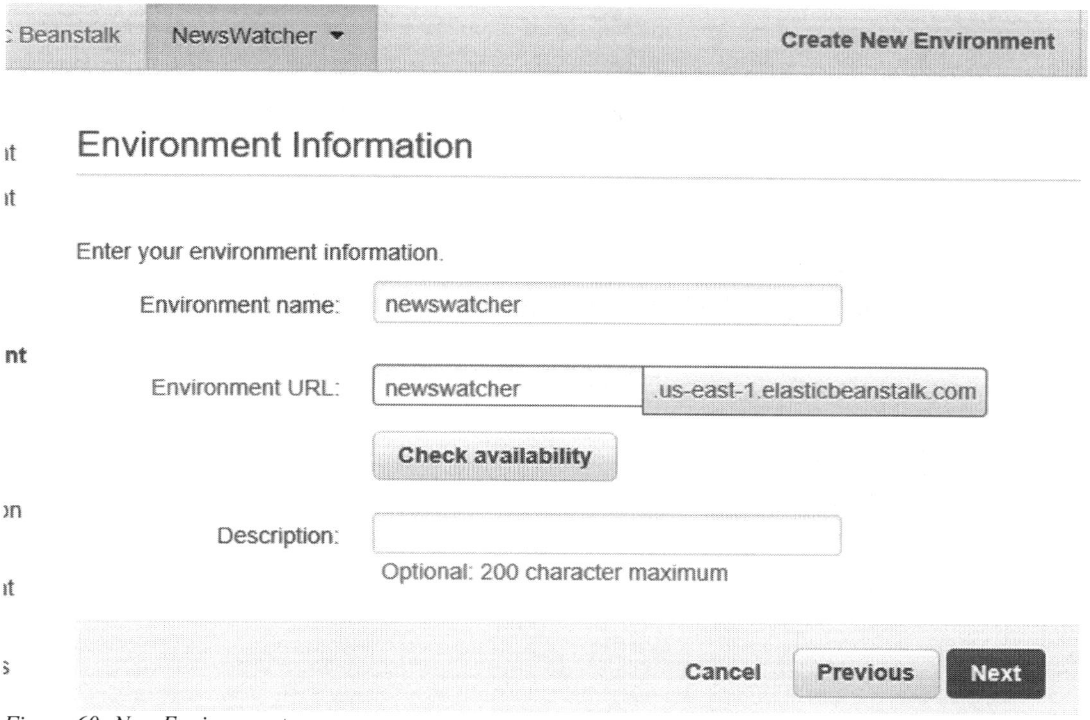
Beanstalk
NewsWatcher
Create New Environment
Environment Information
Enter your environment information.
Environment name:
newswatcher
Environment URL:
newswatcher
.us-east-1.elasticbeanstalk.com
Check availability
Description:
Optional: 200 character maximum
Cancel
Previous
Next

*Figure 60: New Environment name*

11. Leave everything unchecked on the next page that you navigate through and click **Next**.
12. On the next page you navigate through, leave everything unchecked and click **Next** again. The t1.mirco **Instance type** will be free for your usage. You can investigate other types, if you want to later upgrade to something with more performance and pay the monthly fee.
13. On the next page you navigate through, you can also leave everything as is and click **Next**. You will add Key/Value pairs later when you need them.
14. On the next page, you can also leave everything as is and click **Next**.
15. On the final overview page, click **Launch**.

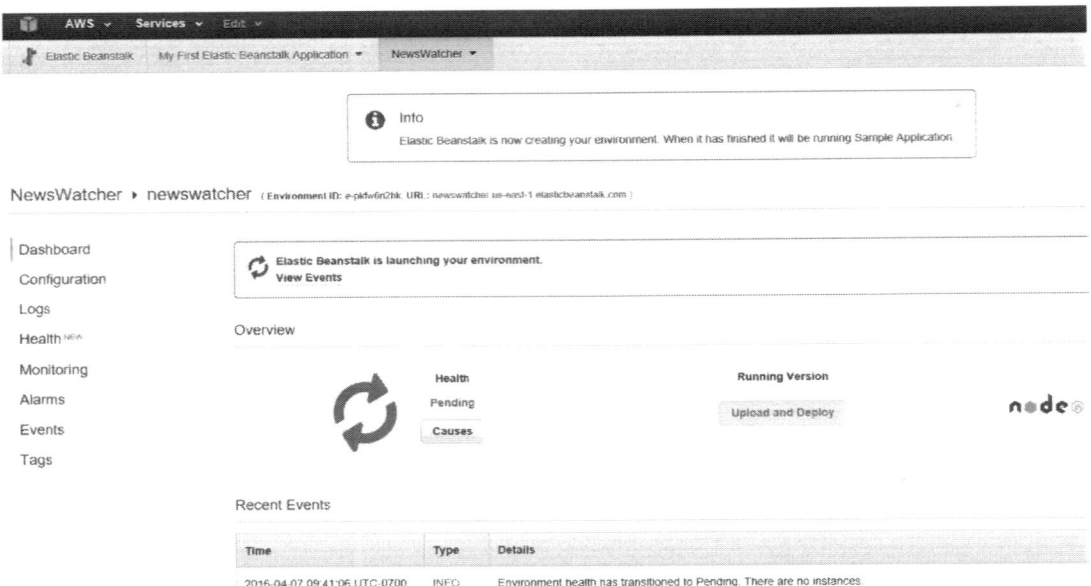

*Figure 61: Elastic Beanstalk configuration*

Once the site is ready, click the URL link on the page to see your site working. Now you can deploy your simple Express application. On a windows machine, this is as follows:

1.  Using the Windows File Explorer, navigate to your project folder.
2.  Select the package.json and server.js files together, then right-click and select **Send to -> Compressed (zipped) folder**. Give the zip file a name and save it.
3.  In the Elastic Beanstalk dashboard for the newswatcher application, click **Upload and Deploy** button and select your zip file.
4.  Wait for the confirmation that the deployment is ready and click the URL again.

Your Node.js application is now working for the whole world to see.

You do not need to zip and send the node_modules folder, as the deployment to Elastic Beanstalk will run 'npm install' for you and create it on the EC2 instances. One thing you should do is to set an environment variable through the Elastic Beanstalk management console so that the node install actually becomes "npm install –production". Set the environment variable as:

```
NPM_CONFIG_PRODUCTION=true
```

This will make the install go much faster as it will not deploy any npm modules that are needed only in test or development environments.

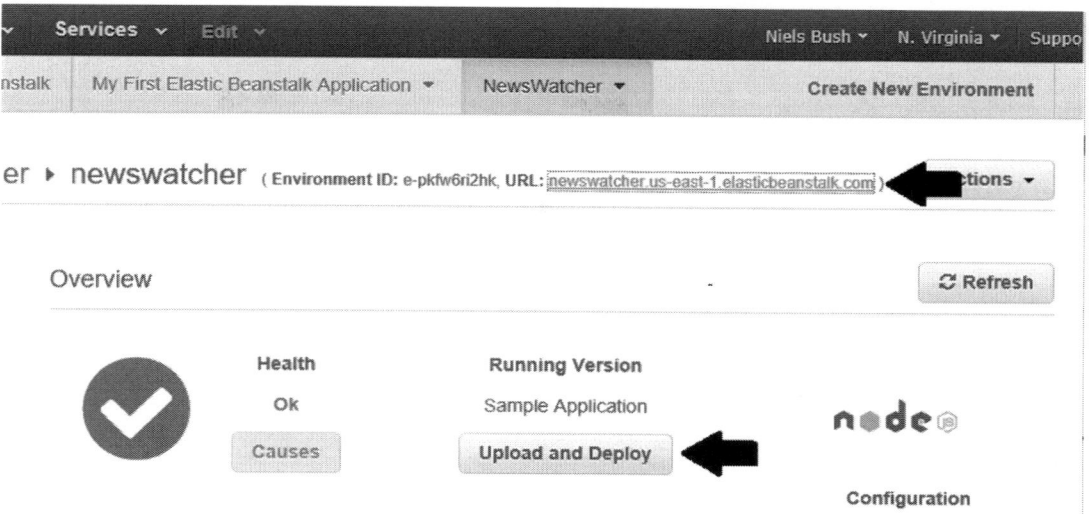

*Figure 62: Upload and deploy the zip file*

You just performed a manual deployment. While a few manual deployments might be tolerable, you eventually want full continuous-integration scripts that run tests and deployments for you. See my blog for information on how to do that.

# 12.4 Basic Project Structure

Now, you can add in the rest of the code for the NewsWatcher application. You first make the change to add in the rest of the Node.js dependencies that you will need. Edit your package.json file to be as follows, then save it:

```
{
  "name": "NewsWatcher",
  "version": "0.0.1",
  "description": "NewsWatcher",
  "main": "server.js",
  "author": {
    "name": "BUSHMAN",
    "email": ""
  },
  "scripts": {
    "start": "node server.js"
  },
  "dependencies": {
    "async": "^1.5.2",
    "aws-sdk": "^2.2.43",
    "bcryptjs": "^2.3.0",
```

```
    "body-parser": "^1.14.2",
    "express": "^4.13.4",
    "express-rate-limit": "^2.2.0",
    "helmet": "^1.3.0",
    "joi": "^8.0.1",
    "jwt-simple": "^0.4.1",
    "kerberos": "0.0.18",
    "mongodb": "^2.1.5",
    "morgan": "^1.6.1",
    "response-time": "^2.3.1",
    "v8-profiler": "^5.5.0"
  },
  "devDependencies": {
    "gulp": "^3.9.1",
    "gulp-bump": "^2.1.0",
    "gulp-git": "^1.7.0",
    "gulp-mocha": "^2.2.0",
    "mocha": "^2.4.5",
    "run-sequence": "^1.1.5",
    "selenium-webdriver": "^2.53.1",
    "supertest": "^1.2.0"
  }
}
```

Now open a command prompt window and type `npm install` at the command prompt. The following figure shows what the folder structure of your application will look like in the VS Code explorer. You will add code to the rest of the files later in this chapter. You can, of course, go to the GitHub project and get all of the code for the NewsWatcher sample application.

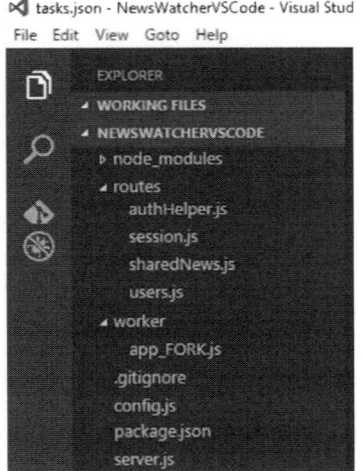

*Figure 63: VS Code explorer*

You are now ready to put your service layer REST web API together.

# 12.5 Where it All Starts (server.js)

You will start by creating the server.js file that tells Node what to do to be initialized and start running. In reality, it could be named anything. Some people prefer to name it app.js. It is in this file that you do things like establish a MongoDB connection, set up the HTTP request handling, set up error handling, and establish the Express listener.

At the top of the server.js file is where you will place the `require` statements that load the needed modules. If you recall, module references inside a file are internal to that file.

Some of the modules you will specify as required are actually used as middleware. This means you set them up with a `require` statement and then don't actually use them directly. They act to intercept calls through an `app.use()` call setting. If needed, you can refer back to the chapter on middleware to review this concept.

Here is the first section of code in the server.js file. I have added comments to briefly describe the purpose of each require statement.

```
var express = require('express'); // Route handlers and templates usage.
var path = require('path'); // Populating the path property of the request
var logger = require('morgan'); // HTTP request logging
var bodyParser = require('body-parser'); // Access to the HTTP request body
var cp = require('child_process'); // Forking a separate Node.js processes
var responseTime = require('response-time'); // Performance logging
var helmet = require('helmet'); // HTTP header hack mitigations
var RateLimit = require('express-rate-limit'); // IP based rate limiter
```

The first require statement provides the object that will be needed for leveraging Express. The path module is basically used to provide a helper object that will be used to manipulate strings for specifying the file paths in your project. The rest of the require statements are for setting up the use of modules that act as middleware.

These next lines needed will pull in modules that you will soon write yourself that provide configuration settings and provide the route handlers:

```
var config = require('./config');
var users = require('./routes/users');
var session = require('./routes/session');
var sharedNews = require('./routes/sharedNews');
```

Your code can now start to implement some of the capabilities. You now make the Express application object available and set a setting on it that will be needed for when it is run in AWS. Since the app is behind an Nginx load balancing with Elastic Beanstalk, you don't want the load balancer IP address being sent in the header requests, but want the IP address of the actual machine that it was acting on behalf of. This is what the trust proxy setting does.

```
var app = express();
app.enable('trust proxy');
```

**Middleware**

Next you can see how the Express middleware is hooked up for some of the modules you are incorporating. Here are those lines:

```
// Set up rate limiting
var limiter = new RateLimit({
  windowMs: 15*60*1000, // 15 minutes
  max: 100, // limit each IP to 100 requests per windowMs
  delayMs: 0 // disable delaying - full speed until the max limit is reached
});

// apply the request limiting to all requests
app.use(limiter);

// Set up the helmet module to mitigate certain security hacks
// Take the defaults to start with and then add in CSP
app.use(helmet());
app.use(helmet.csp({
  // Specify directives for content sources
  directives: {
    defaultSrc: ["'self'"],
    scriptSrc: ["'self'", "'unsafe-inline'", 'ajax.googleapis.com',
'maxcdn.bootstrapcdn.com'],
    styleSrc: ["'self'", "'unsafe-inline'", 'maxcdn.bootstrapcdn.com'],
    fontSrc: ["'self'", 'maxcdn.bootstrapcdn.com'],
    imgSrc: ['*']
    // reportUri: '/report-violation',
  }
}));

// Add an X-Response-Time header to responses to measure response times
app.use(responseTime());

// log all HTTP requests. The "dev" option gives it a specific styling
app.use(logger('dev'));

// Set up the response object in routes to contain a body property with
// an object of what is parsed from a JSON body request payload
// There is no need for allowing a huge body, it might be some type of attack,
// so use the limit option
app.use(bodyParser.json({ limit: '100kb' }));

// This middleware takes any query string key/value pairs and sticks them
// in the body property
//app.use(bodyParser.urlencoded({ extended: false }));
```

182

```
// Simplify the serving up of static content such as HTML, images,
// CSS files, and JavaScript files
app.use(express.static(path.join(__dirname, 'static')));
```

This code takes the modules brought in through the `require()` statements and inserts them as middleware by calling `app.use()`.

The first piece of middleware is what gives protection against DoS attacks. You can look up the module in GitHub to actually see it works as middleware.

The next piece of middleware is Helmet. I covered its use earlier. Helmet is a security mitigation module that tweaks the HTTP headers.

There are five other uses of middleware that are documented in the code to tell you what they do. Each is very useful and you will benefit from them.

You can see the use of the path module to provide functionality to manipulate path strings with the join function. The `__dirname` variable is provided by Node so that you can use it to get the name of the directory that the currently executing script resides in. In this usage, it would return the directory of the server.js file. It will be the local path if you are running it locally, or whatever it is on the AWS production machine if it is running in the deployed environment.

**Forking a Process**

The next code in the server.js file is used to fork off a separate Node.js process and give it a file to execute. This is used to shuttle off any code processing that is more intensive and that you don't want run on your main Node process thread.

```
var node2 = cp.fork('./app_FORK.js');
//var node2 = cp.fork('./app_FORK.js', [], { execArgv: ['--debug=5859'] });
```

Earlier, I explained that you need to be careful with code you wrote that would execute on the main Node.js V8 VM. With NewsWatcher you need to offload a few things to a separate Node process. These involve code for collecting news stories from internet sources into NewsWatcher's master list in MongoDB and doing the filtered matching of stories for users. I will show you the code in the forked process later.

You can see that you use the child_process module to start up the second process. Since Node is ported to many platforms, it will call whatever low-level code is needed to accomplish this for the OS it is running on. Node makes use of some libraries that do this and these have been ported already. You can pass messages back and forth between processes if you like. You will be doing this later in code.

There is an issue when running and attaching a debugger. There ends up being a conflict where both processes try to use the same debug port for debuggers to attach to. This is solved by using a process execution argument to specifically set the debug port of the forked process. If you don't intend to attach a debugger, it is not needed. This is what you see commented out in the code for when you need to attach a debugger.

If the forked process is experiencing runtime errors, it could shut itself down and then the main process could be signaled to start it up again. You could add code in server.js to restart the forked process as follows:

```
node2.on('exit', function (code) {
   node2 = undefined;
   node2 = cp.fork('./worker/app_FORK.js', [],
           { execArgv: ['--debug=5859'] });
});
```

### The MongoDB Data Layer Connection

Most of the code in the service layer deals with interactions with the backend data storage layer. You initialize your MongoDB connection by utilizing the mongodb module that is an NPM download. You use the `connect()` function and then set up the usage of the newswatcher collection. The `connect()` function takes the MongoDB connection URL. You save the connection as a property on an object you set up named **db** to be used later with your Express routes through middleware injection. Watch for that code coming up soon.

```
var assert = require('assert'); // assert testing of values
var db = {};
var MongoClient = require('mongodb').MongoClient;

//Use the connect method to connect to the Server
MongoClient.connect(config.MONGODB_CONNECT_URL, function(err, dbConn) {
    assert.equal(null, err);
    db.dbConnection = dbConn;
    db.collection = dbConn.collection('newswatcher');
    console.log("Connected to MongoDB server");
});
```

The last thing to note about the above code is that you have a configuration file for keeping settings that you want to have in a central place. Some of the values in that file are ones you want to keep secret, so don't post that file for anyone to see. I am keeping needed configuration values this way, but these values could also be set as environment name/value pairs in an Elastic Beanstalk environment.

### Sharing Objects

The node2 and db variables are needed in your routing code. The database connection will be used for all of the CRUD operations, so you need to make that available. You expose these variables through middleware injection. This means that you have a chance to inject the objects into the request processing chain by adding them as properties on the request object.

You stick a middleware function right at the top of the chain that every request will have to pass through first. It is a simple matter of attaching new properties to the request object that is being passed along.

As required, you call `next()` to move the execution along to the rest of the processing chain for the request. Remember that the `use` function applies across all requests, so that a `get`, `put` or any other request is routed through here first.

```
app.use(function (req, res, next) {
  req.db = db;
  req.node2 = node2;
  next();
});
```

### Express Route Handlers

You are almost done with the main application code that sets everything up. The next code you need to put in place is to set up your route handlers. First you need to set up the serving of the main HTML page.

```
app.get('/', function (req, res) {
  res.render('index.html')
});
```

The following are all of the routes for your HTTP/Rest API. This goes back to understanding what your objects are and what verbs each will support. You just list out each object and then, inside each of the supporting modules you will find the verbs and any sub-objects off of them. The users, session and sharedNews are modules you write that each use the Express Router object as was explained in section 9.3.

```
// Rest API routes
app.use('/api/users', users);
app.use('/api/sessions', session);
app.use('/api/sharednews', sharedNews);
```

Next, there is an error handling route that is needed for when invalid URLs come in. This returns a 404 code to signal that the resource was not found. Basically, if none of the other routes kick in, then this one will. For example, if a request came in for /api/blah, it would go here. This then activates an express error handler, because it calls `next(err)`.

185

```
// catch 404 and forward to error handler
app.use(function (req, res, next) {
  var err = new Error('Not Found');
  err.status = 404;
  next(err);
});
```

Here are the error handling routes for when you have an error returned in the code. You get here when a `next(err)` is called in your routing code. There is a handler that only kicks in when running in your development environment. You want to do this so that you can add in what the stack trace is. The second handler is the one that kicks in in the production environment.

```
// development error handler that will add in a stacktrace
if (app.get('env') === 'development') {
  app.use(function (err, req, res, next) {
    res.status(err.status||500).json({message:err.toString(),error:err});
    console.log(err);
  });
}

// production error handler with no stacktraces exposed to users
app.use(function (err, req, res, next) {
  res.status(err.status || 500).json({message:err.toString(), error:{}});
  console.log(err);
});
```

The final lines in server.js contain the standard code that tells Express to be listening for HTTP requests. In production, it picks up the port necessary to run in that hosted environment.

```
app.set('port', process.env.PORT || 3000);
var server = app.listen(app.get('port'), function () {
  console.log('Express server listening on port '+server.address().port);
});
```

If you look at the code in the GitHub project, you will see that I also added route handlers for starting and stopping V8 profiling and for taking memory snapshots. These can then be activated by placing that call, and also deactivated when needed.

# 12.6 A MongoDB Document to Hold News Stories

You need to create a special MongoDB document to store the global news story list in. You do a one-time creation of this in advance through the mLab management portal. This is the master list that is then used by all users to do matching of their news filters with. This way each user does not need to fetch all the news individually. You give this document a distinctive ID that tells you what it is for and also informs you that you should never delete it. This document looks as follows:

```
{
  "_id": "MASTER_STORIES_DO_NOT_DELETE",
  "newsStories": []
}
```

I covered this previously, so you should have already created this document. If not, you can create it at this time. You could create this in code but, since it is a one-time thing, I have chosen to use the mLab management portal to create it.

# 12.7 A Central Place for Configuration (config.js)

You need a module that can hold your configuration values, such as those that are needed to establish the connection to the MongoDB database. You place the config.js file at the top level of the project and require it in most of the rest of the code. You already saw this module being used in the server.js file, where you had a `require` statement for it, and then you used properties from the object it returned.

You can see that it is a fairly simple module. There are no functions, only properties that are exposed. Of course, be aware that I cannot divulge the actual contents of my config.js file as you would then have access to my AWS services. You can edit in the values you need for your own config.js file.

```
var config = {}

config.JWT_SECRET = "<yoursecretkey>";
config.NEWYORKTIMES_API_KEY = "<yoursecretkey>"
config.NEWYORKTIMES_CATEGORIES = ["world", "national", "business"];
config.GLOBAL_STORIES_ID = "MASTER_STORIES_DO_NOT_DELETE";
config.MAX_SHARED_STORIES = 30;
config.MAX_COMMENTS = 30;
config.MAX_FILTERS = 5;
config.MAX_FILTER_STORIES = 15;
config.MONGODB_CONNECT_URL =
"mongodb://<username>:<password>@ds015710.mlab.com:15710/newswatcherdb";

module.exports = config;
```

# 12.8 HTTP/Rest Web Service API

It is now time to furnish the REST Web Service API. The REST API will accept and pass back JSON payloads through HTTP requests.

Eventually, you will create the SPA web page that calls your web service. You would do this once the endpoint is fully tested. If you think about the REST API that you want to expose, it becomes clear that you need to create all the CRUD operations for each resource that is necessary. Your resources are sessions, users, and sharednews.

Here is a table that lists everything the REST API supports. The `id` and `sid` parameters are the identifiers of individual resources for a user and story that are accessed.

| Verb and Path | Result |
|---|---|
| POST /api/sessions | Create a login session token. |
| DELETE /api/sessions/:id | Delete a login session token. |
| POST /api/users | Create a user with the passed in JSON of the HTTP body. |
| DELETE /api/users/:id | Delete a single specified user. |
| GET /api/users/:id | Return the JSON of a single specified user. |
| PUT /api/users/:id | Replace a user with the passed-in JSON of the HTTP body. |
| POST /api/users/:id/savedstories | Save a story for user, content of which is in the JSON body |
| DELETE /api/users/:id/savedstories/:sid | Delete a story that the user had previously saved. |
| POST /api/sharednews | Share a news story as contained in the JSON body |
| GET /api/sharednews | Get all of the shared news stories |
| DELETE /api/sharednews/:sid | Delete a news story that had been shared. |
| POST /api/sharednews/:sid/comments | Add a comment to a specified shared news story |

You may have noticed that some verbs you might have expected to find are missing. For example, you will not see a GET /api/users to get the list of all users. You don't really want other people to see everyone that is a user of NewsWatcher, so don't offer that. You certainly could decide to offer it, but you would then want to place another middleware restriction on it that only allows logged in administrators to have access to it.

Another example of a restricted API route that you do have is `DELETE /api/users/:id`. A user can only delete themselves, so you restrict that to just the logged-in user for deleting their own account and not an account of anyone else. You could allow admins to be able to delete anyone if you like.

Remember that the token is very useful to restrict access with. It is up to you to define what roles and access you will need and then enforce it. In this case, each call only works for that account to access their own data or for whatever is authorized. Perhaps administrators that login can be identified and allowed access to everything.

# Visualizing the code

If you recall, the following lines below are found in the server.js file and are used to set up your Express route handling. The first two Express application calls are used for sending the files back that the client browser application will need. The last three Express application calls are for route handling of everything listed in the REST API resource table.

Here are the lines from the server.js file as a reminder:

```
// serves up of static content such as HTML, images, CSS, and JavaScript
app.use(express.static(path.join(__dirname, 'static')));

// For loading the default HTML page that acts as the SPA Web site
app.get('/', function (req, res) {
   res.render('index.html')
});

// Rest API routes
app.use('/api/users', users);
app.use('/api/sessions', session);
app.use('/api/sharednews', sharedNews);
```

The following is a pictorial representation of how the routing code all hooks together. This does not contain all of the files and details, but just gives you an idea of the routes that are being serviced. I have even included the browser side HTML and Angular code, even though this has not been discussed yet. You can also see that I divide up the code by the architectural layer.

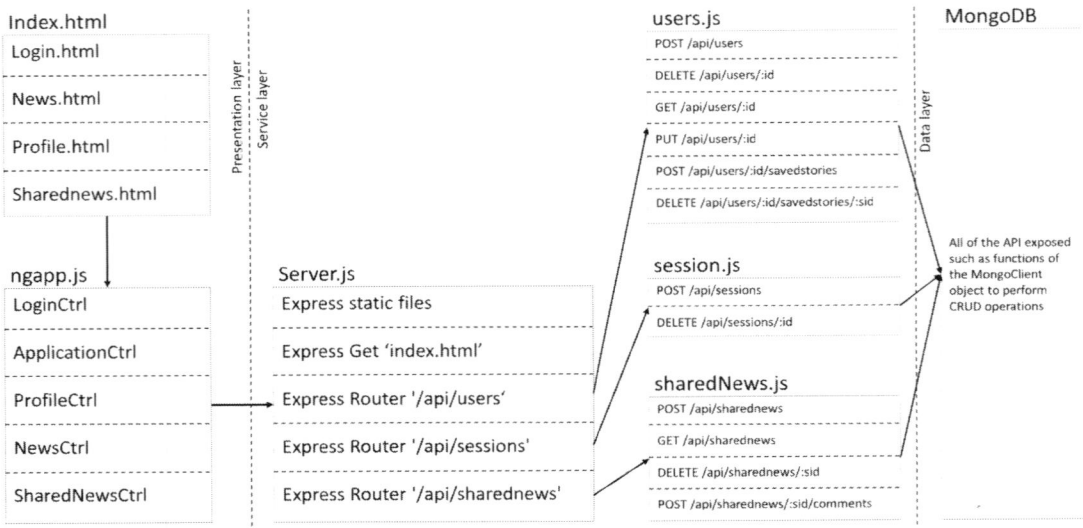

*Figure 64: NewsWatcher file diagram*

You can now look at the individual files used for each of these routes, one at a time. They each exist in their own file and that is where you find the servicing of the individual verbs.

# 12.9 Session Resource Routing (routes/session.js)

The session is used in the API to allow people to log in and out. Here are the specific routes for the session resource:

| Verb and Path | Result |
|---|---|
| POST /api/sessions | Create a login session token. |
| DELETE /api/sessions/:id | Delete a login session token. |

The post operation takes a user's email and password in the request body and basically logs them in. A token is sent back in the response body that the client caller can take and then keep passing back on subsequent calls to identify that person. The token can be stored in client-side storage and used as needed.

The post verb handler needs to first query for the user document to see if they actually have a registered account. The user must exist or they cannot be logged in. If there is a match for the email, then the stored password hash that was stored for them is validated with a hash of the password coming in.

If the password is validated, then a token is created and passed back in the JSON payload. The tokens don't expire, but it would be easy to add a timestamp for one. With that added, you might do something like require a new login every month.

As was discussed, there is a bit of verification that can go on with the token. You check it to make sure it is originating from where the token was originally assigned from. The IP address and the header setting for user-agent are kept with the token as additional verification.

You are not doing any database storage of the token in the NewsWatcher app, so the delete does not really need to do much. There is just a simple check to verify that the person logging out is the same as the one contained in the token.

One of the things you see is the use of the joi module to validate the incoming request body object. Here is the code for session.js:

```
//
// session.js: A Node.js Module for session login and
// logout route handling.
//

"use strict";
var express = require('express');
var bcrypt = require('bcryptjs'); // For password hash comparing
var jwt = require('jwt-simple'); // For token authentication
var joi = require('joi'); // For data validation
var authHelper = require('./authHelper');
var config = require('../config');

var router = express.Router();

//
// Create a security token as the user logs in that can be passed
// to the client and used on subsequent calls.
// The user email and password are sent in the body of the request.
//
router.post('/', function postSession(req, res, next) {
  // Password must be 7 to 15 characters in length and contain
  // at least one numeric digit and a special character
  var schema = {
    email: joi.string().email().min(7).max(50).required(),
    password: joi.string().regex(/^(?=.*[0-9])(?=.*[!@#$%^&*])[a-zA-Z0-
9!@#$%^&*]{7,15}$/).required()
  };

  joi.validate(req.body, schema, function (err, value) {
    if (err)
```

```
      return next(new Error('Invalid field: password 7 to 15 (one number,
one special character)'));

    req.db.collection.findOne({ type: 'USER_TYPE',
              email: req.body.email }, function (err, user)
    {
      if (err) return next(err);

      if (!user) return next(new Error('User was not found.'));

      bcrypt.compare(req.body.password, user.passwordHash,
              function comparePassword(err, match)
      {
        if (match) {
          try {
            var token = jwt.encode({ authorized: true,
                sessionIP: req.ip,
                sessionUA: req.headers['user-agent'],
                userId: user._id.toHexString(),
                displayName: user.displayName },
                config.JWT_SECRET);
            res.status(201).json({ displayName: user.displayName,
                userId: user._id.toHexString(),
                token: token,
                msg: 'Authorized' });
          } catch (err) {return next(err);}
        } else {
          return next(new Error('Wrong password'));
        }
      });
    });
});

//
// Delete the token as a user logs out
//
router.delete('/:id', authHelper.checkAuth, function (req, res, next) {
  // Verify the passed in email is the same as that in the auth token
  if (req.params.id != req.auth.userId)
    return next(new Error('Invalid request for logout'));

  res.status(200).json({ msg: 'Logged out' });
});

module.exports = router;
```

Notice the use of the middleware function authHelper.checkAuth. This is something you will define next that allows you to inject a check first before proceeding on to the final function that does the work. If the authorization fails then the function for the end route handling will not be called.

192

# 12.10 Authorization Token Module (routes/authHelper.js)

You have seen how a user logs in and a token is generated. You now need to create some middleware that will be inserted and run for certain incoming routes. This code will be set up to look at the passed-in token and make sure it is valid. As you know, middleware can be inserted into any route you like and that is what you will be doing.

Each HTTP/Rest call that is made after a person is logged in has an x-auth header token value. Each of the routing modules will make use of the authHelper module to verify that a valid token is being passed in before performing any other action.

You will see this function used in many of the route handlers. The code here will simply verify that there is an x-auth header and, if there is, decode it with your secret, then set the decoded object in a request property named auth for further usage by anything in the processing chain. If the token is missing, has been tampered with, or does not contain what it is supposed to, an error is returned.

When you look at the password sign-in code of session.js, you see where all the information was placed in the token. It really is up to you to decide what to put in there. With this token, you can represent the user being signed in. You certainly do not want, or need, to store the user password (or other sensitive data) in the token. Here is the middleware that verifies that a token is valid:

```
//
// authHelper.js: A Node.js Module to inject middleware that
// validates the request header User token.
//

"use strict";
var jwt = require('jwt-simple');
var config = require('../config');

//
// Check for a token in the custom header setting and verify that it is
// signed and has not been tampered with.
// If no header token is present, maybe the user
// The JWT Simple package will throw exceptions
//
module.exports.checkAuth = function (req, res, next) {
   if (req.headers['x-auth']) {
      try {
         req.auth = jwt.decode(req.headers['x-auth'], config.JWT_SECRET);
```

```
      if (req.auth && req.auth.authorized &&
          req.auth.userId &&
          req.auth.sessionIP === req.ip &&
          req.auth.sessionUA === req.headers['user-agent'])
      {
        return next();
      } else {
        return next(new Error('User is not logged in.'));
      }
    } catch (err) {
      return next(err);
    }
  } else {
    return next(new Error('User is not logged in.'));
  }
};
```

If a user wanted to get their token from the returned login request, they could. If they passed it on to anyone else, their account could possibly be compromised. Thus, the extra tests.

# 12.11 User Resource Routing (routes/users.js)

The user resource represents information for a logged in user. A user document retrieved by their ID will contain information like their profile that has their news filters and also the news stories that have matched. For a given user, you can also make Rest calls to save a story or delete a saved story. Here are the specific routes for the user resource:

| Verb and Path | Result |
|---|---|
| POST /api/users | Create a user with the passed-in JSON of the HTTP body. |
| DELETE /api/users/:id | Delete a single specified user. |
| GET /api/users/:id | Return the JSON of a single specified user. |
| PUT /api/users/:id | Replace a user with the passed-in JSON of the HTTP body. |
| POST /api/users/:id/savedstories | Save a story for user, content of which is in the JSON body |
| DELETE /api/users/:id/savedstories/:sid | Delete a story that the user had previously saved. |

Let's start by looking at the require statements at the very top of users.js. Some of the modules required are ones that you have seen before.

```
"use strict";
var express = require('express');
var bcrypt = require('bcryptjs');
var async = require('async');
var joi = require('joi'); // For data validation
var authHelper = require('./authHelper');
var config = require('../config');
var ObjectId = require('mongodb').ObjectID;

var router = express.Router();

...code cut out...

module.exports = router;
```

Now you can look at the verb handler functions one by one.

**POST /api/users**

The `post` verb takes a JSON payload and creates a new user account as a document in your collection. This happens when a user account is first created. A password is passed in as part of the JSON body and you create a hash of it to store in the document.

This call will fail if the user email already exists in a document in your collection. Relying on an email address to identify a user account is one way to keep user accounts unique and identifiable. The mongodb `findOne()` function is what is used to see if an account existed already.

The code goes ahead and creates all of the properties ever needed in the document with default values that make sense. There is even a sample filter set up for the user.

Notice the call to `node2.send()` that is used to pass a message to the forked Node process to offload the filter processing. This call will take the new account and do the initial matching of stories for the filter. I have not shown you the code for the forked process yet, but you can see that the concept is very simple.

What happens right at the start, is validation of the passed-in JSON body. You want to make sure that there are no extra properties, and also validate that the allowed ones conform to some known types and safe values. The joi NPM module is used to perform your validations. Here is the code for the post verb handler:

```
router.post('/', function postUser(req, res, next) {
    // Password must be 7 to 15 characters in length and contain at
    // least one numeric digit and a special character
    var schema = {
        displayName: joi.string().alphanum().min(3).max(50).required(),
        email: joi.string().email().min(7).max(50).required(),
```

```
   password: joi.string().regex(/^(?=.*[0-9])(?=.*[!@#$%^&*])[a-zA-Z0-
9!@#$%^&*]{7,15}$/).required()
  };

  joi.validate(req.body, schema, function (err, value) {
    if (err)
      return next(new Error('Invalid field: display name 3 to 50
alpanumeric, valid email, password 7 to 15 (one number, one special
character)'));

    req.db.collection.findOne({ type: 'USER_TYPE',
                email: req.body.email },
                function (err, doc)
    {
      if (err)
        return next(err);

      if (doc)
        return next(new Error('Email account already registered'));

      var xferUser = {
        type: 'USER_TYPE',
        displayName: req.body.displayName,
        email: req.body.email,
        passwordHash: null,
        date: Date.now(),
        completed: false,
        settings: {
          requireWIFI: true,
          enableAlerts: false
        },
        newsFilters: [{
            name: 'Technology Companies',
            keyWords: ['Apple', 'Microsoft', 'IBM', 'Amazon', 'Google',
'Intel'],
            enableAlert: false,
            alertFrequency: 0,
            enableAutoDelete: false,
            deleteTime: 0,
            timeOfLastScan: 0,
            newsStories: []
        }],
        savedStories: []
      };

      bcrypt.hash(req.body.password, 10, function getHash(err, hash) {
        if (err)
          return next(err);

        xferUser.passwordHash = hash;
        req.db.collection.insertOne(xferUser,
            function createUser(err, result)
        {
```

```
            if (err)
               return next(err);

            req.node2.send({msg: 'REFRESH_STORIES', doc: result.ops[0]});
            res.status(201).json(result.ops[0]);
          });
        });
      });
});
```

Users are allowed to sign up for an account by having them provide their user name, associated email, and a password. You will not store the actual password, but will instead store an encrypted hashed value of the password. Even if anyone were to get a hold of that for a user, they would still not be able to log in with it as it is extremely difficult to decrypt that into the password.

Once a person is registered as a user, then the /api/session/ path will be used to accept their email and password to get their session going each time they want to log in and use NewsWatcher.

As explained in the chapter on authentication and authorization, you will be sending a token in the header of each HTTP/Rest request. When a user logs in, they get a token that is subsequently used to identify them for all further interactions.

**DELETE /api/users/:id**
With this path, you see the use of a passed-in id. It comes through the mechanism of Express. Specifying the path like this will have Express create a property of req.params.id. What you need to do is to verify that the request for a deletion of a user is actually the id that exists in the token. This way a user cannot delete an account that does not belong to them.

Look at session.js again and you see where the mongodb _id property of the retrieved document is captured. This is what is going to be passed back in the Rest request URL path portion to identify a user.

The middleware function authHelper.checkAuth is injected to do the verification that a valid token exists for the request. That middleware-injected function will return an error if the token is not acceptable and then the route function will never get called.

If everything proceeds correctly, the route function executes, the document is removed from your collection, and the user account is gone. findOneAndDelete() is used as there would be one and only one document with that _id. There is a helper function from the mongodb module to take the string and get it into the proper form needed. Here is the code for the user deletion handler:

```
router.delete('/:id', authHelper.checkAuth, function (req, res, next) {
  // Verify that the passed in id to delete is the same
  // as that in the auth token
  if (req.params.id != req.auth.userId)
    return next(new Error('Invalid request for account deletion'));

  // MongoDB should do the work of queuing this up and retrying if
  // there is a conflict, According to their documentation.
  // This actually requires a write lock on their part.
  req.db.collection.findOneAndDelete({ type: 'USER_TYPE',
             _id: ObjectId(req.auth.userId) },
             function (err, result)
  {
    if (err) {
      console.log("+++CONTENTION ERROR?+++ err:", err);
      return next(err);
    } else if (result.ok != 1) {
      console.log("+++CONTENTION ERROR?+++ result:", result);
      return next(new Error('Account deletion failure'));
    }

    res.status(200).json({ msg: "User Deleted" });
  });
});
```

### GET /api/users/:id
This route handler retrieves a single user by their id. The app would have already called to get a session token first and then have access to the id of the user to pass it in to this API call to retrieve the user document. Since you actually have the _id (object id), you can retrieve the document faster than if you had queried for it some other way. There is always an index created for the _id property.

You do the retrieval and populate a transfer object. Notice that you are also tweaking the HTTP header for the response. That is necessary in order to stop caching from happening. Otherwise, when you got to the Angular code and are trying to retrieve a user, you might not get the most up-to-date one. Here is the code for the user handler to get a single user by their id:

```
router.get('/:id', authHelper.checkAuth, function (req, res, next) {
  // Verify that the passed in id is the same as
  // that in the auth token
  if (req.params.id != req.auth.userId)
    return next(new Error('Invalid request for account fetch'));

  req.db.collection.findOne({ type: 'USER_TYPE',
          _id: ObjectId(req.auth.userId) },
          function (err, doc)
  {
    if (err)
```

```
            return next(err);

        var xferProfile = {
            email: doc.email,
            displayName: doc.displayName,
            date: doc.date,
            settings: doc.settings,
            newsFilters: doc.newsFilters,
            savedStories: doc.savedStories
        };
        res.header("Cache-Control", "no-cache, no-store, must-revalidate");
        res.header("Pragma", "no-cache");
        res.header("Expires", 0);
        res.status(200).json(xferProfile);
    });
});
```

**PUT /api/users/:id**

A put is used to update a user, such as in the case where they have altered a news filter. The code is very similar to what you needed for the initial post of the user, except you now need to worry about a conflict happening upon a database write operation. Here is the code for the user update handler:

```
router.put('/:id', authHelper.checkAuth, function (req, res, next) {
    // Verify that the passed in token is the same as that in the auth token
    if (req.params.id != req.auth.userId)
        return next(new Error('Invalid request for account deletion'));

    // Limit the number of newsFilters
    if (req.body.newsFilters.length > config.MAX_FILTERS)
        return next(new Error('Too many news newsFilters'));

    // clear out leading and trailing spaces
    for (var i = 0; i < req.body.newsFilters.length; i++) {
        if ("keyWords" in req.body.newsFilters[i] &&
                req.body.newsFilters[i].keyWords[0] != "")
        {
            for (var j = 0; j < req.body.newsFilters[i].keyWords.length; j++) {
                req.body.newsFilters[i].keyWords[j] =
                    req.body.newsFilters[i].keyWords[j].trim();
            }
        }
    }

    // Validate the newsFilters
    var schema = {
        name: joi.string().min(1).max(30).regex(/^[-_ a-zA-Z0-
9]+$/).required(),
        keyWords: joi.array().max(10).items(joi.string().max(20)).required(),
        enableAlert: joi.boolean(),
        alertFrequency: joi.number().min(0),
```

199

```
      enableAutoDelete: joi.boolean(),
      deleteTime: joi.date(),
      timeOfLastScan: joi.date(),
      newsStories: joi.array(),
      keywordsStr: joi.string().min(1).max(100)
  };

  async.eachSeries(req.body.newsFilters, function (filter, innercallback){
      joi.validate(filter, schema, function (err, value) {
         innercallback(err);
      });
  }, function (err) {
      if (err) {
         return next(err);
      } else {
         // MongoDB implements optimistic concurrency for us.
         // We need the {returnOriginal: false}, so a test could verify what
         // happened, otherwise the defualt is to return the origional.
         req.db.collection.findOneAndUpdate({ type: 'USER_TYPE',_id:
ObjectId(req.auth.userId) },
                 {$set: { settings: { requireWIFI: req.body.requireWIFI,
enableAlerts: req.body.enableAlerts }, newsFilters: req.body.newsFilters}},
                     { returnOriginal: false },
                     function (err, result) {
            if (err) {
               console.log("+++CONTENTION ERROR?+++ err:", err);
               return next(err);
            } else if (result.ok != 1) {
               console.log("+++CONTENTION ERROR?+++ result:", result);
               return next(new Error('User PUT failure'));
            }

            req.node2.send({ msg: 'REFRESH_STORIES', doc: result.value });
            res.status(200).json(result.value);
         });
      }
  });
});
```

Notice the code to limit the news filter size. You will put code in the UI to limit that as well, but that could be hacked, either in the browser, or by someone sending a bogus put request. You have to guard against potential tampering as you would otherwise have a crash, or at least a failure of the MongoDB update.

There is the use of this fabulous module called async. This allows calls to the joi library to happen over and over and allows waiting for each callback to return for each of the filters for a user. When all are processed, the last anonymous function is called.

The $set operation is used to update only individual properties and not the entire document.

There is a bit of error checking code in there to detect any contention error. I had tried over and over and had never seen one yet.

**POST /api/users/:id/savedstories**
In the user document there is an array used for saving stories that a user wants to keep around. This route will take the JSON of the passed-in request body as the story to save. The id in the route is the id of the user that is requesting the saving of the story.

There are a few checks that need to go on before saving a story. You need to verify that the story is not already inserted. There is also a limit on the number of stories that can be saved, so that has to be checked.

Stories have an id associated with them to be able to identify them in cases like this where you don't want duplicates saved or shared. You will later see the code that creates that id. Here is the code for the user posting a story to be save:

```
router.post('/:id/savedstories', authHelper.checkAuth, function (req, res,
next) {
  // Verify that the passed in id is the same as that in the auth token
  if (req.params.id != req.auth.userId)
    return next(new Error('Invalid request for saving story'));

  // Validate the body
  var schema = {
    contentSnippet: joi.string().max(200).required(),
    date: joi.date().required(),
    hours: joi.string().max(20),
    imageUrl: joi.string().max(300).required(),
    keep: joi.boolean().required(),
    link: joi.string().max(300).required(),
    source: joi.string().max(50).required(),
    storyID: joi.string().max(100).required(),
    title: joi.string().max(200).required()
  };

  joi.validate(req.body, schema, function (err, value) {
    if (err)
      return next(err);

    // This uses the MongoDB operators to test the savedStories array
    // to make sure
    // A. Story is not aready in there.
    // B. We limit the number of saved stories to 30
    // We can just let addToSet take care of the comparison and silently
    // fail as the user does not need to know if the story was
    // really already there
    req.db.collection.findOneAndUpdate({ type: 'USER_TYPE', _id:
ObjectId(req.auth.userId), $where: 'this.savedStories.length<29' },
        { $addToSet: { savedStories: req.body } },
```

```
              { returnOriginal: true },
              function (err, result) {
         if (result.value == null) {
           return next(new Error('Over the save limit, or story already
saved'));
         } else if (err) {
           console.log("+++CONTENTION ERROR?+++ err:", err);
           return next(err);
         } else if (result.ok != 1) {
           console.log("+++CONTENTION ERROR?+++ result:", result);
           return next(new Error('Story save failure'));
         }

         res.status(200).json(result.value);
     });
   });
});
```

## DELETE /api/users/:id/savedstories/:sid

This is similar to the other functions and accomplishes the verification of the story existing before being able to delete it. The $pull operator is used with the array property of the document to delete the story entry. Here is the code for deleting a saved story:

```
router.delete('/:id/savedstories/:sid', authHelper.checkAuth, function
(req, res, next)
{
   // Verify that the passed in user is the same as that in the auth token
   if (req.params.id != req.auth.userId)
     return next(new Error('Invalid request for deletion of saved story'));

   req.db.collection.findOneAndUpdate({ type: 'USER_TYPE', _id:
ObjectId(req.auth.userId) },
     { $pull: { savedStories: { storyID: req.params.sid } } },
     { returnOriginal: true },
     function (err, result) {
        if (err) {
          console.log("+++CONTENTION ERROR?+++ err:", err);
          return next(err);
        } else if (result.ok != 1) {
          console.log("+++CONTENTION ERROR?+++ result:", result);
          return next(new Error('Story delete failure'));
        }
        res.status(200).json(result.value);
   });
});
```

# 12.12 Shared News Routing (routes/sharedNews.js)

Shared news stories are those that are seen by all users. People can save, view and comment on news stories. Here are the specific routes for the sharedNews resource:

| Verb and Path | Result |
|---|---|
| POST<br>/api/sharednews | Share a news story as contained in the JSON body |
| GET<br>/api/sharednews | Get all of the shares news stories |
| DELETE<br>/api/sharednews/:sid | Delete a news story that has been shared. |
| POST<br>/api/sharednews/:sid/comments | Add a comment to a specified shared news story |

At the top and bottom of the file is the usual code as shown here:

```
"use strict";
var express = require('express');
var joi = require('joi'); // For data validation
var authHelper = require('./authHelper');
var config = require('../config');
var ObjectId = require('mongodb').ObjectID;

var router = express.Router();

...this part left out...

module.exports = router;
```

Here are each of the route path handlers.

**POST /api/sharednews**
This code is very similar to the code you already saw for saving a story in user.js. The only difference is that now, the story is being copied into a different document where all NewsWatcher users can view stories and comment on them.

There is a limit set for the number of possible shared stories. There is a test to make sure the story was not already shared. If all looks good, the document is created. Here is the code for sharing a story:

```
router.post('/', authHelper.checkAuth, function (req, res, next) {
  // Validate the body
  var schema = {
```

```
      contentSnippet: joi.string().max(200).required(),
      date: joi.date().required(),
      hours: joi.string().max(20),
      imageUrl: joi.string().max(300).required(),
      keep: joi.boolean().required(),
      link: joi.string().max(300).required(),
      source: joi.string().max(50).required(),
      storyID: joi.string().max(100).required(),
      title: joi.string().max(200).required()
   };

  joi.validate(req.body, schema, function (err, value) {
     if (err)
        return next(err);

     // We first make sure we are not at the count limit.
     req.db.collection.count({ type: 'SHAREDSTORY_TYPE' }, function (err,
count) {
        if (err)
           return next(err);

        if (count > config.MAX_SHARED_STORIES)
           return next(new Error('Shared story limit reached'));

        // Make sure the story was not already shared
        req.db.collection.count({ type: 'SHAREDSTORY_TYPE', _id:
req.body.storyID }, function (err, count) {
           if (err)
              return next(err);
           if (count > 0)
              return next(new Error('Story was already shared.'));

           // Now we can create this as a shared news story Document.
           // Note that we don't need to worry about simultaneous post
           // requests creating the same story
           // as the id uniqueness will force that and fail other requests.
           var xferStory = {
              _id: req.body.storyID,
              type: 'SHAREDSTORY_TYPE',
              story: req.body,
              comments: [{
                  displayName: req.auth.displayName,
                  userId: req.auth.userId,
                  dateTime: Date.now(),
                  comment: req.auth.displayName + " thought everyone might
enjoy this!"
              }]
           };

           req.db.collection.insertOne(xferStory, function createUser(err,
result)
           {
              if (err)
```

```
        return next(err);

          res.status(201).json(result.ops[0]);
        });
      });
    });
  });
});
```

## GET /api/sharednews

Retrieving all shared stories is done by directly getting the documents of type SHAREDSTORY_TYPE as follows:

```
router.get('/', authHelper.checkAuth, function (req, res, next) {
  req.db.collection.find({ type: 'SHAREDSTORY_TYPE' }).toArray(function
(err, docs) {
    if (err)
      return next(err);

      res.status(200).json(docs);
  });
});
```

You know there will not be more than 30 so it is ok to have an array returned and not use a cursor to iterate through the results. The array also works great, as you can send that back in the response and then Angular can bind to lists with it on the client side.

## DELETE /api/sharednews/:sid

Individual shared stories can be deleted. You will not actually be calling this from the presentation layer, but need it just for testing purposes to clean up after yourself. It can either be commented out or have some checks done to only allow an admin account to call it. The code is as follows:

```
router.delete('/:sid', authHelper.checkAuth, function (req, res, next) {
  req.db.collection.findOneAndDelete(
    { type: 'SHAREDSTORY_TYPE', _id: req.params.sid },
    function (err, result)
    {
      if (err) {
        console.log("+++CONTENTION ERROR?+++ err:", err);
        return next(err);
      } else if (result.ok != 1) {
        console.log("+++CONTENTION ERROR?+++ result:", result);
        return next(new Error('Shared story deletion failure'));
      }

      res.status(200).json({ msg: "Shared story Deleted" });
  });
});
```

**POST /api/sharednews/:sid/comments**
To add a comment, you need the id of the story and the body JSON with the comment. Since you have a partially normalized design here with separate documents for each story, you will not have as much concurrent access. There will still be concurrent access issues for each individual story as multiple comment additions will possibly conflict. This is why the findOneAndUpdate() call is used, as it will handle this for you.

Notice that this can fail if there are already 30 comments added. There are three different parts to the query criteria used. The first two narrow it down to exactly what is being searched for. Then the $where operator is used and the actual JavaScript object is accessed to check the array length. The shared story document is added as follows:

```
router.post('/:sid/Comments', authHelper.checkAuth, function (req, res,
next) {
  // Validate the body
  var schema = {
    comment: joi.string().max(250).required()
  };

  joi.validate(req.body, schema, function (err, value) {
    if (err)
      return next(err);

    var xferComment = {
      displayName: req.auth.displayName,
      userId: req.auth.userId,
      dateTime: Date.now(),
      comment: req.body.comment.substring(0, 250)
    };

    req.db.collection.findOneAndUpdate({ type: 'SHAREDSTORY_TYPE', _id:
req.params.sid, $where: 'this.comments.length<29' },
        { $push: { comments: xferComment } },
        function (err, result) {
      if (result.value == null) {
        return next(new Error('Comment limit reached'));
      } else if (err) {
        console.log("+++CONTENTION ERROR?+++ err:", err);
        return next(err);
      } else if (result.ok != 1) {
        console.log("+++CONTENTION ERROR?+++ result:", result);
        return next(new Error('Comment save failure'));
      }

      res.status(201).json({ msg: "Comment added" });
    });
  });
});
```

# 12.13 Forked Node Process (app_FORK.js)

You never want to have any compute-intensive code in your main Node.js process. If you do, it will overwhelm the V8 JavaScript processing thread and your web service will become unresponsive. There are reasonable solutions to this, such as forking off other processes from your one main process and having code execute there.

In order to architect your application correctly, you need to consider what needs to be moved off to the secondary processes. In the case of NewsWatcher, you can identify a few pieces of code that really need to be sent off to be run on a second Node.js process that is waiting to do any processing.

You can create a file named app_FORK.js and put a few pieces of code in there. One section of code would be that which is periodically run on a timer for any batch type of work. For example, you need to populate the master news document with the latest news stories every once in a while and then run something to match all of the filters of the users.

The other code would be signaled to run by sending a message to this second Node process from the main process. For example, if a user ever alters their filters, you need to run code to update the stories that match.

Let's start with the top of the app_FORK.js file and look at the initialization code. The first lines will set up what is required for your module usage. One thing to note is that the database connection cannot be shared across processes, so you need to establish that here.

```
"use strict";

var config = require('../config');
var bcrypt = require('bcryptjs');
var http = require("http");
var async = require('async');
var assert = require('assert');
var ObjectId = require('mongodb').ObjectID;
var MongoClient = require('mongodb').MongoClient;

var db = {};
MongoClient.connect(config.MONGODB_CONNECT_URL, function (err, dbConn) {
    assert.equal(null, err);
    db.dbConnection = dbConn;
    db.collection = dbConn.collection('newswatcher');
    console.log("Connected to MongoDB server");
});
```

# PART II: The Service Layer (Node.js)

Let's look at how you communicate back and forth between Node processes. There is a global variable made available in Node.js named `process`. It is used for accessing process-related properties and functions. One of those functions is `send()`. It is used to send messages back to the parent process that forked us. The `on()` function is for handling messages sent to this forked process from the main process.

```
process.on('message', function (m) {
  if (m.msg) {
    if (m.msg == 'REFRESH_STORIES') {
      setImmediate(function (doc) {
        refreshStoriesMSG(doc, null, null);
      }, m.doc);
    }
  } else {
    console.log('Message from master:', m);
  }
});
```

The one message sent from the main process is to handle changes to a user's filter. You schedule the handling of that and return immediately from the event. It is better to do this as you have other scheduled timer functions that may fire off, as well as other message requests coming all of the time from different users. The `setImmediate()` function sets up callbacks to run after I/O handling.

### Refresh of a user's filters

Now, you can look at the function that reacts to a user who has just updated their filters and is run in response to your message handling. The basic algorithm is to loop through each filter a user has. For each filter, the code can see if there are any stories in the master news list that match the key words. There is a limit to the number of stories that can be matched.

When the update of the user document happens, the `$set` operator is used and only a single property of the document is updated, just the array property that holds the news filters.

There is code in here for testing purposes. This is here, to be able to verify you have a known news story to use in your tests for a special predetermined keyword string. You will later see how this is used when the test code is presented. Here is the code:

```
function refreshStoriesMSG(doc, globalNewsDoc, callback) {
  if (!globalNewsDoc) {
    db.collection.findOne({ _id: config.GLOBAL_STORIES_ID }, function
(err, gDoc) {
      // TODO: Save this so not getting it on every filter change!
      if (err) {
        console.log('FORK_ERROR: global news read err:' + err);
        if (callback)
          return callback(err);
```

```
            else
               return;
         } else {
            refreshStories(doc, gDoc, callback);
         }
      });
   } else {
      refreshStories(doc, globalNewsDoc, callback);
   }
}

function refreshStories(doc, globalNewsDoc, callback) {
   // Loop through all newsFilters and seek matches for all stories
   for (var filterIdx = 0; filterIdx<doc.newsFilters.length; filterIdx++) {
      doc.newsFilters[filterIdx].newsStories = [];

      for (var i = 0; i < globalNewsDoc.newsStories.length; i++) {
         globalNewsDoc.newsStories[i].keep = false;
      }

      // If there are keyWords, then filter by them
      if ("keyWords" in doc.newsFilters[filterIdx] &&
          doc.newsFilters[filterIdx].keyWords[0] != "")
      {
         var storiesMatched = 0;
         for (var i=0; i<doc.newsFilters[filterIdx].keyWords.length; i++) {
            for (var j = 0; j < globalNewsDoc.newsStories.length; j++) {
               if (globalNewsDoc.newsStories[j].keep == false) {
                  var s1 = globalNewsDoc.newsStories[j].title.toLowerCase();
                  var s2 =
globalNewsDoc.newsStories[j].contentSnippet.toLowerCase();
                  var keyword =
doc.newsFilters[filterIdx].keyWords[i].toLowerCase();
                  if (s1.indexOf(keyword) >= 0 || s2.indexOf(keyword) >= 0) {
                     globalNewsDoc.newsStories[j].keep = true;
                     storiesMatched++;
                  }
               }
               if (storiesMatched == config.MAX_FILTER_STORIES)
                  break;
            }
            if (storiesMatched == config.MAX_FILTER_STORIES)
               break;
         }

         for (var k = 0; k < globalNewsDoc.newsStories.length; k++) {
            if (globalNewsDoc.newsStories[k].keep == true) {
               doc.newsFilters[filterIdx].newsStories.push(
                  globalNewsDoc.newsStories[k]);
            }
         }
      }
   }
}
```

```
// For the test runs, inject news stories that will be controlled
if (doc.newsFilters.length == 1 &&
        doc.newsFilters[0].keyWords.length == 1
        && doc.newsFilters[0].keyWords[0] == "testingKeyword") {
    for (var i = 0; i < 5; i++) {
        doc.newsFilters[0].newsStories.push(globalNewsDoc.newsStories[0]);
        doc.newsFilters[0].newsStories[0].title = "testingKeyword title"+i;
    }
}

// Do the replacement of the news stories in the document
db.collection.findOneAndUpdate({ _id: ObjectId(doc._id) },
    { $set: { "newsFilters": doc.newsFilters } },
    function (err, result) {
        if (err) {
            console.log('FORK_ERROR Replace of newsStories failed:', err);
        } else if (result.ok != 1) {
            console.log('FORK_ERROR Replace of newsStories failed:', result);
        } else {
            if (doc.newsFilters.length > 0) {
                console.log({ msg: 'MASTERNEWS_UPDATE first filter news length
= ' + doc.newsFilters[0].newsStories.length });
            } else {
                console.log({ msg: 'MASTERNEWS_UPDATE no newsFilters' });
            }
        }
        if (callback)
            return callback(err);
    });
}
```

This second function is used elsewhere, so there needed to be a way to allow another call of it where the global news document had already been fetched.

**Timer event to populate the master news list**
Every few hours, a function runs that fetches all news stories from the source news service provider. This mean that it works on a batch of data and could take some time before it finishes. This function was placed in this second Node.js process because it is long-running. It is still significant enough that it is better to place it there so as to not upset the main Node process core CPU usage. This could even eventually be offloaded to a completely different machine.

The first thing that happens is an HTTP request is sent to a news feed API provided by the New York Times API service. The results from that are placed into formatted news elements in the master document `newsStories` array. Notice the use of the async module to be able to loop a number of times and also set a .5 second delay between each batch news request from NYT. This is because there is a restriction with the usage that you can't call it more than five times a second, or they may disable your IP address from accessing them.

210

There is an id needed for each story. A GUID could have been generated, but the problem is that the same story might appear again in the next batch of news and that would cause problems if you thought it was a new news story. A hash of the link will turn out to be the best way to uniquely identify a story. The link itself would be unusable later in a URL to pass in as an ID, but the hash value works, as long as you replace certain characters of it.

Once all of the news stories are in place, you can go through all of the user documents and, for each user, do the story matching against the news filters there. This is done in a somewhat tricky way. The `async.doWhilst()` functionality is used. This way, it can handle the difficulty of managing multiple async calls, one at a time, in a simple way. The code will keep running as long as there is processing to do.

You have to consider the throughput capability on the MongoDB side and not overwhelm it, so it is good to have this processing serialized. You need to keep plenty of headroom for your normal user interactions. Here is the code:

```
var count = 0;
newsPullBackgroundTimer = setInterval(function () {
  // Use the NYT news API service, several categories to loop through
  var date = new Date();
  console.log("app_FORK: datetime tick: " + date.toUTCString());
  async.timesSeries(10, function (n, next) {
    setTimeout(function () {
      try {
        https.get({
          host: 'api.nytimes.com',
          path: '/svc/topstories/v2/' +
            config.NEWYORKTIMES_CATEGORIES[n] + '.json',
          headers: { 'api-key': config.NEWYORKTIMES_API_KEY }
        }, function (res) {
          var body = '';
          res.on('data', function (d) {
            body += d;
          });
          res.on('end', function () {
            next(null, body);
          });
        }).on('error', function (err) {
          // handle errors with the request itself
          console.log(err.message);
          return;
        });
      }
      catch (err) {
        count++;
        if (count == 3) {
          console.log('app_FORK.js: shutting down err:' + err);
          clearInterval(newsPullBackgroundTimer);
          clearInterval(staleStoryDeleteBackgroundTimer);
```

```
          process.disconnect();
        }
        else {
          console.log('app_FORK.js error. err:' + err);
        }
      }
    }, 1500);
  }, function (err, results) {
    if (err) {
      console.log('failure');
    } else {
      console.log('success');

      // Do the replacement of the master Document holder or news
      db.collection.findOne({ _id: config.GLOBAL_STORIES_ID }, function
(err, globalNewsDoc) {
        if (err) {
          console.log(JSON.stringify(err.body, null, 4));
        } else {
          globalNewsDoc.newsStories = [];
          for (var i = 0; i < results.length; i++) {
            // JSON.parse is syncronous and it will throw an exception
            try {
              var news = JSON.parse(results[i]);
            } catch (e) {
              console.error(e);
              return;
            }
            for (var j = 0; j < news.results.length; j++) {
              var xferNewsStory = {
                link: news.results[j].url,
                title: news.results[j].title,
                contentSnippet: news.results[j].abstract,
                source: news.results[j].section,
                date: new Date(news.results[j].updated_date).getTime()
              };
              // Only take stories with images
              if (news.results[j].multimedia.length > 0) {
                xferNewsStory.imageUrl =
                        news.results[j].multimedia[0].url;
                globalNewsDoc.newsStories.push(xferNewsStory);
              }
            }
          }

          async.eachSeries(globalNewsDoc.newsStories, function (story,
innercallback) {
            bcrypt.hash(story.link, 10, function getHash(err, hash) {
              if (err)
                innercallback(err);

              story.storyID = hash.replace(/\+/g, '-').replace(/\//g,
'_').replace(/=+$/, '');
```

212

```
                    innercallback();
                });
            }, function (err) {
                if (err) {
                    console.log('failure on story id creation');
                } else {
                    console.log('story id creation success');
                    setImmediate(function (doc) {
                        refreshAllUserStories(doc, null, null);
                    }, globalNewsDoc);
                }
            });
        }
    });
    });
}
}, 120 * 60 * 1000);

function refreshAllUserStories(globalNewsDoc) {
    db.collection.findOneAndUpdate({ _id: globalNewsDoc._id }, { $set: {
newsStories: globalNewsDoc.newsStories } }, function (err, result) {
        if (err) {
            console.log('FORK_ERROR Replace of global newsStories failed:',
err);
        } else if (result.ok != 1) {
            console.log('FORK_ERROR Replace of global newsStories failed:',
result);
        } else {
            // For each NewsWatcher user, do news matching on their newsFilters
            var cursor = db.collection.find({ type: 'USER_TYPE' });
            var keepProcessing = true;
            async.doWhilst(
                function (callback) {
                    cursor.next(function (err, doc) {
                        if (doc) {
                            refreshStories(doc, globalNewsDoc, function (err) {
                                callback(null);
                            });
                        } else {
                            keepProcessing = false;
                            callback(null);
                        }
                    });
                },
                function () { return keepProcessing; },
                function (err) {
                    console.log(err);
                });
        }
    });
}
```

*Note: Anytime you use these async functions, you have to be really careful of how they operate with their async and sync capabilities and make sure you call the required callbacks correctly in the right place. Error handling can also be a bit tricky.*

### Deleting old stories
Shared stories that are old are deleted. This becomes another timer that goes off periodically to do this processing. The code is as follows:

```
staleStoryDeleteBackgroundTimer = setInterval(function () {
   db.collection.find({ type: 'SHAREDSTORY_TYPE' }).toArray(function (err,
docs) {
      if (err) {
         console.log('Fork could not get shared stories. err:', err);
         return;
      }

      async.eachSeries(docs, function (story, innercallback) {
         // Go off the date of the time the story was shared
         var d1 = story.comments[0].dateTime;
         var d2 = Date.now();
         var diff = Math.floor((d2 - d1) / 3600000);
         if (diff > 72) {
            db.collection.findOneAndDelete({ type: 'SHAREDSTORY_TYPE', _id:
story._id }, function (err, result) {
               innercallback(err);
            });
         } else {
            innercallback();
         }
      }, function (err) {
         if (err) {
            console.log('stale story deletion failure');
         } else {
            console.log('stale story deletion success');
         }
      });
   });

}, 48 * 60 * 60 * 1000);
```

# 12.14 Securing with HTTPS

At this point I need to discuss an important security measure that needs to be put into place. You just can't host your REST API endpoint without encrypting traffic back and forth. You fix this by only permitting HTTPS connections. That way all traffic is encrypted and signed so as to be tamper-resistant and harder to eavesdrop on.

Since the Node.js service is exposed through the Elastic Beanstalk app, you don't need to make any changes to your Node.js code. If your Node.js instance was exposed directly to the Internet and serving up the traffic directly, then you would do some simple configuration on the Node.js side to install a certificate and key files and then make a few modifications to the Node code.

In this case, Elastic Beanstalk keeps Node from being directly exposed. The Elastic Beanstalk service acts as a reverse proxy and that is where you need to set SSL up. You will need to get your own domain name and install a certificate for your Elastic Beanstalk service.

*Note: When you launch your application through VS Code, it will not accept HTTPS locally on your machine. However, tests run against a production deployment must be altered to use HTTPS. You need to be aware of that in your test code and make the appropriate changes to the URL.*

### Securing communications to MongoDB
For performance reasons, you will want to place your database in the same AWS datacenter as your Elastic Beanstalk Node app. As an added bonus of doing this, the ability to secure the communication between your Node.js service and your database becomes easier. This is because everything is sent over the internal datacenter network and never gets out over the public Internet. As a further measure of security, you can also communicate over an SSL connection if you use a dedicated plan from mLab.

With a dedicated plan you also define custom firewall rules so that your database access is limited to specific IP address ranges and/or to specific AWS EC2 security groups.

## DNS and certificate setup
In the Introduction, you saw a physical topology diagram (see figure 4) that showed you having your own domain name that was routed through a DNS server with a certificate to enable HTTPS. You can now go about setting that up.

First go to the Route 53 service management console. Click **Register Domain** on the far right side of the page to start the process of getting your own domain. If you already have your own domain name and want to use it, you can do that but it's not covered in this book. Here is the Route 53 management console:

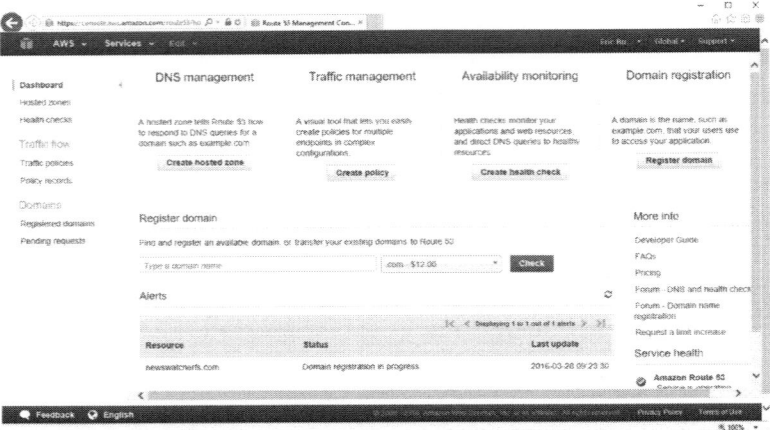

*Figure 65: Route 53 service management console*

You can type in different names to try and you will be able to find one that is available. There is an initial charge as well as a small recurring fee when you purchase a domain name. For this implementation of the NewsWatcher sample app, I settled on newswatcherfs.com since newswatcher.com was already taken. I figured fs at the end could stand for Full Stack.

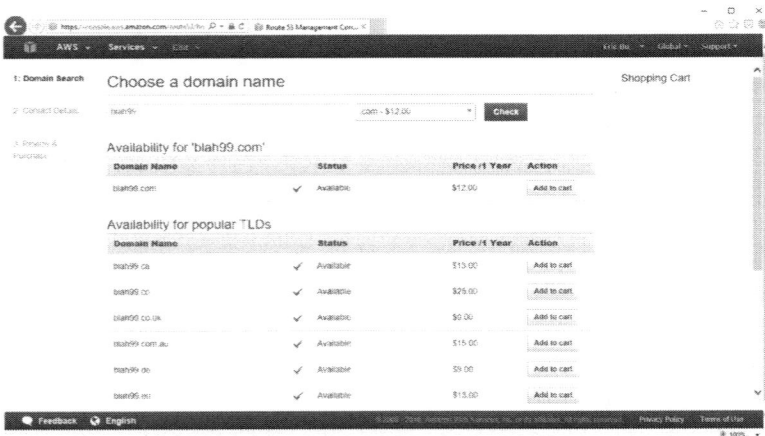

*Figure 66: Route 53 domain availability*

It can take an hour or longer before everything is ready and you can use your new domain name. Once it is ready, you can get a certificate set up using the AWS Certificate Manager Service. You go to that service and enter the domain name variations you want supported. You can use wildcards and have the flexibility you need. Here is the initial screen:

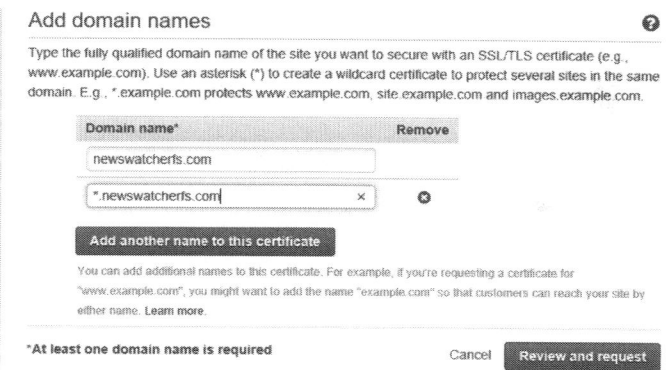

Figure 67: Add domain names to AWS Certificate Manager

After this screen, there are a few more to click through. At some point, you will also need to validate this action through an email exchange that verifies that you are the owner of the domain name that the certificate is being set up for.

Now you can set up the certificate on the Elastic Beanstalk load balancer. You can do this through the AWS management portal. Here are the steps:

1. Log in and open the AWS Elastic Beanstalk console in the browser.
2. Open your Elastic Beanstalk environment and on the left select **Configuration**.
3. Click the gear icon next to **Load Balancing**.
4. Select your certificate from the **SSL certificate ID** drop down.
5. Click **Apply** at the bottom of the page.

Now you can watch the status there until it indicates that the configuration change is successful.

Recent Events

| Time | Type | Details |
|------|------|---------|
| 2016-04-07 13:46:48 UTC-0700 | INFO | Environment update completed successfully. |
| 2016-04-07 13:46:48 UTC-0700 | INFO | Successfully deployed new configuration to environment. |
| 2016-04-07 13:45:01 UTC-0700 | INFO | Updating environment newswatcher's configuration settings. |
| 2016-04-07 13:44:48 UTC-0700 | INFO | Environment update is starting. |

Figure 68: Elastic Beanstalk status

Now you can set up DNS routing to your Elastic Beanstalk load balancer. Go back into the Route 53 management console and click the DNS management hosted zone that will show up in the upper left. Then click **Create Record Set**.

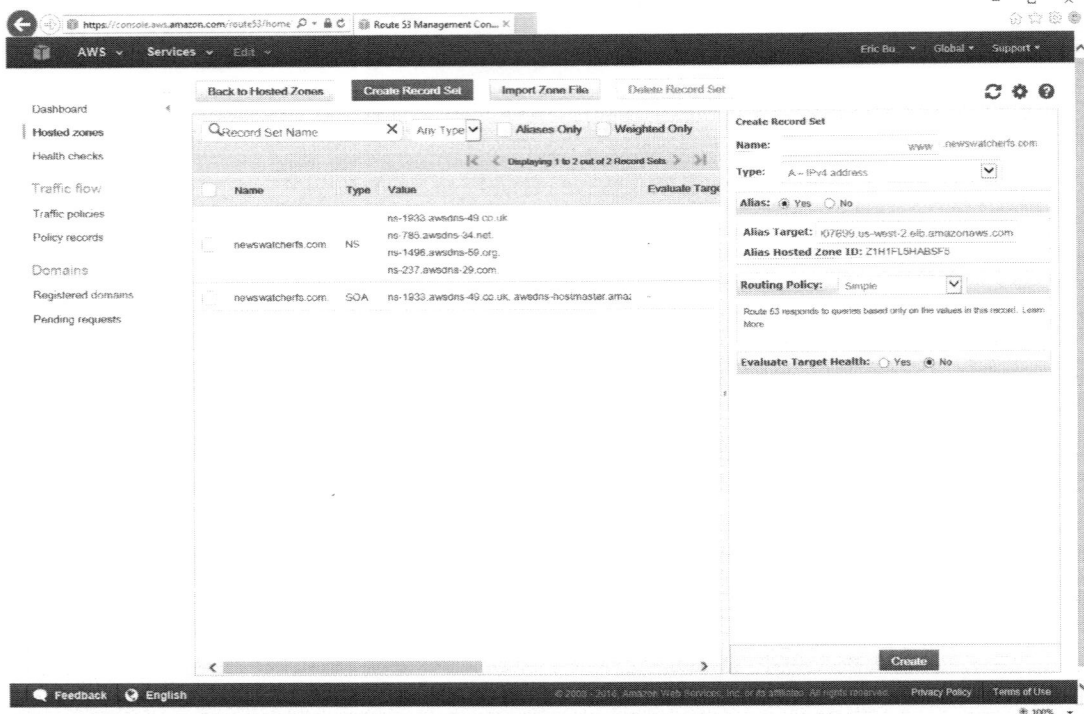

*Figure 69: AWS Certificate Management Create Record Set*

Fill out the form on the right. For **Alias Target**, select your load balancer.

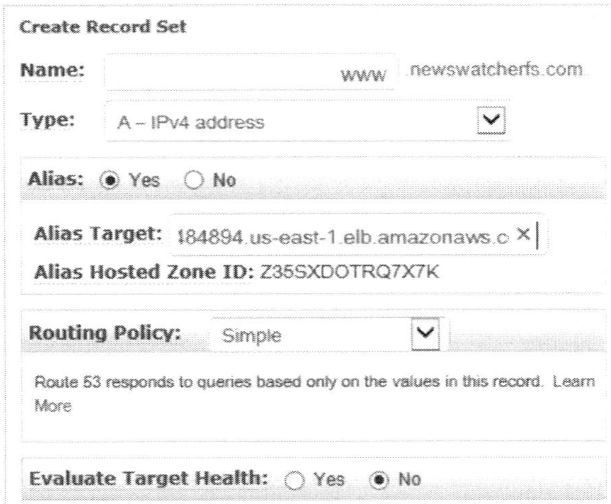

**Create Record Set**

**Name:** www .newswatcherfs.com

**Type:** A – IPv4 address

**Alias:** ⦿ Yes ◯ No

**Alias Target:** 184894.us-east-1.elb.amazonaws.c ✕

**Alias Hosted Zone ID:** Z35SXDOTRQ7X7K

**Routing Policy:** Simple

Route 53 responds to queries based only on the values in this record. Learn More

**Evaluate Target Health:** ◯ Yes ⦿ No

*Figure 70: Route 53 create record set*

You are almost done. You need to turn off HTTP access at the load balancer. To do that:
1. Go to the EC2 service management console and click **1 Load Balancers**.
2. Click the **Listeners** tab, then click **Edit**.
3. Delete the HTTP entry, then click **Save**.

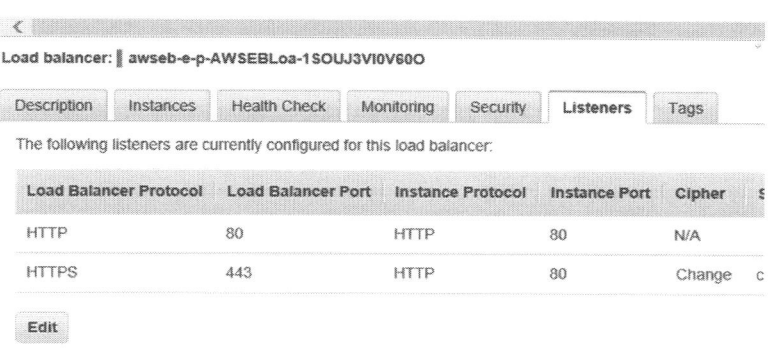

*Figure 71: EC2 service Listeners tab*

Back at the Elastic Beanstalk environment page, if you click on the URL at the top, it will no longer work. In your browser, change the URL to start with `https:` and you will be told the certificate does not match. Now type in the URL to the domain name you registered and you will see everything up and working as it should. HTTPS is now working So, https://www.newswatcherfs.com/ will work, but http://www.newswatcherfs.com/ will not work.

# 12.15 Deployment

At this point you have everything in place to start trying out your middle-tier web service API that is implemented as an HTTP/Rest endpoint. You obviously would not build a service like this without testing it along the way. For the purposes of being clear in presenting the material in this book, all of the testing is discussed in the next chapter.

Don't get the wrong impression. I certainly wrote the code in small iterations and tested each and every bit of it along the way. Good developers iterate and test everything as they go.

At this point, you can zip up your code and deploy it up to AWS similarly to the deployment described in section 12.3. Before doing so, you can test things out with some tests that will be described in chapter 13. You will actually want to test on your local machine as well as deploy to some known staging cloud location and test there as well. You would be running the test code from your local machine to go against a staging site that is hosted in AWS.

# PART II: The Service Layer (Node.js)

Here are the folders and files I select to have zipped up on my Windows machine:

Name

- .git
- .vscode
- node_modules
- routes
- static
- test
- worker
- .gitignore
- config.js
- gulpfile.js
- LICENSE
- package.json
- README.md
- server.js

*Figure 72: Selections to make to zip*

# Chapter 13: Testing the NewsWatcher Rest API

Now comes the exciting part. You will actually get to see the HTTP/Rest Web API exercised thoroughly. You will prove that the service is up and running locally before you deploy and verify everything again in production. Once sufficiently proven, you can move on to the final task of creating a UI for NewsWatcher and be assured that the integration will go fairly smoothly.

This chapter will present several practices that you will want to follow for exercising your code in order to fully test it. It is a lot simpler to test and debug issues locally. The next chapter will then show you how to employ techniques for debugging issues in production.

# 13.1 Debugging During Testing

Let's first talk about debugging techniques. You will need to do some of that as you run tests and need to examine the execution of your code.

In some cases, output logging to the Node console window will provide you with enough clues to track down an issue. This means that you must log important things that are happening in the application. Beyond this, you will need a few tools to help you do your investigations.

One tool at your disposal is the VS Code debugger. Before deploying anything, you will be running your code locally. You can use VS Code to debug your Node.js project code or even debug your test code.

If you want to debug your Node.js code, you open your project, and launch the Node.js project by pressing F5. You can set up your breakpoints in advance, or add ones as needed that you want hit. Once your project is running, you run Mocha from the command line and exercise your code through tests you have written. Then you can step through your code.

To set up debugging in VS code, click the debug icon. You will see a gear icon at the top of the window that you can click to create the launch.json file. This is the file that instructs VS Code how to proceed. By default, it will have two configurations in the file. One will be for launching your node process with debugging capability. The other entry is for attaching to an already running Node process. When you click the gear icon, select the Node selection and create the file. Your file will look as follows:

```
{
  "version": "0.2.0",
  "configurations": [
    {
      "name": "Launch",
      "type": "node",
      "request": "launch",
      "program": "server.js",
      "stopOnEntry": false,
      "args": [],
      "cwd": ".",
      "runtimeExecutable": null,
      "runtimeArgs": [
        "--nolazy"
      ],
      "env": {
        "NODE_ENV": "development"
      },
      "externalConsole": false,
      "sourceMaps": false,
      "outDir": null
    },
    {
      "name": "Attach",
      "type": "node",
      "request": "attach",
      "port": 5858
    }
  ]
}
```

To the left of the gear is the start button (you can also press F5). The dropdown menu will show you the config section options to use that exist in your launch.json file. The far right greater-than symbol in the box opens the output console window. It is a good idea to always have that open to view any statements or errors that get displayed.

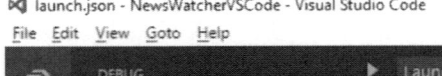

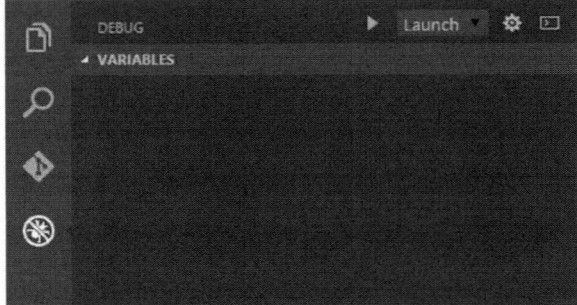

*Figure 73: Visual Studio Code*

You can open the launch.json file and look at it, but you do not need to make any adjustments to it as the defaults are just what you need. Here is a table that lists what each of the settings are for.

| Setting: | Purpose: |
|---|---|
| name | What shows up in the selection dropdown. F5 will run the selected one. |
| type | The type of debugging that is allowed. You want "node", of course. |
| request | If you want to launch or attach. |
| program | The file that node will be launched with to run. |
| stopOnEntry | If you want to break in the debugger on the very first line. |
| args | Any parameters you want passed in. |
| cwd | The working directory to execute in. |
| runtimeArgs | Those that get sent to Node. "nolazy" means that delayed parsing is off, so that code is read and available to set breakpoints on up front. |
| env | Environment variables to set that your program can access. |
| sourceMaps | Used for languages like TypeScript so you can relate the compiled JavaScript back to your TypeScript code. |
| outDir | The generated code directory for the source maps. |
| port | The debug port that was surfaced that you want to connect to. |

To place a breakpoint, open a JavaScript file and click out to the left of the margin, or click on the line and press F9. Once you hit a breakpoint while running code, you get full access to inspect the call stack and variables.

# 13.2 Tools to Make an HTTP/Rest Call

You will probably want to use a tool to make individual calls to your API. That way, you can take small steps to get everything verified before you throw a test harness into the mix. I have installed both Fiddler and Curl.exe on my machine for that purpose. There are many of these such tools. Some of them are used as browser plugins. With these types of tools, you can send calls to your service and view the returned results.

From one of the recommended tools, you can set up the verb to call with, as well as the headers and the JSON body content. You can do a send and then look at the returned response. Let's look at the UI of Fiddler and I will explain the basics of how to use it to call your API.

You can send an HTTP request to the route handler that registers a user. This is an obvious first place to start. To do that, you know you have the `app.use('/api/users', users)`

call in your server.js file that takes you to the users.js function of `router.post('/',
function (req, res, next) {}`. This is the code that creates a new registration.

You want to make a post verb call and pass in a JSON body that contains the display name, email and password. You then expect a 201 return code to be given back to indicate a successful creation. In the return response would be the returned document that you could inspect.

You can now start up your node service with your project open and press F5 to debug, or press Ctrl+F5 to run without debugging. The first thing you notice is that you get a console app window that opens. That represents your node process running and the executing of your server.js file. You will see all of your console logging appear in this window. Here is what the console window might look like:

*Figure 74: Console window*

As you see, your server is running as a local process. To make an HTTP request you can connect to localhost with the port number of 3000 and interact with the Rest API. You can open Fiddler and try this out. The first thing to do is to limit what traffic Fiddler sees going back and forth. Otherwise you will get lost in the stream of traffic. To do this and also make an HTTP request do the following:

1. In the Fiddle Web Debugger, click the **Filters** tab.
2. In the top section, check **Use Filters.**
3. In the **Request Headers** section, check **Show only if URL contains** and type in "localhost".

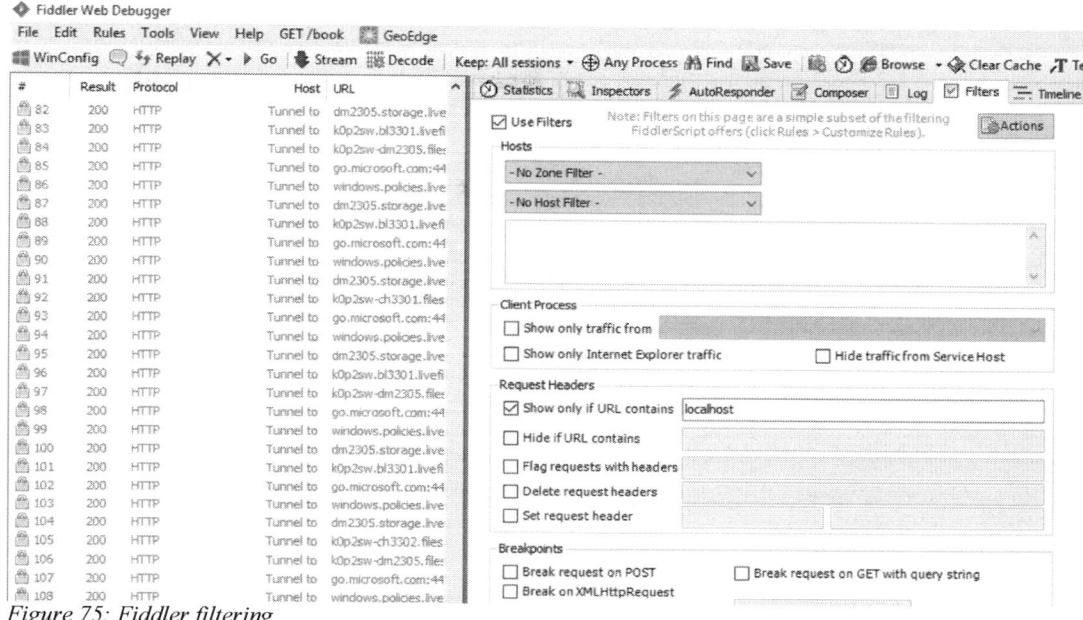
*Figure 75: Fiddler filtering*

4. Click the dropdown menu **X -> Remove all** to get rid of all old traffic.

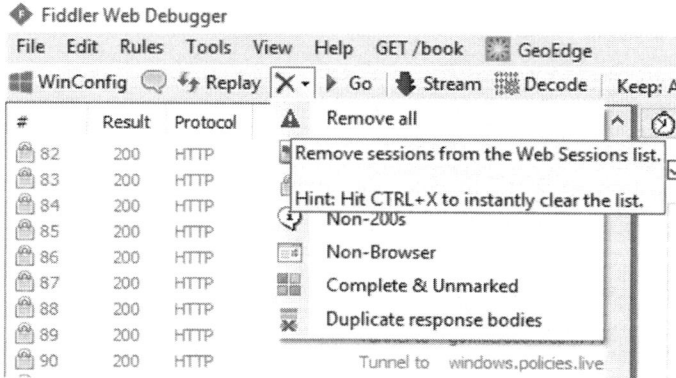
*Figure 76: Fiddler remove all*

5. Click the **Composer** tab, then click the **Options** sub-tab under that and make sure it looks as follow:

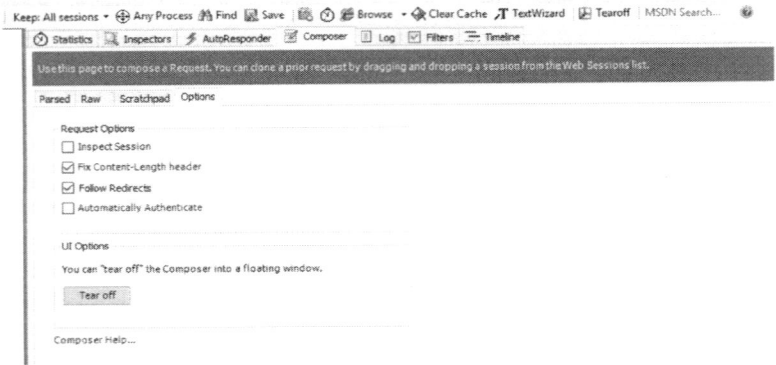

*Figure 77: Options*

You want Fiddler to figure out the content header length value for you.

6. Click the **Raw** tab, and enter the following request:

```
POST http://localhost:3000/api/users HTTP/1.1
User-Agent: Fiddler
Host: localhost:3000
Content-Type: application/json
Content-Length: 85

{
"email" : "bush@sample.com",
"displayName" : "Bushman",
"password" : "abc123"
}
```

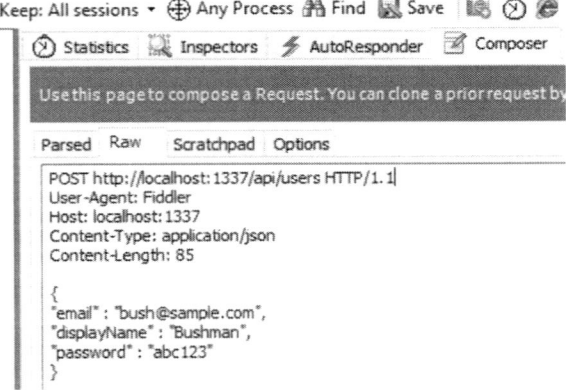

*Figure 78: Fiddler RAW request*

7. Click **Execute.**

If you look in the left-hand pane, you will see the request being sent and a response returned. If you double click the 201 response, you can examine it and see that it worked. It should look as follows if you click on **Raw** or **JSON** view:

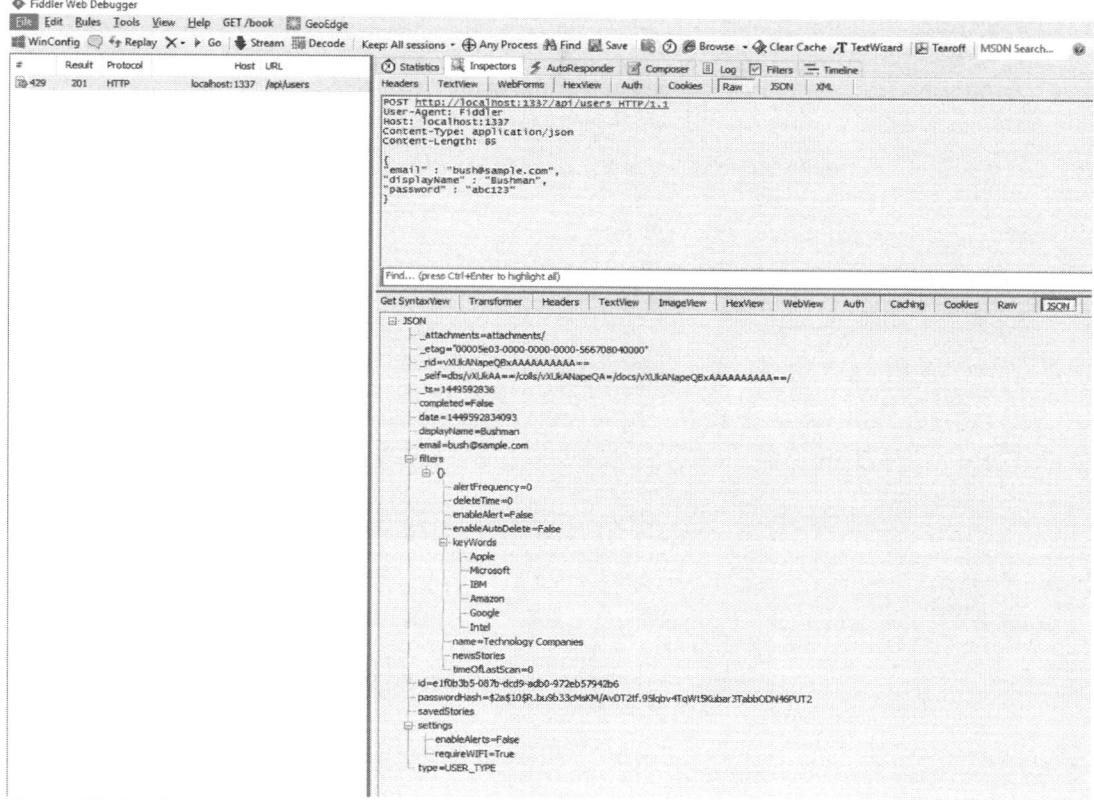

*Figure 79: Fiddler request and response*

You have now successfully seen your API exercised. Go to the mLab Management Portal and you can also see that there is a new document created. In the mLab portal, you will see something like the following:

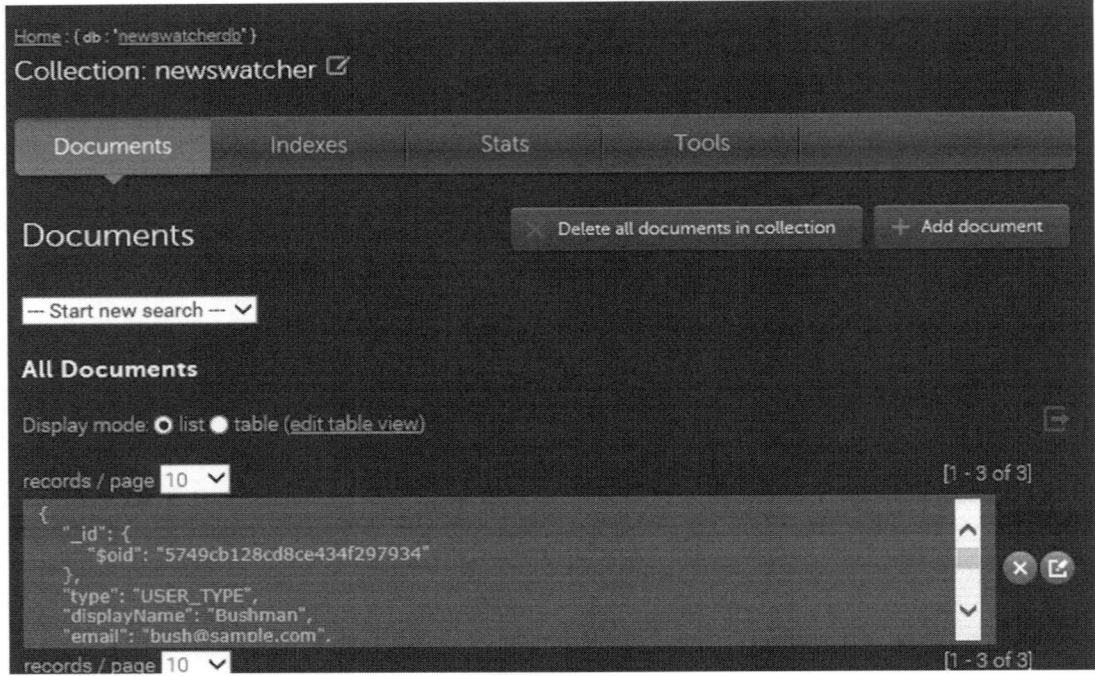

*Figure 80: mLab management portal with a new document*

You can now enter every single request through Fiddler to prove them all. Next, try to log in and get a token back:

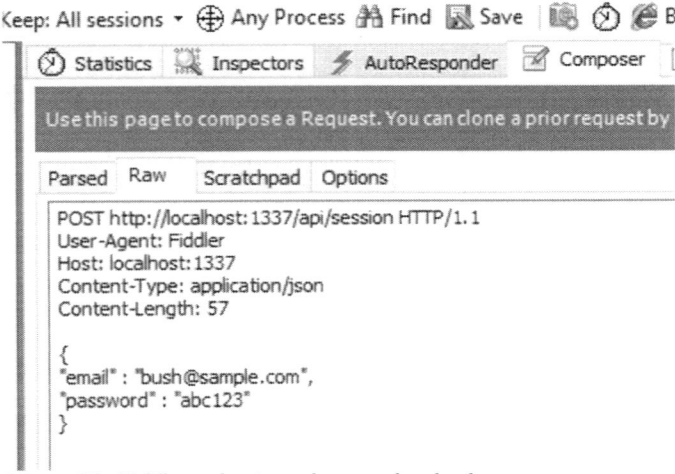

*Figure 81: Fiddler to log in and get a token back*

Look at the result and you will see a token in the response if you open it up. You will need this token to use in the next requests. You can next make a call to retrieve the user document and see if there are any news stories that have matched the filter.

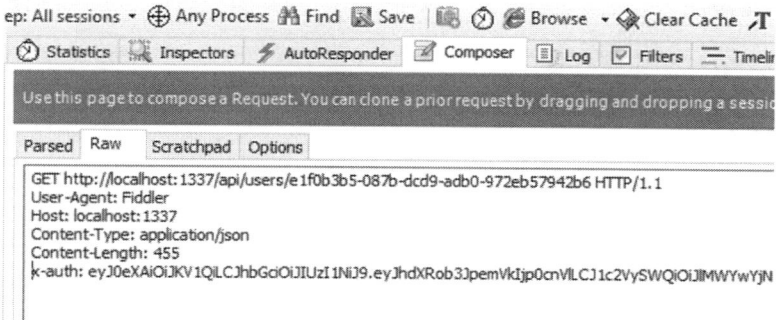

*Figure 82: Fiddler to see the token*

In Fiddler, Click **Execute** and you will see a response with the returned user document and possibly some news stories. This is great progress, and you can continue to try all of your API calls and debug each one if needed. As you get each one working, you can create a test case for each.

As was mentioned, you might find a tool other than Fiddler that you like. Curl is a nice option because you just open a command prompt and execute it there. It has a simple syntax that you use to formulate your requests.

# 13.3 A Functional Test Suit with Mocha

Now you will take the next step of automating the testing of the API using a test suite. This will then become your functional test pass. You can start by implementing some of the same operations that were already tried when you used Fiddler. To start with, you need to add a new folder to your VS Code project to hold the tests. You can also set up the added node modules you need for the tests.

*Note: NPM lets you download different types of modules. Like many modules I've shown you, you download them and then use a* require *statement to utilize them as code modules. Others, like Mocha, are not code modules, but are command-line tools. What you do is write a JavaScript file that Mocha will interpret and run. You then launch a command-line to execute Mocha, and it does its work. Mocha is installed as a local part of your project. This means the executable will be referenced from that location. Mocha can also be installed globally, if you like.*

Add the following to the package.json file:

```
"devDependencies": {
  "gulp": "^3.9.1",
  "gulp-bump": "^2.1.0",
  "gulp-git": "^1.7.0",
  "gulp-mocha": "^2.2.0",
  "mocha": "^2.4.5",
  "run-sequence": "^1.1.5",
  "selenium-webdriver": "^2.53.1",
  "supertest": "^1.2.0"
}
```

The devDependencies section is reserved for non-production modules that you will not need to deploy to a production build. They are only needed to be able to run your test code locally.

Here is the added folder with the files you will be needing for your test code:

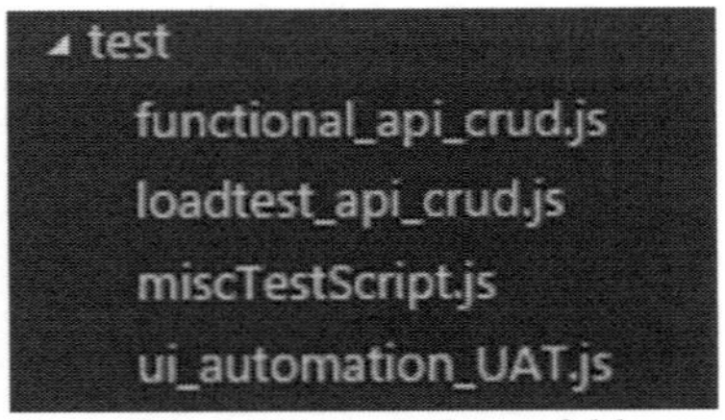

*Figure 83: VSCode with test folder*

# Writing mocha tests (functional_api_crud.js)

You will make use of the supertest module and the assert module. Set up the require() calls for those. The next code in the test file will be the code that makes use of mocha.

The request object is what you set up from the supertest module. With that, you can call the post verb and register a user.

You will use the describe keyword for a major test block and use the individual it keywords for each test inside of that. With just one test to run, it would look like the following example code:

```
var assert = require('assert');
var request = require('supertest')('http://localhost:3000');

describe('User cycle operations', function () {
  it("should create a new registered User", function (done) {
    request.post("/api/users")
    .send({
```

```
            email: 'bush@sample.com',
            displayName: 'Bushman',
            password: 'abc123'
        })
        .end(function (err, res) {
            assert.equal(res.status, 201);
            assert.equal(res.body.displayName, "Bushman", "Name of user should
be as set");
            done();
        });
    });
});
```

*Note: Mocha actually supports several different styles of syntax, so don't be confused if you see other projects using Mocha and it does not look exactly like the code in this book.*

I will go through the previous code to make sure you understand it. To start with, you have the usual Node.js require statements at the top. For the supertest module, you specify that you are going to hit the local running web server endpoint of your Node project. The strings you have as parameters to describe() and it() are for your purposes in understanding the output from a run as you see the results and recall what was tested. You should use text that helps you remember what you were testing.

With this code, you have a test that will verify that you can register a user. The it block takes a string to describe what you are testing and then a function to run. There is a done() function that you call to signal to mocha that it can move on to the next it block. These tests are each run sequentially. If you don't call done(), the test will eventually time out.

To use supertest, you specify a verb operation to use. This one is using post. You string together the function calls send() and end(). Each one will get called in sequence. The send function does the HTTP/Rest request and has the body set.

The end() function can get the response and validate the return code and values from the returned body. You use the assert module for validations.

There are some cases where you have a second test that relies on the results of the first test. This can be tricky if there is delayed processing of the first test code. You can either stack one test inside the other, or use a JavaScript setTimeout() call to delay your second test run by a bit and then have it run.

For example, for NewsWatcher, when a user changes their news filters, that operation will return and complete. This means that the test code will move on to the next test. The way NewsWatcher works though, is that it sends a message to the forked process to now update the news stories. If you wanted to test that a change to a filter retrieved new news stories, you would have to guess that it would take a second to do that in the background and do a delay until you ran the next piece of test code.

The following code shows using a delay of three seconds before running the test.

```
it("should allow access if logged in ", function (done) {
    setTimeout(function () {
        request.get("/api/users/" + userId)
        .set('x-auth', token)
        .end(function (err, res) {
            assert.equal(res.status, 200);
            savedDoc = res.body.newsFilters[0].newsStories[0];
            console.log(JSON.stringify(savedDoc, null, 4));
            done();
        });
    }, 3000);
});
```

Here is a more complete set of tests that registers a user and then makes sure they can log in and then deletes the account to clean things up. The test right at the start is to verify that a person cannot log in if they don't first register.

There may be negative tests you can put into place to verify your error handling code. In this code below, I make use of local valuables inside the describe block to pass these between tests such as the token vriable. For example, you need to capture the token at sign in time and keep using it on subsequent rest calls that you are testing.

```
var assert = require('assert');
var request = require('supertest')('http://localhost:3000'); // For local
testing

describe('User cycle operations', function () {
    var token;
    var userId;
    var savedDoc;

    it("should deny unregistered user a login attempt", function (done) {
        request.post("/api/sessions").send({
            email: 'bush@sample.com',
            password: 'abc123*'
        })
        .end(function (err, res) {
            assert.equal(res.status, 500);
            done();
        });
    });

    it("should create a new registered User", function (done) {
        request.post("/api/users")
```

```
      .send({
       email: 'bush@sample.com',
       displayName: 'Bushman',
       password: 'abc123*'
    })
       .end(function (err, res) {
       assert.equal(res.status, 201);
       assert.equal(res.body.displayName, "Bushman", "Name of user should
be as set");
       done();
    });
  });

  it("should not create a User twice", function (done) {
    request.post("/api/users")
     .send({
       email: 'bush@sample.com',
       displayName: 'Bushman',
       password: 'abc123*'
    })
     .end(function (err, res) {
       assert.equal(res.status, 500);
       assert.equal(res.body.message, "Error: Email account already
registered", "Error should be already registered");
       done();
    });
  });

  it("should detect incorrect password", function (done) {
    request.post("/api/sessions")
     .send({
       email: 'bush@sample.com',
       password: 'wrong1*'
    })
     .end(function (err, res) {
       assert.equal(res.status, 500);
       assert.equal(res.body.message, "Error: Wrong password", "Error
should be already registered");
       done();
    });
  });

  });

  it("should allow registered user to login", function (done) {
    request.post("/api/sessions")
     .send({
       email: 'bush@sample.com',
       password: 'abc123*'
    })
     .end(function (err, res) {
       //<Session&Cookie code>cookies = res.headers['set-cookie'];
       token = res.body.token;
       userId = res.body.userId;
```

```
          assert.equal(res.status, 201);
          assert.equal(res.body.msg, "Authorized", "Message should be
AUthorized");
          done();
      });
  });

  it("should allow registered user to logout", function (done) {
      request.del("/api/sessions/" + userId)
        .set('x-auth', token)
        .end(function (err, res) {
          assert.equal(res.status, 200);
          done();
      });
  });

  it("should not allow access if not logged in", function (done) {
      request.get("/api/users/" + userId)
        .end(function (err, res) {
          assert.equal(res.status, 500);
          done();
      });
  });

  it("should allow registered user to login", function (done) {
      request.post("/api/sessions")
        .send({
          email: 'bush@sample.com',
          password: 'abc123*'
      })
        .end(function (err, res) {
          token = res.body.token;
          userId = res.body.userId;
          assert.equal(res.status, 201);
          assert.equal(res.body.msg, "Authorized", "Message should be
AUthorized");
          done();
      });
  });

  it("should delete a registered User", function (done) {
      request.del("/api/users/" + userId)
        .set('x-auth', token)
        .end(function (err, res) {
          assert.equal(res.status, 200);
          done();
      });
  });
});
```

You run your Mocha test suite from a command prompt. On Windows machines, use your keyboard, click **Windows Logo+Q** and type Node. You should see **Node.js command**

**prompt** as a selection. I like to pin it to my taskbar for easy access. Once you are in the command prompt, you **cd** (change directory) to navigate to the location of your project.

Start up the node.js application locally. Then you can run Mocha from the local project in the Node command prompt:

```
.\node_modules\.bin\mocha --timeout 15000 test\functional_api_crud.js
```

You may need to play around with the timeout argument. It is possible to get false failures because of Mocha timing-out and moving on to next it test too quickly. The output for the complete functional test suite look as follows:

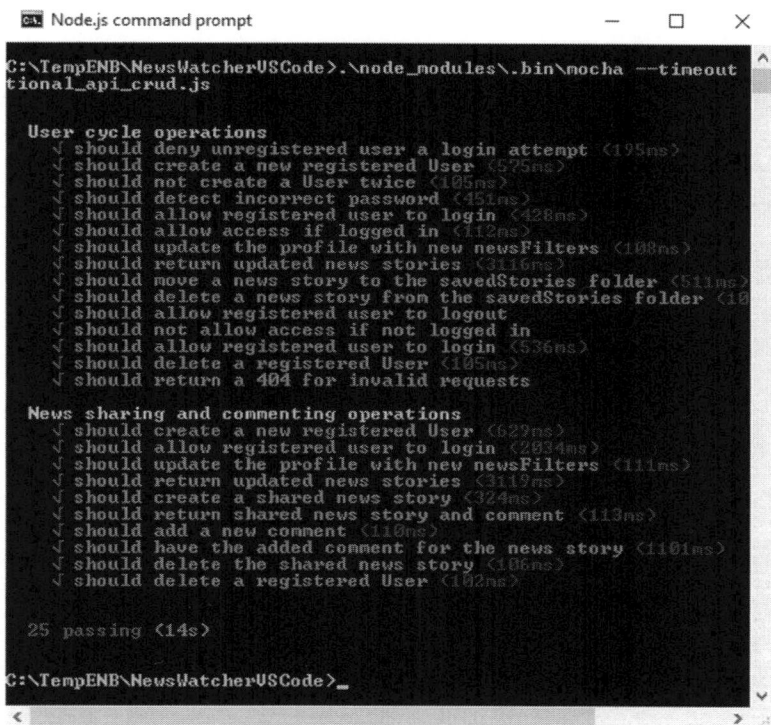

*Figure 84: Mocha functional test output*

**Note**: *You should realize that, even if you are running against your local Node.js service, you are still hitting the real AWS hosted MongoDB database. You might need to go to the mLab management portal and delete unwanted documents that you created through your tests. The tests included with the NewsWatcher sample are written to clean up after themselves.*

To run against the deployed Node.js application in AWS, you can change the supertest usage to go against the production URL, such as https://www.newswatcherfs.com.

# 13.4 Performance and Load Testing

Writing an application that can serve a single user is not a big challenge. The real challenge comes when multiple people are all hitting the web service REST API at the same time.

To write the NewsWatcher sample app and get it to work for a single user was just two weeks of work for me. To get it to scale and handle the simulated load of many users, required months to work out all the issues. You certainly don't want to wait until your big production rollout to find that your code falls flat on its face when more than one person uses it.

How are you going to accomplish testing at scale? The only way to accomplish that is with a test suite that can provide usage in parallel and also simulate multiple users.

There are UI testing tools that can record your usage of a web site and replay it. They can be replayed more than once at the same time to simulate lots of interaction happening. This might work well for some sites that serve static content and have no concept of people logging in and causing some unique workflow to happen in the backend service layer.

The problem is that you need to have real-life exercising of your middle and back end tiers to cause certain bugs to manifest themselves. The UI interaction recording tools cannot mimic multiple logins that do random operations. You could record multiple people logging in, but it still plays the same usage over and over. So how would you mimic hundreds of unique people logging in and doing random things? That is a tough question to answer.

The command line load testing tools and modules I investigated all had the shortcoming of not being able to truly mimic multi-user usage logins for real world scenario workflows.

Short of writing your own tool, I recommend you make use of a most ingenious node module named "async". It was not specifically created as a testing framework, but I find it quite useful at actually fulfilling the requirements of one. It is incredibly flexible and will help you put together a test suite of code to exercise your backend in realistic ways.

The file loadtest_api_crud.js contains your load testing code and has the ability to be configured with parameters to change it. The knowledge from this section alone will be worth your time reading this book.

Here is the top of the load testing file. It has your required modules and makes use of the async module. Supertest is used to make the HTTP calls. You also see you have some variables that you can tweak to alter how the load testing proceeds. You can alter the number of simulated users and also specify how many users are interacting simultaneously.

You first set up an array for each user so they will have the needed information to register and to log them in and out. You can also change the URL to actually go against your production or staged deployment. Here is the code to initialize the simulated users:

```
var async = require('async');
var assert = require('assert');

var request = require('supertest')('http://localhost:3000');

var NUM_USERS = 50;
var MAX_PARALLEL_WORKLOAD = 6;
var NUM_WORK_LOOPS = 10;

var usersP = [];
for (var i = 0; i < NUM_USERS; i++) {
   usersP.push({ idx: i,
                email: 'testrunPPP4980' + i + '@example.com',
                displayName: 'testrunPPP4980' + i, password: 'password',
                token: null,
                userId: null,
                savedDoc: null });
}
```

Follow along carefully as I describe how the structure of the load testing code works as it might seem a little tricky the first time you see it. The main structure is set up to run a series of code segments that are necessary for your load test suit. You use the `async.series` capability for that. The overall abbreviated code consists of seven steps.

1. Register all users.
2. Log in all users.
3. Create a news filter setting for each user to ensure a test news story exists.
4. Save away a document to share and save for each user.
5. Run the test workflows.
6. Delete all of the test shared stories.
7. Delete all the accounts.

Each step, in and of itself, uses some functionality from the async module. The first two steps use `async.eachLimit` which means it loops through the user array to execute something for each entry. You set it up to actually run two at a time in parallel until all are done in the array. Note that the login step saves the login token. The third step runs through the same array to execute a function for each, but only does so one at a time. I omitted that code as it is similar to steps one and two.

At one point I had step four combined with step three. In other words, I put code in the return of the profile update to turn around and do a get of the updates news stories because of the update of the filter. The problem is that the processing of the filter is done through a message sent to the forked process and you cannot tell how long it will take to update. It could be 50 milliseconds or two seconds. I was occasionally hitting a case where it was taking too long, so I moved it out so that this is a separate step that can happen at a time when all the processing has certainly finished.

Step five runs the workload tests for the specified number of times using async.timesSeries. Inside of that looping, there is an async.eachLimit that allows you to run through each user and simulate them running a random action. With this async capability you can specify the parallelism for how many people are doing something at the exact same time. Here is the overall structure of the code with some code left out to make it easier to follow:

```
console.time('LOAD TEST DURATION');
async.series({
  one: function (callback) { // Account creations
    async.eachLimit(usersP, 2, function (user, innercallback) {
      request.post("/api/users")
      .send({
        email: usersP[user.idx].email,
        displayName: usersP[user.idx].displayName,
        password: usersP[user.idx].password
      })
      .end(function (err, res) {
        assert.equal(res.status, 201);
        innercallback();
      });
    }, function (err) {
      callback(err, 1);
    });
  },
  two: function (callback) { // login all users
    async.eachLimit(usersP, MAX_PARALLEL_BEFOREAFTER, function (user,
innercallback) {
      request.post("/api/sessions")
      .send({
        email: usersP[user.idx].email,
        password: usersP[user.idx].password
      })
      .end(function (err, res) {
        usersP[user.idx].token = res.body.token;
        usersP[user.idx].userId = res.body.userId;
        assert.equal(res.status, 201);
        innercallback();
      });
    }, function (err) {
      callback(err, 1);
    });
  },
  three: function (callback) { // Filter settings
    async.eachSeries(usersP, function (user, innercallback) {
```

```
        ...code left out...
      });
    },
    four: function (callback) { // Save away a document for each user
      async.eachSeries(usersP, function (user, innercallback) {
        ...code left out...
      });
    },
    five: function (callback) { // Do the test work flows
      async.timesSeries(NUM_WORK_LOOPS, function (n, next) {
        async.eachLimit(usersP, MAX_PARALLEL_WORKLOAD, function (user,
innercallback) {
          array_of_scenarioFcns[Math.floor(Math.random() *
array_of_scenarioFcns.length)](user, innercallback);
        }, function (err) {
          next(err, 1)
        });
      }, function (err, users) {
        callback(err, 1);
      });
    },
    six: function (callback) { // Delete shared news stories
      ...
    },
    seven: function (callback) { // User account deletions
      console.log("STEP: Delete all test user accounts");
      async.eachLimit(usersP, MAX_PARALLEL_BEFOREAFTER, function (user,
innercallback) {
        request.del("/api/users/" + usersP[user.idx].userId)
        .set('x-auth', usersP[user.idx].token)
        .end(function (err, res) {
          assert.equal(res.status, 200);
          innercallback();
        });
      }, function (err) {
        callback(err, 1);
      });
    }
  },
  function (err, results) {
    console.log("END: load testing");
    console.timeEnd('LOAD TEST DURATION');
});
```

Notice how there are two calls made to be able to time the whole load test. You place the `console.time()` call and then follow that with a `console.timeEnd()` call to get the total elapsed time. That way you can do some benchmarking of the overall performance and then, as you make changes to your code, you can see the change that might occur because of that.

# PART II: The Service Layer (Node.js)

The possible actions for the testing workloads are found in an array. I actually took them straight from the Mocha functional test suite and modified them a bit to work in this load testing suite. Here is part of that array:

```
var array_of_scenarioFcns = [
  function (user, innercallback) {
    console.log("It should not create a User twice")
    request.post("/api/users")
        .send({
      email: usersP[user.idx].email,
      displayName: usersP[user.idx].displayName,
      password: usersP[user.idx].password
    })
        .end(function (err, res) {
      assert.equal(res.status, 500);
      assert.equal(res.body.message, "Error: Email account already
gistered", "Error should be already registered");
      innercallback();
    });
  },
  function (user, innercallback) {
    console.log("It should detect incorrect password")
    request.post("/api/sessions")
        .send({
      email: usersP[user.idx].email,
      password: 'wrong1*'
    })
        .end(function (err, res) {
      assert.equal(res.status, 500);
      assert.equal(res.body.message, "Error: Wrong password", "Error ould
be already registered");
      innercallback();
    });
  },
  function (user, innercallback) {
    console.log("It should log someone out and then back in")
    request.del("/api/sessions/" + usersP[user.idx].userId)
      .set('x-auth', usersP[user.idx].token)
      .end(function (err, res) {
      assert.equal(res.status, 200);
      request.post("/api/sessions")
              .send({
        email: usersP[user.idx].email,
        password: usersP[user.idx].password
      })
              .end(function (err, res) {
        usersP[user.idx].token = res.body.token;
        usersP[user.idx].userId = res.body.userId;
        assert.equal(res.status, 201);
        innercallback();
      });
    });
```

240

```
    },
    function (user, innercallback) {
      console.log("It should create a shared news story")
      request.post("/api/sharednews")
            .send(usersP[user.idx].savedDoc)
            .set('x-auth', usersP[user.idx].token)
            .end(function (err, res) {
        // res.status could be 201 or 500. depending on if the story s
added already or not
            assert.equal((res.status == 201 || res.status == 500), true);
            innercallback();
      });
    },
    function (user, innercallback) {
      console.log("It should get shared news stories and comment on random
one")
      request.get("/api/sharednews")
            .set('x-auth', usersP[user.idx].token)
            .end(function (err, res) {
        assert.equal(res.status, 200);
        if (res.body.length > 0) {
          var storyChoice = Math.floor(Math.random() * res.body.length)
          var storyID = res.body[storyChoice].story.storyID;
          //var storyID = res.body[0].story.storyID;
          request.post("/api/sharednews/" + storyID + "/Comments")
                    .send({ comment: "This is amazing news!" })
                    .set('x-auth', usersP[user.idx].token)
                    .end(function (err, res) {
              // Accept a 201, or a 500 if message is "Comment limit
reached"
              if (res.status == 500) {
                //console.log(res.body);
                assert.equal(res.body.message, "Error: Comment limit
reached", "Limit message was expecetd");
              } else {
                assert.equal(res.status, 201);
              }
              innercallback();
          });
        } else {
          console.log("NO NO NO NO NO stories returned! NONONONONO NONONO
NO NO")
          innercallback();
        }
      });
    },
  ...and many other tests...
]
```

# PART II: The Service Layer (Node.js)

The output of the load testing is quite informative. When run, you might see output such as:

```
GET /api/users/e641e9b5-9ed9-3475-10ca-2337fbe8b3bf 200 256.078 ms - 6213

POST /api/users/e641e9b5-9ed9-3475-10ca-2337fbe8b3bf/savedstories 200
324.725 ms - 7381

DELETE /api/users/e641e9b5-9ed9-3475-10ca-
2337fbe8b3bf/savedstories/$2a$10$jPBpM
qS5uFc1_Vkc9XsVOOfFnpEhv_OvHFf9oeDNi4bE7aFnsW5l. 200 281.427 ms - 6577
```

What this is showing you are the response times and anything else you want to log. A careful examination of all of this would be valuable.

This load testing enables you to prove the scaling of your application. You also use this to measure your SLA values under a constant load. You can experiment by increasing the testing numbers until you find the breaking point. This will tell you the absolute peak values you can run under. To do this, you need to alter the URL to be that of the production or cloud staging environment.

Running the load testing suit can also help you test out your Elastic Beanstalk scaling strategies and topology. It will of course also be useful in verifying any sharding you have set up with MongoDB.

The complete load testing code is available in the GitHub project. There was just too much of it to include here.

# Chapter 14: DevOps Service Layer Tips

It is a fabulous accomplishment to get the code all tested and deployed to production. Don't get too comfortable though, as it is quite another matter to manage the operations of a full-stack application. This chapter will present some key skills that will make your life easier when it comes to running the 24x7 operations for your service layer.

Chances are that you will experience some type of catastrophic failure before too long. First off, you absolutely want to do everything up front to put preventative measures in place. As the old saying goes "An ounce of prevention is worth a pound of cure."

You also need to put a plan into place for handling a crisis when it comes. You want to be in a position to have all of the information at your fingertips to make it possible to recover in the shortest amount of time. There are some general techniques that will be presented here, but you will have to come up with your own specific strategies that fit your own environment.

Let me make a brief comment about continuous integration and continuous delivery (CI/CD). If you are working on any kind of substantial project that will be going on for a while, or has multiple people contributing, you definitely need to implement CI/CD. Manually performing the tasks of building, testing, and deploying code gets old fast. Always remember that doing these things manually is prone to human error. If your DevOps process is not automated with full integration testing, then it is not really complete.

There is a wise saying that states "You have to slow down to speed up." You can interpret that to mean that a little investment up front pays huge dividends over and over. This ability to centrally coordinate CI/CD really helps groups with an agile process iterate more rapidly. Productivity goes up because of this automation and team downtime is reduced because integration bugs are not spread across the rest of the team. It is much more expensive in time and money to catch bugs in production, so there is a huge savings to be had here.

# 14.1 Console Logging

Writing messages to a console output or log file is an age-old practice that might be useful if you can avoid being overwhelmed by too much logging and then be able to interpret the information to solve problems.

Node has the Console module that is used to write to the trace output. The module is available in your application already, so you don't need to use a `require` statement. Here are some useful methods you can use that are found on the console object:

| | |
|---|---|
| `log()`<br>`info()`<br>`error()`<br>`warn()` | Basic method for outputting text. It comes in several different forms all with the same function signature.<br><br>`console.log("we made it here %d", someVarNumber);` |
| `dir()` | It is useful to view an object you might have in your code. There are options available for this, for example to recurse further than the default depth of 2 levels.<br><br>`console.dir(someObject);` |
| `time()` and `timeEnd()` | To log elapsed time, you use these two methods. You will get the elapsed time when you do the following:<br><br>`console.time("start");`<br>`// some code operations that you want to time…`<br>`console.timeEnd("start");` |
| `trace()` | For showing a stack trace from the point in your code where this is called.<br><br>`console.trace("someLabel");` |
| `assert()` | This is the standard assertion usage commonly available.<br><br>`console.assert(valid, "Hi");` |

Logging can definitely be handy. You can set up logging to go into a file that can be looked at. Sometimes logging will point you in the general direction and then you can use the debugger to further diagnose an issue. You could also simply send every log message to a special collection in MongoDB. You can even set up MongoDB documents to have a time to live (TTL) before they are automatically deleted for you.

# 14.2 CPU Profiling

The V8 engine can provide you with CPU usage reports. The simplest way to do this is to launch your node process with the profile flag set, after running your test code, you stop the process and you will have a file available to view. You would launch Node as follows on your local machine:

```
Node -prof server.js
```

If you then run some test code, such as your load testing suite, you can get some idea of where your code might be spending most of its time. Once you have run your test code for a bit, you stop the node process and a file named something like "isolate-000001D213C4D490-v8.log" will be saved.

Next, open your browser and navigate to the Chrome V8 profiling log processor site at http://v8.googlecode.com/svn/trunk/tools/tick-processor.html. You can open your log file with this tool and see a nice, crisp layout of your code calls listed in order of where most of the time was spent. There is a command line version of the tick processor also available for download.

You will see reports that look as follows:

```
Statistical profiling result from null, (4298 ticks, 3285 unaccounted, 0 excluded).

[Shared libraries]:
   ticks  total  nonlib   name

[JavaScript]:
   ticks  total  nonlib   name
    938  21.8%   21.8%  LazyCompile: *_encipher C:\TempENB\NWDocDBQ\NewsWatcher\node_modules\bcryptjs\dist\bcrypt.js:90
     43   1.0%    1.0%  LazyCompile: ~now native date.js:201:17
     39   0.9%    0.9%  LazyCompile: ~createWriteReq net.js:697:24
     37   0.9%    0.9%  LazyCompile: *_key C:\TempENB\NWDocDBQ\NewsWatcher\node_modules\bcryptjs\dist\bcrypt.js:950:18
     11   0.3%    0.3%  LazyCompile: ~next C:\TempENB\NWDocDBQ\NewsWatcher\node_modules\bcryptjs\dist\bcrypt.js:1055:22
      9   0.2%    0.2%  LazyCompile: ~Socket._writeGeneric net.js:622:42
      8   0.2%    0.2%  LazyCompile: ~runInThisContext node.js:901:28
      8   0.2%    0.2%  LazyCompile: *exports.runInThisContext vm.js:52:36
      8   0.2%    0.2%  LazyCompile: *exports.runInThisContext vm.js:52:36
      6   0.1%    0.1%  LazyCompile: ~parse native json.js:43:19
      3   0.1%    0.1%  LazyCompile: ~socketOnData _http_client.js:308:22
      3   0.1%    0.1%  LazyCompile: ~Mime.define C:\TempENB\NWDocDBQ\NewsWatcher\node_modules\mime\mime.js:21:34
      3   0.1%    0.1%  LazyCompile: ~EventEmitter.init events.js:36:29
```

*Figure 85: V8 Report sample*

```
[Summary]:
   ticks  total  nonlib   name
   1262  29.4%   29.4%  JavaScript
      0   0.0%    0.0%  C++
      6   0.1%    0.1%  GC
      0   0.0%           Shared libraries
   3285  76.4%           Unaccounted

[C++ entry points]:
   ticks   cpp   total   name

[Bottom up (heavy) profile]:
 Note: percentage shows a share of a particular caller in the total
 amount of its parent calls.
 Callers occupying less than 2.0% are not shown.

   ticks parent  name
    938  21.8%  LazyCompile: *_encipher C:\TempENB\NWDocDBQ\NewsWatcher\node_modules\bcryptjs\dist\bcrypt.js:907:23
    613  65.4%    LazyCompile: *_key C:\TempENB\NWDocDBQ\NewsWatcher\node_modules\bcryptjs\dist\bcrypt.js:950:18
    613 100.0%      LazyCompile: ~next C:\TempENB\NWDocDBQ\NewsWatcher\node_modules\bcryptjs\dist\bcrypt.js:1055:22
    442  72.1%        LazyCompile: processImmediate timers.js:367:26
    171  27.9%        LazyCompile: ~_crypt C:\TempENB\NWDocDBQ\NewsWatcher\node_modules\bcryptjs\dist\bcrypt.js:1022:20
    171 100.0%          LazyCompile: ~_hash C:\TempENB\NWDocDBQ\NewsWatcher\node_modules\bcryptjs\dist\bcrypt.js:1110:1
    101  59.1%            LazyCompile: ~bcrypt.hash C:\TempENB\NWDocDBQ\NewsWatcher\node_modules\bcryptjs\dist\bcrypt.j
     70  40.9%            LazyCompile: ~<anonymous> C:\TempENB\NWDocDBQ\NewsWatcher\node_modules\bcryptjs\dist\bcrypt.j
    324  34.5%    LazyCompile: *next C:\TempENB\NWDocDBQ\NewsWatcher\node_modules\bcryptjs\dist\bcrypt.js:1055:22
    243  75.0%      LazyCompile: processImmediate timers.js:367:26
     81  25.0%      LazyCompile: ~_crypt C:\TempENB\NWDocDBQ\NewsWatcher\node_modules\bcryptjs\dist\bcrypt.js:1022:20
     81 100.0%        LazyCompile: ~_hash C:\TempENB\NWDocDBQ\NewsWatcher\node_modules\bcryptjs\dist\bcrypt.js:1110:19
     62  76.5%          LazyCompile: ~bcrypt.hash C:\TempENB\NWDocDBQ\NewsWatcher\node_modules\bcryptjs\dist\bcrypt.js:
     62 100.0%            LazyCompile: ~bcrypt.compare C:\TempENB\NWDocDBQ\NewsWatcher\node_modules\bcryptjs\dist\bcryp
     19  23.5%          LazyCompile: ~<anonymous> C:\TempENB\NWDocDBQ\NewsWatcher\node_modules\bcryptjs\dist\bcryp
     19 100.0%            LazyCompile: <anonymous> C:\TempENB\NWDocDBQ\NewsWatcher\node_modules\bcryptjs\dist\bcrypt.js
```

*Figure 86: V8 Report sample*

You can also utilize the V8-profiler using a Node module to start it up in your code if you set up route handlers and want to profile things in production. The V8 engine, which is one of the components that Node.js is built on, lets you run analysis of production running code. Profiling data can be sent to an external file that you can later open and view the results with. Here is the code to accomplish a profile run:

```
var fs = require('fs');
var profiler = require('v8-profiler');
profiler.startProfiling();

...do some processing...

var profileResult = profiler.stopProfiling();

profileResult.export()
  .pipe(fs.createWriteStream('profile.json'))
  .on('finish', function() {
    profileResult.delete();
  });
```

Here is a screen shot of the Chrome Dev Tool (press F12 while running Chrome) that is capable of reading the profile file.

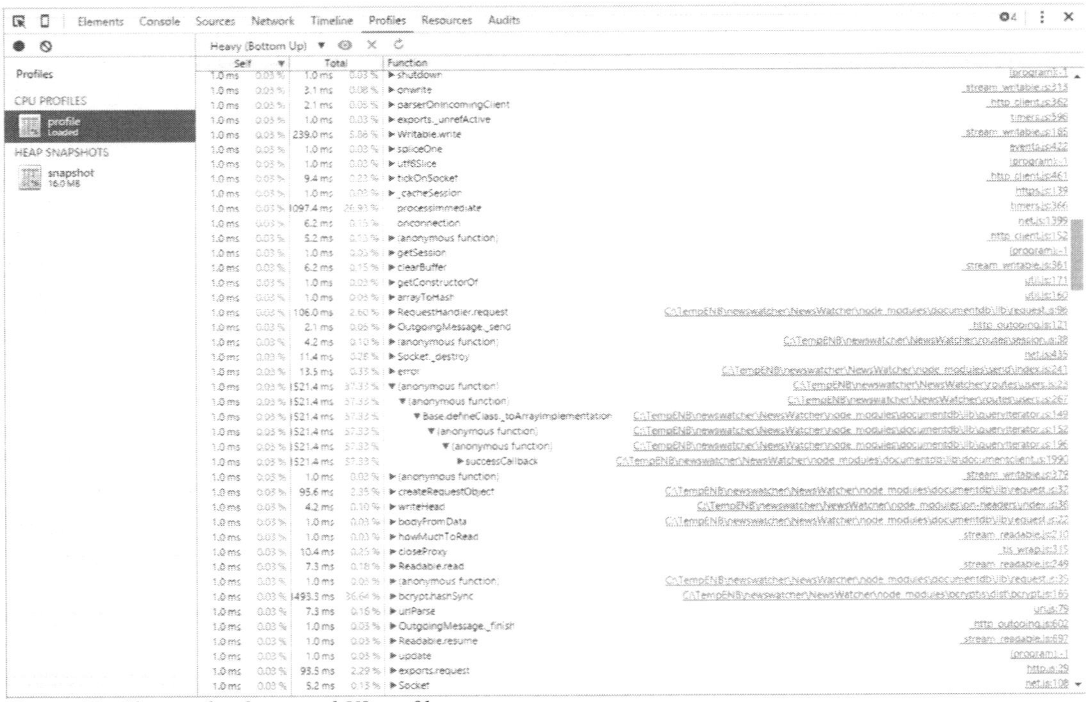

*Figure 87: Chrome developer tool V8 profile report*

To read in your file, Click the **Profiles** tab, then click the **Profiles** pane and click **Load** to load your file(s).

With profiling turned on while a load test was run, I was able to produce a report that showed a few issues I could address. One of them turned out to be the use of `bcrypt` for password hashing. As seen in the profile analysis, you see a bottom-up view of the calling tree. If you expand until you see your functions, you can then understand where the call is being made from. Here, you see that the `bcrypt.hashSync()` function call took 19% of the time.

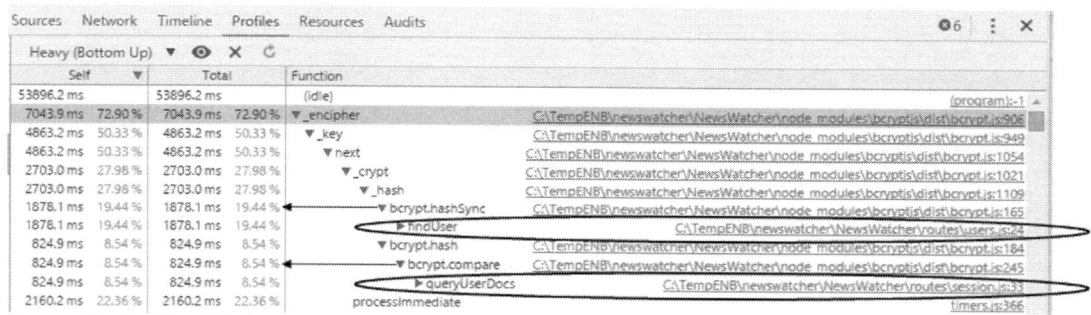

*Figure 88: Profile drill-down*

Here is the code for what you see listed for the first issue:

```
findUserByEmail(req.db, req.body.email, function findUser(err, doc) {
    ...
        passwordHash: bcrypt.hashSync(req.body.password, 10),
```

It was obvious, given the name of the function, that I was not using the async version of the hash-generation function. Go figure, I should have known that `hashSync()` was not a good idea to call. As you know, you want to minimize CPU usage on the main Node thread. Checking the documentation, I found the async version and made the change to use it:

```
bcrypt.hash('bacon', 8, function(err, hash) {
});
```

***Note**: It is helpful to give names to all anonymous functions, otherwise you will just see a lot of "anonymous" functions and it is harder to pinpoint what functions are in the profile listing.*

# 14.3 Memory Leak Detection

In a managed language framework, you don't directly allocate memory and subsequently free it up. You can do a `new` and `delete` of an object, but you still don't have control over that memory, such as the actual reclaiming of it, or doing things like having memory pointers into it. Instead, there is a garbage collector that keeps track of memory references and the GC decides when to run and when memory can be recycled.

The truth is, that with garbage collection running, you can still run into memory leaks that will eventually cause your application to either run slowly, to completely freeze, or crash.

You can obviously create a memory growth problem if you had something as simple as an array that you continually pushed data into and never free up. If you held on to an object reference permanently after you no longer needed it, the garbage collector will not ever reclaim it. A thorough code review of callbacks, closures, constructor functions, and arrays can be a starting point to finding memory leaks.

Ultimately, your brain might not be able to trace through all of the intricacies of your code and you will need to take memory snapshots that can be compared across time. Node.js applications are always built with several, if not dozens, of downloaded modules. You have to be suspicious of those, as well, as they might contain memory leaks.

You can watch the OS reporting of memory for your Node.js process over time and see what kind of graph you have and, if you see an ever-increasing amount of memory being taken up, you can then dive in and investigate. It is even not unheard of for people to resort to restarting their Node.js processes every day just to circumvent any memory leak problems. You might, in reality, not have a leak if, over time, you can see the garbage collector kick in and do its job. Compare memory snapshots over a 24-hour time span.

You can use the v8-profiler module that was previously used for CPU profiling to take memory snapshots. You can likewise having the output files viewed in the Chrome debugger.

```
var fs = require('fs');
var profiler = require('v8-profiler');
var snapshot = profiler.takeSnapshot();

snapshot.export()
  .pipe(fs.createWriteStream('snapshot.json'))
  .on('finish', snapshot.delete);
```

*Note: Remember to never run your CPU profiling at the same time as you take heap snapshots. The overhead memory usage for the CPU profiler will inundate you.*

I have set up a specific route through Express that can trigger a memory snapshot. That way I can insert this ability into my tests and have it available for me as part of a load testing run. Here is a screen shot of a memory snapshot file that is loaded into the Chrome browser debugger.

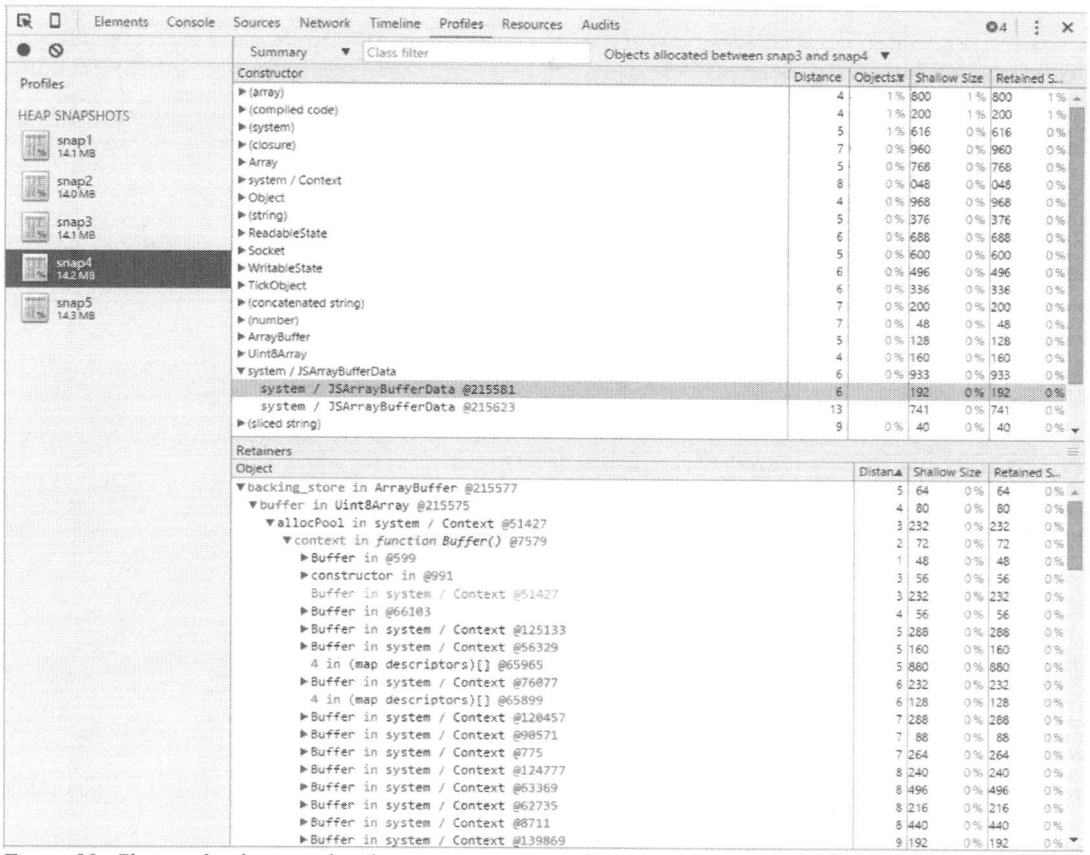

*Figure 89: Chrome developer tool with memory snapshot*

The Distance column shows you how many steps removed from the root object the memory reference is. You can usually assume that the object with the shortest distance is the one causing a memory leak. The Shallow Size is just what this one usage is taking. Retained Size gives you all of the space that would be freed up that this object is referencing and thus holding on to. This only true if those objects are also no longer referenced by anything else.

There are different views you can try out, such as Containment, which helps you also view low-level memory internals.

# 14.4 Monitoring and Alerting

The AWS Elastic Beanstalk management portal has a Monitoring page with which you can view key machine performance metrics. You definitely want to open the portal and look at what is available to be monitored. Not only can you look at trending charts, but you can also set up alerts that send you emails, or even get text messages in the case of thresholds being crossed. Here is the Monitoring page:

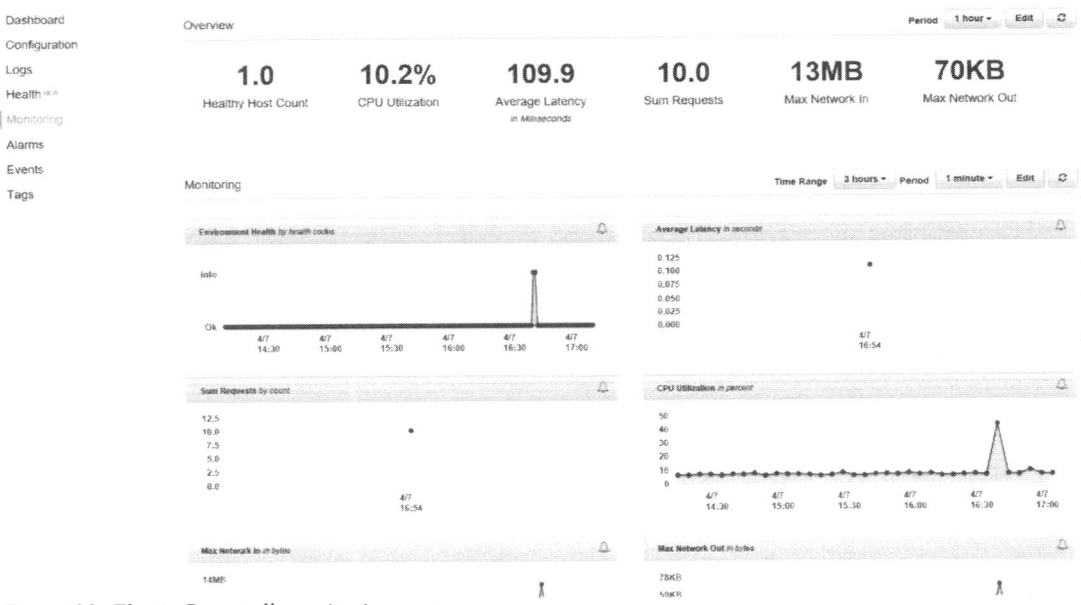

*Figure 90: Elastic Beanstalk monitoring page*

You can click **Edit** and select what you want to be graphed out. You can also click the alarm bell icon and create an alarm that would notify you if you crossed some threshold.

Alternatively, you can open up the CloudWatch management console in AWS and explore similar capabilities for metric viewing, logs, events and alarms.

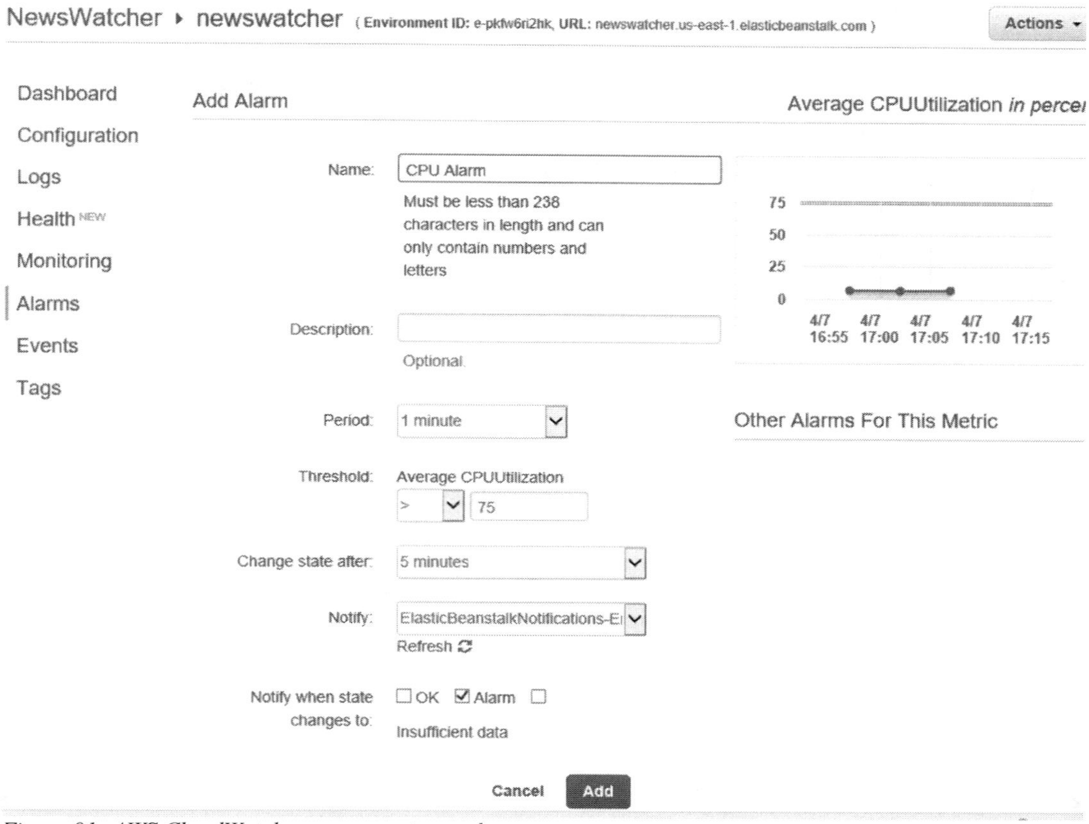

*Figure 91: AWS CloudWatch management console*

One thing to know is that the Node.js process can crash and if that happens, it needs to be restarted. In an IaaS environment, you would be responsible to have some mechanism to detect this and restart your Node.js process.

There are NPM downloads such as "forever" and PM2 that do this. With AWS Elastic Beanstalk, it uses Nginx and the restarting is handled automatically for you. This is another example of how PaaS really done right can make your life easier.

If your application is not available, reliable, and performant, then your customers and your business will suffer. The goal of monitoring and alerting is to maintain application availability, reliability, and performance. You do this by implementing Application Performance Monitoring (APM). This allows you to discover problems before anyone else does and then to achieve resolutions in the least amount of time.

251

# PART II: The Service Layer (Node.js)

To begin implementing an APM strategy, you need to instrument your code and surface events, logs, and metrics. Then you use an APM tool to chart out performance metrics and set up alarms.

You need metrics so that you are not flying blind. A pilot can fly a plane in the dark because of his instrumentation and telemetry. The last thing you want to have to do is remote into individual servers and start poking around to search for a "needle in a haystack". Instrumentation and monitoring is the only way you will be able to scale and survive.

# PART III: The Presentation Layer (AngularJS/HTML)

Part three of this book will teach you about the presentation layer. In doing so, you will be extending the sample application in order to bring it to a state where the UI is fully functional. You will need at least a basic understanding of HTML. I will present the technology of AngularJS as a framework that fits nicely into the overall architecture as a way to bind data to and from the service layer web service.

There are many decisions that go into creating a presentation layer. The very first step involves planning for what type of interactions your users would want to take. An initial sketch of the UI of your application would most likely happen long before you even conceived of what code is required for the service layer. It is wise to pursue a simultaneous bottom-up and top-down approach.

You will use the already built and tested service layer for the UI to connect to. This is very convenient, as your Node.js code can also perform the dual role of servicing not only the HTTP/Rest API, but also of serving up your HTML and associated files to a browser.

*Note: It is not the intention of this book to be a comprehensive guide to UX design or SPA web design. I will only touch on some concepts and then stick to a narrow technology presentation. Even the information on Angular will not be as complete as what I have presented for MongoDB and Node.js. The main purpose of this book is to present the data and service layers, as they are the topics that are not as well understood and affect your ability to develop something that is truly a scalable, enterprise-worthy architecture. In this part of the book, I will only be covering the bare essentials of what will be used in getting the NewsWatcher sample application features fulfilled.*

# Chapter 15: Fundamentals

I will now go over the fundamental concepts of the top tier in a three-tier architecture. You will see what capabilities are essential and find a list of questions to consider when doing your design. You can then get into the specifics of AngularJS for how they will be used with the NewsWatcher sample application. Angular was chosen as a technology to fulfill the needs of this top layer of the application architecture, and being that it uses JavaScript, it fits in perfectly with the overall development stack.

*Note: Most people refer to AngularJS simply as Angular, and I will do the same.*

# 15.1 Definition of the Presentation Layer

Any application that requires user interaction will need a presentation layer. It would not be feasible to ask a user to open a command prompt and use curl.exe to submit REST requests to the service layer. Neither would you have users connect directly to the backend database. User interfaces accomplish the backend interactions for users.

Humans need a presentation layer to view data and to allow them to input data. For example, an online bookstore would want to present the list of books to a user to browse through. Each book selection presented might contain a photo of the book and the data associated with it, such as the title, author, description, publication date, cost, and reviews. Input gathered from the user would be things like book orders and customer service questions.

## MV* and SPA designs

You need to employ the techniques of abstraction and componentization in all of the layers. This is accomplished with the coding of the presentation layer.

One of the benefits of choosing a framework for your presentation layer is that most frameworks are set up to employ some type of MV* pattern that lends itself to an organized set of components that make up your code.

Make yourselves acquainted with MV* design patterns and also with what a Single Page Application (SPA) design entails. There are several excellent books available and plenty of online material to study. There are many things about SPA designs that make them a great choice today.

## Presentation layer planning

Knowing what operations and workflows are needed is the first step in fleshing out a presentation layer. The following questions are useful to help you determine the design of a presentation layer:

- Have you done any of the following: sketching, prototyping, storyboards, surveys, contextual inquiry, stakeholder interviews, A/B testing, wireframes, sitemaps, personas, scenarios. What about human interaction, usability, and accessibility studies?
- What are your data security and privacy requirements?
- How do people sign in and become authorized?
- Are there multiple steps that are progressively revealed, one after another?
- Is there a need for a customizable UI?
- What are your globalization and localization requirements?
- What devices are you targeting, such as desktop and mobile platforms?
- How can you keep data presentation to a minimum to not overwhelm the user?
- What form is data best presented in?
- What is the business need that can be accomplished?
- What accessibility requirements are there?
- What are the navigation levels of the UI? Can you map out how the navigation works?
- Do you need a user feedback mechanism?
- Do you have offline requirements?
- How will the UI be deployed and updated?
- How will users enter data and what tests are needed to validate it?
- Can you map out the multi-step data entry forms and show the branching conditions?

The answers to these questions should be carefully considered. Before you roll anything out into your production environment, have experts reviewing everything.

# 15.2 Introducing Angular

Angular is a framework that greatly enhances the capabilities of what HTML can accomplish. To do this, Angular provides new attributes and syntax that you put inside your HTML markup. You also write JavaScript to go along with your HTML. This JavaScript code leverages the Angular library to do things like access the middle-tier through HTTP/Rest requests that then bind the returned data to your HTML elements. The overall capabilities of Angular provide the mechanisms to enable you to build a SPA.

There have been other similar frameworks that appeared at the same time as Angular such as Knockout,js, Ember.js, React, NativeScript, and Backbone.js. Angular is my choice in this book as it has many things going for it, such as being widely adopted, and also because it is officially sponsored by Google as an open-source project. You can be up and running on the desktop, mobile web, and native mobile applications in a short amount of time.

Angular frees you up from some of the laborious code you used to have to write to do Domain Object Model (DOM) manipulation. Because of its ability to bind and affect DOM elements, you no longer need to utilize libraries such as jQuery.

HTML was always great at serving up static data. Angular now extends this to make HTML dynamic so that data values flow back and forth for you. To use AngularJS, you alter your HTML with special attributes and expressions and then provide the JavaScript code that goes along with it. Be aware however, that Angular does not provide new control elements or styling for you as that is left to other libraries such as Bootstrap.

Angular is run completely on the client-side through an SDK library that is delivered as JavaScript files that run in a browser context. The SDK is written and consumed by placing a script instruction in your HTML file to consume the script file that provides the library.

*Note: You might recall that the Node.js Express module has the concept of serving up templates of "HTML-like" files and binding data to them on the server side, so that they arrive on the client side all filled out. Express supports many template formats such as Jade, EJS, mustache, and handlebars. I don't recommend this server-side data binding technique in this book for the NewsWatcher application. Instead, I give preference to simply serving the HTML that works as a SPA application, with the client side using Angular to request data through a Rest API with JSON and then doing the binding on the client side. This alleviates the back-and-forth HTML page requests. All of the navigation and page rendering is done on the client side, not on the server side. This is similar to what you would need to do if you were to develop a native mobile application. You can also stick with HTML instead of having to learn a new template markup syntax such as Jade.*

# 15.3 The Basics of Directives and Expressions

One basic concept of Angular is that you alter your HTML markup using attributes and expressions defined by Angular. Angular uses the term "directive" for the attributes that you can use in your HTML. An expression syntax is also used where you place double curly brackets to indicate to Angular to look inside those and render values appropriately.

Here is a simple example that shows some of the attribute directives and the curly brace expression syntax. I have bolded the important additions that Angular implements. Angular documentation refers to this HTML, which has now been modified with directives and expressions, as a "template".

```
<div ng-init="name='Jack'">
  <div>
    Name: <input type="text" ng-model="name">
  </div>
  <div>
    <b>Welcome:</b> {{name}}
  </div>
</div>
```

An `ng-app`, shown later, is the directive that actually kicks off the whole process of Angular being involved in the rendering of your page. When your page is loaded, Angular is loaded and parses the content and renders the view for you. It will see the `ng-model` that sets up a variable named `name` that it will bind the text input to.

There is an `ng-init` attribute at the top that sets a default value for the `name` variable. The expression syntax with the curly braces tells Angular to render whatever the value is for the `name` variable. As you type characters into the text control, the expression rendering keeps up and changes the value you see.

With these three directives you can see the power of Angular. Besides these directives, there are many others to become acquainted with. I will cover some of them, but you should refer to Angular's documentation for complete information on these and others.

# 15.4 HTML Backed with JavaScript Modules and Controllers

You never just provide an HTML file when you use Angular — you also need to provide some JavaScript along with it. Your SPA application will need to make calls to backend services to retrieve data that can be presented on your pages. Angular has organized the creation of this JavaScript for you. You simply follow their pattern for creating it.

The two main JavaScript objects you create with the Angular SDK are the module and the controller. The module is your main object; you typically have only one of those, and it can be thought of as existing application wide.

From the module object, you create one or more controller objects. Typically, one for each HTML template that you have. The following is an illustration of this:

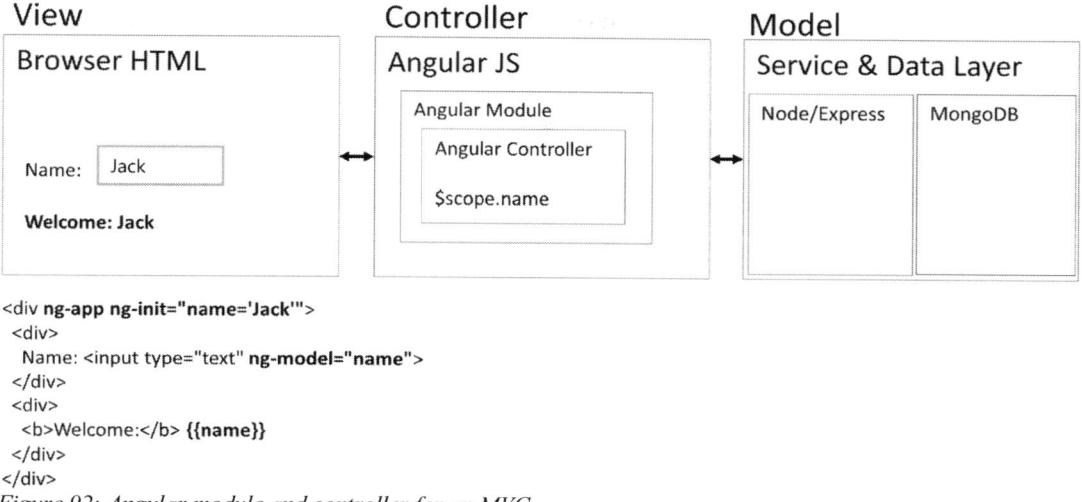

```
<div ng-app ng-init="name='Jack'">
 <div>
  Name: <input type="text" ng-model="name">
 </div>
 <div>
  <b>Welcome:</b> {{name}}
 </div>
</div>
```

*Figure 92: Angular module and controller for an MVC*

Controllers have the ability to set values on properties and also provide functions that are then used in binding values into the HTML elements. The code logic can be written in JavaScript, Dart, or TypeScript. I will stick with JavaScript. Here is a complete example that illustrates the concepts:

```
// index.html
<!DOCTYPE html>
<html ng-app='app'>
<head>
  <meta charset="UTF-8">
  <title>Example</title>
</head>
<body ng-controller='myCtrl'>
  <div ng-init="name='Jack'">
    <div>
      Name: <input type="text" ng-model="name">
    </div>
    <div>
      <b>Welcome:</b> {{name}}
    </div>
    <div>
      Food selection:
      <select ng-model="favorite">
        <option ng-repeat="food in foods">{{food}}</option>
      </select>
    </div>
    <div>
```

259

```
        <button class="btn" ng-click="shoutIt()">Shout it!</button>
      </div>
    </div>
    <script
src='https://ajax.googleapis.com/ajax/libs/angularjs/1.4.7/angular.min.js'>
</script>
    <script src='ngapp.js'></script>
</body>
</html>
```

I demonstrated the ng-controller, ng-repeat and ng-click directives in this example.

The ng-controller addition tells Angular which controller to use for hooking up your JavaScript.

The ng-repeat is a handy way to iterate over an array from your JavaScript controller.

The ng-click is for hooking up functions that get called in response to the user interaction. You tell it which function to call.

The JavaScript that goes along with this example will set up the module that is your overall application object and the one controller for the one page you have here. Here is the code to set up the module and the controller:

```
// ngapp.js
'use strict';
angular.module('app', [])
  .controller('myCtrl', ['$scope', function ($scope) {
    $scope.foods = ["Pizza", "Oatmeal", "Broccoli"];
    $scope.shoutIt = function () {
      window.alert($scope.name + " loves " + $scope.favorite + "!");
    };
  }]);
```

The function signature for module() takes an optional array of dependency modules that you want to have exposed. You are not requiring any here, but will see some used later in the NewsWatcher code.

The controller function is being called on the module object. It takes two parameters. The first is the name you give the controller. The second parameter is an array that first lists all of the dependent services and then, as the last entry in the array, you enter your function that acts as the constructor that is called to set it up. This function is where all of your controlling code resides. This makes use of what is called the $scope service.

260

# 15.5 $scope

You use the `$scope` service to hang your properties and functions off of. Properties and functions that exist on `$scope` can then be used in the binding expressions in your HTML. This means that in your function code, you set properties and functions on $scope. Angular directives can use the properties and functions. As you see, you set up `$scope.foods` in your controller and then can use `foods` in the HTML.

You might use more than one controller in a page, as they can act in a hierarchy as you have them spread throughout your DOM. There can end up being a hierarchy of them where one would take precedence over the other in the hierarchy.

There is also a `$rootScope` service that is always there for you to use, if you need it. This represents the top of the scope hierarchy. It is then accessible across all controllers and can be used to share properties and functions across all of the controllers.

# 15.6 Services

You saw the use of the `$scope` service, but that is just scratching the surface. There are many more services that Angular provides for your consumption to make the code in the controllers very powerful. For example, `$window` gives you access to the browser window object. `$q` gives you an implementation of asynchronous promises in JavaScript. `$location` gives you control over the URL in the browser address bar to force navigation to happen.

`$http` is a service you can use to make remote HTTP calls such as to utilize the browser's `XMLHttpRequest` object or via JSONP. `$filter` is used to create data filters you can insert into an Angular expression.

One amazing thing that you can accomplish with this design is the mocking out of a service such as `$http` to return your own staged data for testing purposes.

You can even create your own services. The reason you would want to do this is to expose functionality as modular pieces and also to be able to mock up your own services. Let's say you were going to provide some service that accessed your Node.js middle tier. Instead of putting this code directly into your page controller, you can encapsulate it all into a service to be injected.

To create a service, you first create a module to hold the service, and then use the `factory()` function. The following example shows the previous controller, but this time makes use of the service that you could create that would exist in a separate file.

```
// ngapp.js
'use strict';
angular.module(app, ['helperModule'])
.controller('myCtrl', [$scope, 'myService', function ($scope, 'myService')
{
     $scope.foods = myService.GetFoods();

     $scope.shoutIt = function () {
        window.alert("$scope.name loves " + $scope.favorite + "!");
     };
  }]);

// myService.js
angular.module('helperModule', [])
  .factory('myService', ['$http', function ($http) {
     var getFoods = function () {
        $http({
           method: 'GET',
           url: '/api/foods',
           responseType: 'json'
        }).then(function successCallback(response) {
           return response.data;
           $scope.$emit('msg', "News fetched");
        });
     };

     return {
        getFoods: getFoods
     };
  }]);
```

# 15.7 Client-Side Routing and ng-view

One important mechanism of Angular is that of accomplishing navigation between views. To set up an Angular SPA web page, you can provide the master index.html file that provides the framework that all other views render into. The HTML needs to contain some type of menu or tab selections and then a div is filled in for each navigation that happens. There would probably be some default page put in the view upon an initial load of the page.

To do this navigation, Angular has a separate JavaScript file you need to include. You include this JavaScript library as follows:

```
<script src='https://ajax.googleapis.com/ajax/libs/angularjs/1.4.7/angular-
route.js'></script>
```

In the body of your index.html file you place the navigation links and also the one special div with the `ng-view` directive on it. It would look as follows:

```
<script src="script.js"></script>
<body ng-app="myApp">
  <div ng-controller="myController">
    Choose:
    <a href="Books/CPlusPlus">C++</a> |
    <a href="Book/JavaScript ">JavaScript</a><br/>

    <div ng-view></div>
  </div>
</body>
```

The script.js file then contains the code required to initialize the module and set up the navigation in the `config()` function. You would have something like the following:

```
angular.module('myApp', ['ngRoute'])
.config(function ($routeProvider) {
    $routeProvider
    .when('/Book/:bookId', { controller: 'BookController', templateUrl:
'book.html' })
});
```

# 15.8 Content Visibility and Enabling

One nice capability of Angular is the ability to manipulate the DOM. In many cases, you just need to provide the directives and the variable binding takes care of the rest for you.

Examples of things you can do are plentiful. You can do things such as show or hide elements on a page. Look at the following two list items. They both show and hide themselves depending on the boolean value of the variable `loggedIn`:

```
<li ng-show="loggedIn"><a id="logoutLink" href="javascript:void(0)" ng-
click="logout()">Logout</a></li>

<li ng-hide="loggedIn"><a href="javascript:void(0)" ng-
click="changeView('/')">Login</a></li>
```

Similar element manipulation can be done with `ng-if`, `ng-class`, and `ng-disabled`.

# Chapter 16: NewsWatcher App Development

Now I can go over the construction of the NewsWatcher web site. As I explained, there are no tools to install in order to use Angular 1.x. You can just use the editing capabilities of VS Code to bring it all together.

*Note: Don't forget that you can access all of the code for the sample NewsWatcher project at https://github.com/eljamaki01/NewsWatcherAWS.*

Your existing Node.js project is already capable of serving up your UI. You may have noticed that you had a placeholder index.html file that your Node.js service was serving up. This is your starting point and it will actually not require any new server side Node application code.

In the previous two parts of this book, you had to step through the development process in great detail as some steps required going to the AWS management portal, while other steps required installing Node.js modules. Here, you don't have to do any of that. You will simply learn about the files necessary as they exist in the project and how each one is pieced together. Once your files are in place, you simply deploy them and run. Once everything is in place, the project folders will look as follows:

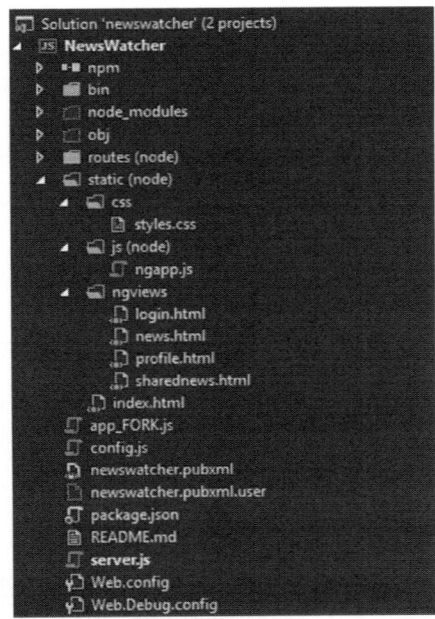

*Figure 93: VS Code file tree*

# 16.1 The Brains Behind It All (static/js/ngapp.js)

The overall structure of the Angular application is actually very simple. So simple in fact, that I placed all of the code into one single file and chained the controller functions together.

The abbreviated code below shows the overall structure:

```
angular.module('app', ['ngRoute'])
.config(function ($routeProvider) {
    $routeProvider
  .when('/', { controller: 'LoginCtrl', templateUrl: './ngviews/login.html'
})
  .when('/news', { controller: 'NewsCtrl', templateUrl:
'./ngviews/news.html' })
  .when('/news/:saved', { controller: 'NewsCtrl', templateUrl:
'./ngviews/news.html' })
  .when('/sharednews', { controller: 'SharedNewsCtrl', templateUrl:
'./ngviews/sharednews.html' })
  .when('/profile', { controller: 'ProfileCtrl', templateUrl:
'./ngviews/profile.html' })
})
.controller('ApplicationCtrl', ['$rootScope', '$scope', '$http',
'$location', '$window', function ($rootScope, $scope, $http, $location,
$window) {
    ...code left out...
}])
.controller('LoginCtrl', ['$rootScope', '$scope', '$http', '$location',
'$window', function ($rootScope, $scope, $http, $location, $window) {
    ...code left out...
}])
.controller('ProfileCtrl', ['$rootScope', '$scope', '$http', '$location',
'$window', function ($rootScope, $scope, $http, $location, $window) {
    ...code left out...
}])
.controller('NewsCtrl', ['$rootScope', '$scope', '$http', '$routeParams',
function ($rootScope, $scope, $http, $routeParams) {
    ...code left out...
}])
.controller('SharedNewsCtrl', ['$scope', '$http', function ($scope, $http)
{
    ...code left out...
}]);
```

The first line is using the angular library to set up the overall application. You have simply provided the identifying name of "app". After that, you call the config() function that allows you to set up your navigation routes for your site. This is using the $routeProvider service. This will set up each path with a controller and the required HTML to render each view.

The last portion of the ngapp.js file is the list of each of the controller functions that correspond to the HTML files that are part of your UI navigation. Each controller will be filled in with its detail when I show each individual HTML file. Here are each of them.

# 16.2 Where it All Starts (static/index.html)

Back when I covered the Node.js web service development, you put two lines of code into your server.js file that served up a get request to your main HTML page. This allowed you to open a browser and display your site.

The route servicing for that file was separated from those providing access to your API. Here are the lines from service.js for the route handling that serves up the index.html file:

```
app.use(express.static(path.join(__dirname, 'static')));

// For loading the default HTML page that acts as the SPA Web site
app.get('/', function (req, res) {
    res.render('index.html')
});
```

The first app.use() call sets up middleware so that you never have to specify a router path for all of the static files. You simply tell it that you have this directory named "static" and that is where they all get found.

The next lines give a specific route for a get request to your root site and states that you would always serve up your index.html file for that.

This is really all you need to do and you are ready to put in the HTML, CSS and JavaScript code that makes use of Angular.

Now I'll show you what is in the index.html file. You will not get a complete understanding of it until you see what is in the accompanying JavaScript behind it.

**Main HTML element containers**
Let's look at the main elements of the index.html file. You really have just two sections to fill out: head and body. It is on the html tag that you add your first piece of AngularJS notation. Study the following HTML:

```
<!DOCTYPE html>
<html ng-app='app'>
<head>
    <meta name="viewport" content="width=device-width, initial-scale=1">
    <link rel='stylesheet'
href='https://maxcdn.bootstrapcdn.com/bootstrap/3.3.5/css/bootstrap.min.css
'>
    <link rel='stylesheet' href='./css/styles.css'>
</head>
<body ng-controller='ApplicationCtrl'>
...to be filled in soon...
</body>
</html>
```

The attribute `ng-app` is digested by Angular to instruct it to look for a module to match up with this file. Angular then knows to use this as the app context for this element hierarchy. You will soon see the code in the JavaScript file that calls into the Angular SDK to set up your application.

The `head` element contains the standard type of link instructions to include the needed styling. In this case, you are making use of Bootstrap. This gives you a really responsive application that is even good on smaller mobile screens. You also see a reference to your own CSS file that will give you any tweaks necessary. The `body` element is shown here, but not filled out.

**The body element**

The body requires a similar Angular attribute as the main html. This Angular design is set up to have the one overall application, with sub-controllers where all of the interaction code goes.

Here, on your main page, you set up a controller named `ApplicationCtrl`. It will only apply to what is rendered here and deals with the few things necessary to support your overall page navigation. The following line specifies the controller:

```
<body ng-controller='ApplicationCtrl'>
```

**Navigation bar**

You first set up the main navigation bar that will exist for users to get access to the menus and see a status message. The HTML makes use of some handy bootstrap styling. You can investigate the particulars about how it all works on your own. This is standard HTML that you can find available for your use. Here is an image of what would be rendered on a smartphone device. It shows the UI state when the menu is opened.

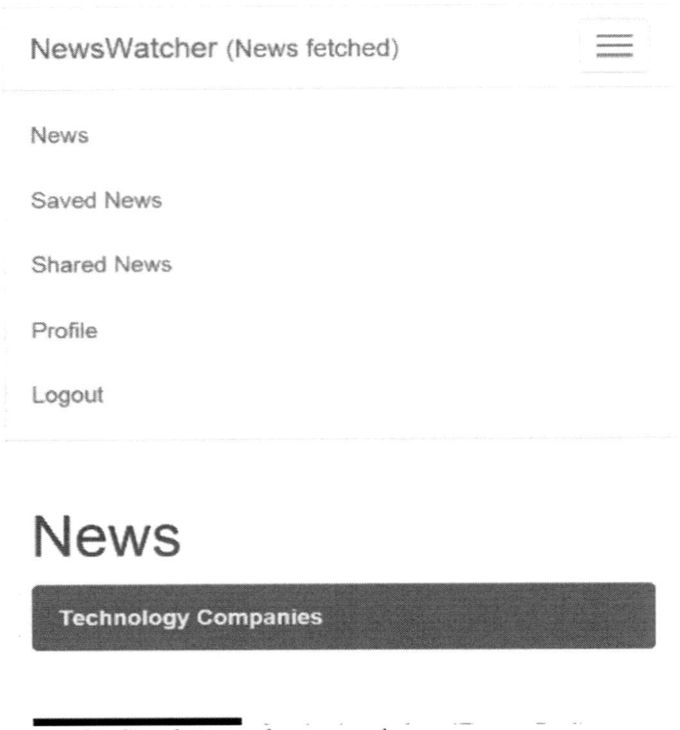

NewsWatcher (News fetched)    ≡

News

Saved News

Shared News

Profile

Logout

# News

Technology Companies

*Figure 94: Sample image for a smartphone*

The HTML for the navigation bar creates a button that will be used to provide a dropdown menu when it is being run on a mobile smartphone. If you run it in a desktop browser, it does not appear this way, but is spread out. Bootstrap classes adapt to the size of the display.

The actual menu selections are in individual li entries. As part of the header of the navbar, there is an element used to display messages you want the user to see. For example, if their login fails, you want to notify the user.

Each li entry represents the menu selections that a user can use to navigate around the application. They can do things like go to the shared news story feed, or alter their news story filters, etc. There is a clever way to show or hide each entry depending on the state of the app. The ng-show and ng-hide attributes bind to a property you can define in your JavaScript code. By toggling that, you control the visibility of what menu items you want. For example, when a user is logged in, you want all of the menu selections visible. Until then, they are hidden.

The actual navigation click-handling is done through a shared function that accepts the path of navigation. The changeView() function will be covered when I show the JavaScript behind this in the controller code. Here is the HTML that controls the navigation selection.

268

```
<nav class='navbar navbar-default'>
   <div class='container-fluid'>
      <div class="navbar-header">
         <button type="button"
          class="navbar-toggle collapsed"
          data-toggle="collapse"
          data-target="#myNavbar">
            <span class="icon-bar"></span>
            <span class="icon-bar"></span>
            <span class="icon-bar"></span>
         </button>
         <a class="navbar-brand">
            NewsWatcher
            <span ng-if='currentMsg'>
               <small id="currentMsgIndex">
                  ({{currentMsg}})
               </small>
            </span>
         </a>
      </div>
      <div class="navbar-collapse collapse"
       id="myNavbar"
       data-toggle="collapse"
       data-target=".navbar-collapse.in">
         <ul class='nav navbar-nav'>
            <li ng-show="loggedIn">
               <a id="newsLink"
                href="javascript:void(0)"
                ng-click="changeView('/news')">
                  News
               </a>
            </li>
            <li ng-show="loggedIn">
               <a id="savedLink"
                href="javascript:void(0)"
                ng-click="changeView('/news/saved')">
                  Saved News
               </a>
            </li>
            <li ng-show="loggedIn">
               <a id="sharedLink"
                href="javascript:void(0)"
                ng-click="changeView('/sharednews')">
                  Shared News
               </a>
            </li>
            <li ng-show="loggedIn">
               <a id="profileLink"
                href="javascript:void(0)"
                ng-click="changeView('/profile')">
                  Profile
               </a>
            </li>
```

```
<li ng-show="loggedIn">
  <a id="logoutLink"
   href="javascript:void(0)"
   ng-click="logout()">
     Logout
  </a>
</li>
<li ng-hide="loggedIn">
    <a href="javascript:void(0)"
     ng-click="changeView('/')">
       Login
    </a>
  </li>
 </ul>
  </div>
  </div>
</nav>
```

You may have noticed that I skipped over what the id attribute is used for. You probably know that the id is standard for HTML and is used to give a unique id in order to place specific CSS styling on an element. It is similar to the class attribute, except that class does not need to be unique. You will actually not be using the id for any styling, but will instead be using it later when you set up some UI automation testing. The testing harness will be able to interact with the DOM and control the UI because you can pinpoint each UI element you need to interact with by knowing its id.

The href="javascript:void(0) is a neat little way to disable the cursor from changing when you mouse over the menu selections in a browser.

**Container**

Next up in your html body section, you need to place an area that will serve as a location to render your pages as you navigate to them. The container you see in the following div element is a styling provided by bootstrap that provides a responsive, fixed-width container. The ng-view identifies the div as something Angular can render into as you navigate through menu selections. This might look kind of magical as you won't see any specific code to directly reference it. It is all done behind the scenes in the Angular library.

```
<div class='container' ng-view></div>
```

**JavaScript libraries**

The last section to go over is the script section. This is at the end to make your page more responsive at load time. You pull in the JavaScript libraries for Bootstrap and for Angular. You also see the usage of jQuery. Don't be alarmed. I certainly did not want to "taint" the project and bring in something such as that, as it could be considered an older and competing technology to what Angular does. jQuery is required by bootstrap because of modal dialogs being used. You will see where they are used later.

270

```
<script
src="https://ajax.googleapis.com/ajax/libs/jquery/1.11.3/jquery.min.js">
</script>
<script
src='https://maxcdn.bootstrapcdn.com/bootstrap/3.3.5/js/bootstrap.min.js'>
</script>
<script
src='https://ajax.googleapis.com/ajax/libs/angularjs/1.4.7/angular.min.js'>
</script>
<script src='https://ajax.googleapis.com/ajax/libs/angularjs/1.4.7/angular-
route.js'>
</script>
<script src='./js/ngapp.js'>
</script>
```

## ApplicationCtrl controller

The Angular controller code that goes along with this main HTML page is in the ngapp,js file. This code only runs once and is executed when the index.html file is initially loaded. Thus, at the start, you run some code to look at the local storage to see if the user's login token has been saved. If it is found, then you can assume you should set that up so that further calls utilize the token in the HTTP header correctly. You can then take the user directly to their own news page. Otherwise, you load the login page.

Even though this controller and page only get loaded once, it stays active while other pages and controllers come and go that are views inside this page.

As with all controllers, you list the services you need to utilize in that controller. $scope is the local controller scope that you hang your properties and functions on to bind to the HTML page using that controller.

$rootScope is a global scope object that works across everything. You set properties on that to share them across controllers.

$http is for placing HTTP requests and is how you connect up to the HTTP/Rest web service API of your service layer.

The $window service gives you access to things like your browser local storage.

This controller sets up the functions you saw referenced in the HTML. One is for logging out and the other for navigation view changing. To navigate, you use the $location service to change the path and trigger the route path code into action to navigate.

Notice the use of the $scope.$on() function to pass messages back and forth across controllers. This can accept an incoming message from a view and use that to set the text for the user on the main HTML page. Other controllers will call `$scope.$emit()` to have their messages sent here to be displayed. Here is the controller code for index.html:

```
.controller('ApplicationCtrl', ['$rootScope', '$scope', '$http',
'$location', '$window', function ($rootScope, $scope, $http, $location,
$window) {
   // Check for token in local HTML5 client side storage
   var retrievedObject = $window.localStorage.getItem("userToken");
   if (retrievedObject) {
      $rootScope.session = JSON.parse(retrievedObject);
      $scope.remeberMe = true;
      $rootScope.loggedIn = true;
      $http.defaults.headers.common['x-auth'] = $rootScope.session.token;
      $scope.$emit('msg', "Signed in as " + $rootScope.session.displayName);
      $location.path('/news').replace();
   } else {
      $scope.remeberMe = false;
      $location.path('/').replace();
   }

   $scope.$on('msg', function (event, msg) {
      $scope.currentMsg = msg;
   });

   $scope.logout = function () {
      $http({
         method: 'DELETE',
         url: "/api/sessions/" + $rootScope.session.userId,
         headers: {
            'Content-Type': 'application/json'
         },
         responseType: 'json'
      }).then(function successCallback(response) {
         $rootScope.loggedIn = false;
         $rootScope.session = null;
         $http.defaults.headers.common["x-auth"] = null;
         $window.localStorage.removeItem("userToken");
         $scope.$emit('msg', "Signed out");
         $location.path('/').replace();
      }, function errorCallback(response) {
         $scope.$emit('msg', "Sign out failed. " + response.data.message);
      });
   }

   $scope.changeView = function (view) {
      $location.path(view).replace();
   }

   $scope.dismissError = function () {
      $scope.currentMsg = null;
   }
}])
```

272

# 16.3 The Login Page (static/ngviews/login.html)

To log a user in, their email and password needs to be accepted. Emails are unique in the system, so no duplicates are allowed in the data layer. The form for the login page contains a checkbox for the user to specify that they want their local device to store their login token for them. If they are not registered yet, they can click to bring up a popup modal dialog form to register with.

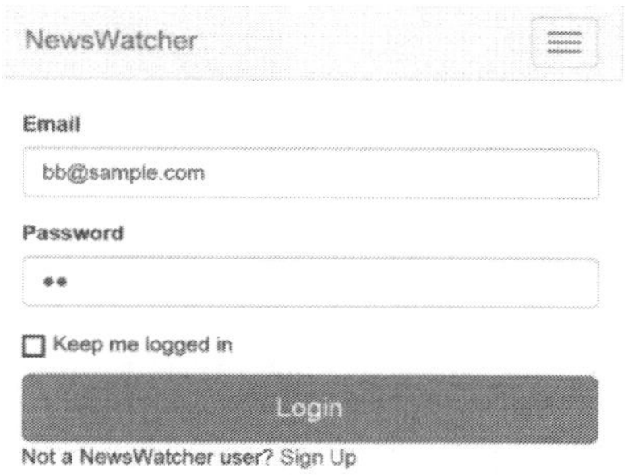

*Figure 95: NewsWatcher login form*

This HTML is for a standard form that has an angular directive to take action on the submit and call the `login()` controller function. You see the `ng-model` directives that bind to specific properties of the controller. Just outside of the form is a link to click to open the modal registration dialog. Here is the HTML for the main login form:

```
<form ng-submit="login(email, password)">
   <div class="form-group">
      <label>Email</label>
      <input id="emailLogin" class="form-control" type="text"
          maxlength="50" ng-model="email">
   </div>
   <div class="form-group">
      <label>Password</label>
      <input id="passwordLogin" class="form-control" type="password"
         maxlength="50" ng-model="password">
   </div>
   <div class="checkbox">
      <label><input type="checkbox" value="" checked ng-model="remeberMe">
         Keep me logged in
      </label>
   </div>
   <input id="btnLogin" class="btn btn-success btn-lg btn-block"
      type="submit" value="Login">
</form>
```

The modal registration dialog looks as follows:

*Figure 96: NewsWatcher Modal Registration*

There is nothing really unusual here, just the use of the `ng-model` and `ng-click` directives. Here is the HTML for that:

```
<div class="modal fade" id="myRegModal" role="dialog">
   <div class="modal-dialog">
      <div class="modal-content">
         <div class="modal-header" style="padding:35px 50px;">
            <button type="button" class="close" data-
dismiss="modal">&times;</button>
            <h4><span class="glyphicon glyphicon-lock"></span> Register</h4>
         </div>
         <div class="modal-body" style="padding:40px 50px;">
            <form role="form">
               <div class="form-group">
                  <label for="displayNameRegister">
                     <span class="glyphicon glyphicon-user"></span>
                     Display Name
                  </label>
                  <input id="displayNameRegister" type="text" maxlength="50"
                     class="form-control" placeholder="Enter display name"
                     ng-model="displayNameReg">
               </div>
```

274

```
            <div class="form-group">
               <label for="emailRegister"
                  <span class="glyphicon glyphicon-user"></span>
                   Email
               </label>
               <input id="emailRegister" type="text" maxlength="50"
                  class="form-control" placeholder="Enter email"
                  ng-model="emailReg">
            </div>
            <div class="form-group">
               <label for="passwordRegister">
                  <span class="glyphicon glyphicon-eye-open"></span>
                   Password
               </label>
               <input id="passwordRegister" type="password" maxlength="15"
                  class="form-control" placeholder="Enter password"
                  ng-model="passwordReg">
            </div>
            <button id="btnRegister" type="submit"
               class="btn btn-success btn-block" data-dismiss="modal"
               ng-click="register()">
               <span class="glyphicon glyphicon-off"></span>
                Register
            </button>
         </form>
      </div>
      <div class="modal-footer">
         <button id="btnCancelRegister" type="submit"
            class="btn btn-danger btn-default pull-left"
            data-dismiss="modal">
            <span class="glyphicon glyphicon-remove"></span>
             Cancel
         </button>
      </div>
   </div>
 </div>
</div>
```

## LoginCtrl controller

Let's now look at the controller for the Login page. The `login()` and `register()` functions should look familiar. It is practically the same code you have used in the test code. The `openRegModal()` function is used for opening up the modal dialog.

```
.controller('LoginCtrl',
   ['$rootScope', '$scope', '$http', '$location', '$window',
    function ($rootScope, $scope, $http, $location, $window)
   {
   $scope.login = function (email, password) {
      $http({
         method: 'POST',
         url: '/api/sessions',
```

```
      cache: false,
      headers: {
        'Content-Type': 'application/json'
      },
      responseType: 'json',
      data: { email: email, password: password }
    }).then(function successCallback(response) {
      $rootScope.loggedIn = true;
      $rootScope.session = response.data;
      $http.defaults.headers.common['x-auth'] = response.data.token;
      $scope.$emit('msg', "Signed in as " + response.data.displayName);
      // Set the token in client side storage if the user desires
      if ($scope.remeberMe) {
        var xfer = {
          token : response.data.token,
          displayName: response.data.displayName,
          userId: response.data.userId
        };
        $window.localStorage.setItem("userToken", JSON.stringify(xfer));
      } else {
        $window.localStorage.removeItem("userToken");
      }
      $location.path('/news').replace();
    }, function errorCallback(response) {
      $scope.$emit('msg', "Sign in failed. " + response.data.message);
    });
  }

  $scope.register = function () {
    $http({
      method: 'POST',
      url: '/api/users',
      cache: false,
      headers: {
        'Content-Type': 'application/json'
      },
      responseType: 'json',
      data: { email: $scope.emailReg,
              displayName: $scope.displayNameReg,
              password: $scope.passwordReg }
    }).then(function successCallback(response) {
      $scope.$emit('msg', "Registered");
    }, function errorCallback(response) {
      $scope.$emit('msg', "Failed to Register. " +
response.data.message);
    });
  }

  $scope.openRegModal = function () {
    angular.element('#myRegModal').modal('show');
  }
}])
```

# 16.4 Displaying the News (static/ngviews/news.html)

This page serves double duty. It will display the main news page as well as the page to show the news stories that the user has saved. The news page looks as follows:

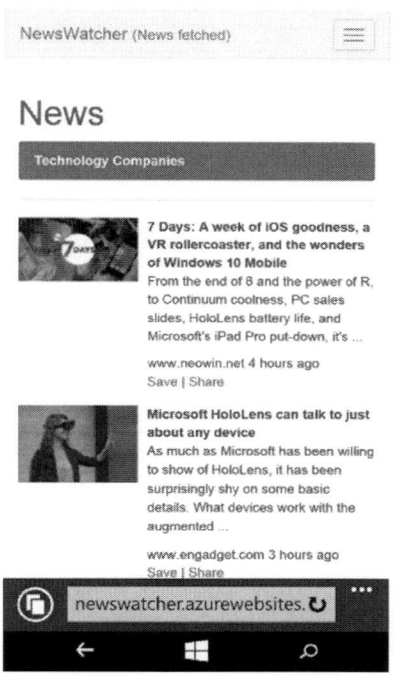

*Figure 97: NewsWatcher news page*

Pay attention to the usage of the `ng-if` directive that causes different UI to be shown in each case. If it is the main page of news, then there is a list that displays the filters to select between. The `ng-repeat` directive is used to ingest the array of filters. Each one is given text from the `filter.name` property as set by the `ng-repeat="filter in user.newsFilters"` statement. You set up the selection handling and activation through the `ng-click` and `ng-class` directives. Here is the HTML:

```
<div ng-if="showSavedNews == null">
   <h1>News</h1>
</div>
<div ng-if="showSavedNews">
   <h1>Saved News</h1>
</div>
<div ng-if="showSavedNews == null" class="list-group">
```

```
    <button ng-repeat="filter in user.newsFilters" type="button"
     class="list-group-item" ng-click="selectOne($index)"
     ng-class="{active: $index == selectedIdx}">
       <strong>{{ filter.name }}</strong>
    </button>
</div>
<hr />
<ul class="media-list">
    <li class="media" ng-repeat="story in news">
      <div class="media-left">
        <a href="{{ story.link }}" target="_blank">
           <img class="media-object" ng-src="{{ story.imageUrl }}">
        </a>
      </div>
      <div class="media-body">
        <h class="media-heading"><b>{{ story.title }}</b></h>
        <p>{{ story.contentSnippet }}</p>
        {{ story.source }}    <span>{{ story.hours }}</span>
        <div ng-if="showSavedNews == null" class="media-body">
          <a href="javascript:void(0)" ng-click="saveStory($index)">
            Save
          </a>
           |  <span>
            <a href="javascript:void(0)" ng-click="shareStory($index)">
              Share
            </a>
          </span>
        </div>
        <div ng-if="showSavedNews" class="media-body">
          <a href="javascript:void(0)" ng-click="deleteSavedStory($index)">
            Delete
          </a>
           |  <span>
            <a href="javascript:void(0)" ng-click="shareStory($index)">
              Share
            </a>
          </span>
        </div>
      </div>
    </li>
</ul>
```

The list of stories is set up with an `ng-repeat` directive. Each `div` in the list has HTML elements to set the news picture and display the news title and text. There is also the ability to click on Save and Share, and to Delete stories for each element.

### NewsCtrl controller
When the page is opened, code is run to do the fetching of the news stories. Then there are the `selectOne()`, `saveStory()`, `deleteSavedStory()`, and `shareStory()` functions that do what you have already seen in the test code.

278

```
.controller('NewsCtrl', ['$rootScope', '$scope', '$http', '$routeParams',
function ($rootScope, $scope, $http, $routeParams) { // Retrieve
NewsWatcher news
    $scope.selectedIdx = 0;
    $scope.showSavedNews = $routeParams.saved;

    $http({
        method: 'GET',
        url: "/api/users/" + $rootScope.session.userId,
        cache: false,
        headers: {
            'Cache-Control': 'no-cache',
            'Pragma': 'no-cache',
            'If-Modified-Since': '0'
        },
        responseType: 'json'
    }).then(function successCallback(response) {
        $scope.user = response.data;
        if ($routeParams.saved) {
            $scope.news = response.data.savedStories;
            for (var i = 0; i < $scope.news.length; i++) {
                $scope.news[i].hours = toHours($scope.news[i].date);
            }
        }
        else {
            $scope.news =
                $scope.user.newsFilters[$scope.selectedIdx].newsStories;
            for (var i = 0; i < $scope.user.newsFilters.length; i++) {
                for (var j = 0;
                    j < $scope.user.newsFilters[i].newsStories.length;
                    j++)
                {
                    $scope.user.newsFilters[i].newsStories[j].hours =
                        toHours($scope.user.newsFilters[i].newsStories[j].date);
                }
            }
        }

        $scope.$emit('msg', "News fetched");
    }, function errorCallback(response) {
        $rootScope.loggedIn = false;
        $rootScope.session = null;
        $http.defaults.headers.common["x-auth"] = null;
        $window.localStorage.removeItem("userToken");
        $scope.$emit('msg', "News fetch failed. " + response.data.message);
        $location.path('/').replace();
    });

    $scope.selectOne = function (index) {
        $scope.selectedIdx = index;
        $scope.news =
            $scope.user.newsFilters[$scope.selectedIdx].newsStories;
    }
```

```
    $scope.saveStory = function (index) {
    $http({
        method: 'POST',
        url: "/api/users/" + $rootScope.session.userId + "/savedstories",
        headers: {
            'Content-Type': 'application/json'
        },
        responseType: 'json',
        data: $scope.news[index]
    }).then(function successCallback(response) {
        $scope.$emit('msg', "Story saved");
    }, function errorCallback(response) {
        $scope.$emit('msg', "Story save failed. " + response.data.message);
    });
}

$scope.deleteSavedStory = function (index) {
    $http({
        method: 'DELETE',
        url: "/api/users/" +
            $rootScope.session.userId +
            "/savedstories/" +
            $scope.news[index].storyID,
        headers: {
            'Content-Type': 'application/json'
        },
        responseType: 'json'
    }).then(function successCallback(response) {
        $scope.news.splice(index, 1);
        $scope.$emit('msg', "Story deleted");
    }, function errorCallback(response) {
        $scope.$emit('msg',
                "Story delete failed. " + response.data.message);
    });
}

$scope.shareStory = function (index) {
    $http({
        method: 'POST',
        url: '/api/sharednews',
        headers: {
            'Content-Type': 'application/json'
        },
        responseType: 'json',
        data: $scope.news[index]
    }).then(function successCallback(response) {
        $scope.$emit('msg', "Story shared");
    }, function errorCallback(response) {
        $scope.$emit('msg', "Story share failed. " +response.data.message);
    });
}
}])
```

280

Here is this little helper function that is being used to format the text to display how old a news story is:

```
function toHours(date)
{
   var d1 = date;
   var d2 = Date.now();
   var diff = Math.floor((d2 - d1) / 3600000);
   if (diff == 0 || diff < 2) {
     return "1 hour ago";
   } else {
     return diff.toString() + " hours ago";
   }
}
```

# 16.5 Shared News Page (static/ngviews/sharednews.html)

The shared news story has the same type of news listing capability you have seen before. Here is that HTML:

```
<h1>Shared News</h1>
<ul class="media-list">
   <li class="media" ng-repeat="sharedStory in news">
     <div class="media-left">
        <a href="{{ sharedStory.story.link }}" target="_blank">
           <img class="media-object"
                 ng-src="{{ sharedStory.story.imageUrl }}">
        </a>
     </div>
     <div class="media-body">
        <h class="media-heading">
           <b id="{{ sharedStory.story.storyID }}">
              {{ sharedStory.story.title }}
           </b>
        </h>
        <p>{{ sharedStory.story.contentSnippet }}</p>
        {{ sharedStory.story.source }}
        <span>{{ sharedStory.story.hours }}</span>
        <a href="javascript:void(0)" ng-click="openModal($index)">
           Comments
        </a>
     </div>
   </li>
</ul>
```

The difference is that there is a capability to comment on each story. That is done through a modal dialog similar to the one used for user registration. Here is the image and HTML:

*Figure 98: NewsWatcher add comment dialog*

```
<div class="modal fade" id="mySharedModal" role="dialog">
  <div class="modal-dialog">
    <div class="modal-content">
      <div class="modal-header" style="padding:35px 50px;">
        <button type="button" class="close" data-dismiss="modal">
          &times;
        </button>
        <h4><span class="glyphicon glyphicon-lock"></span> Add
Comment</h4>
      </div>
      <div class="modal-body" style="padding:40px 50px;">
        <form role="form">
          <div class="form-group">
            <label for="usrname">
              <span class="glyphicon glyphicon-user"></span> Comments
            </label>
            <ul style="height: 10em; overflow: auto; overflow-x:
hidden">
              <li ng-repeat="comment in
news[selectedStoryIdx].comments">
                <div>
```

```
                         <p>'{{ comment.comment }}' - {{
comment.displayName }} </p>
                    </div>
                </li>
            </ul>
        </div>
        <div ng-show="showAddComment()">
            <div class="form-group">
                <label for="usrname">
                    <span class="glyphicon glyphicon-user"></span> Comment
                </label>
                <input id="txtComment" type="text" maxlength="250"
                    class="form-control" placeholder="Enter your comment"
                    ng-model="comment">
            </div>
            <button id="btnComment"
             type="submit" class="btn btn-success btn-block"
             data-dismiss="modal" ng-click="addStoryComment($index)">
                <span class="glyphicon glyphicon-off"></span> Add
            </button>
        </div>
    </form>
</div>
<div class="modal-footer">
    <button type="submit"
     class="btn btn-danger btn-default pull-left"
     data-dismiss="modal">
        <span class="glyphicon glyphicon-remove"></span> Cancel
    </button>
</div>
        </div>
    </div>
</div>
```

## SharedNewsCtrl controller

Again, you run some code upon opening this view and then have the `addStoryComment()` and `openModal()` functions available. There is also some detection to make sure that no more than 30 comments can be added or shown.

```
.controller('SharedNewsCtrl', ['$rootScope', '$scope', '$http', function
($rootScope, $scope, $http) { // Retrieve shared NewsWatcher stories
    $scope.selectedStoryIdx = null;

    $http({
        method: 'GET',
        url: '/api/sharednews',
        cache: false,
        headers: {
            'Cache-Control': 'no-cache',
            'Pragma': 'no-cache',
            'If-Modified-Since': '0'
```

```
    },
    responseType: 'json'
  }).then(function successCallback(response) {
    $scope.news = response.data;
    for (var i = 0; i < $scope.news.length; i++) {
      $scope.news[i].story.hours = toHours($scope.news[i].story.date);
    }
    $scope.$emit('msg', "News fetched");
  }, function errorCallback(response) {
    $scope.$emit('msg', "News fetch failed. " + response.data.message);
  });

  $scope.addStoryComment = function (index) {
    $http({
      method: 'POST',
      url: "/api/sharednews/" +
$scope.news[$scope.selectedStoryIdx].story.storyID + "/Comments",
      headers: {
        'Content-Type': 'application/json'
      },
      responseType: 'json',
      data: { comment: $scope.comment }
    }).then(function successCallback(response) {
      $scope.news[$scope.selectedStoryIdx].comments.push({ displayName:
$rootScope.session.displayName, comment: $scope.comment });
      $scope.$emit('msg', "Comment added");
    }, function errorCallback(response) {
      $scope.$emit('msg', "Comment add failed. " +
response.data.message);
    });
  }

  $scope.openModal = function (index) {
    $scope.selectedStoryIdx = index;
    angular.element('#mySharedModal').modal('show');
  }

  $scope.showAddComment = function () {
    if ($scope.selectedStoryIdx != null)
      return $scope.news[$scope.selectedStoryIdx].comments.length < 30;
    else
      return false;
  }
}]);
```

# 16.6 Profile Page (static/ngviews/profile.html)

The profile page allows the user to create one or more news filters. Each filter has a title and a list of keywords. You have the same type of button dropdown you have seen before. Then you have the form and the three buttons to save, delete, and create a new filter. The image and HTML are as follows:

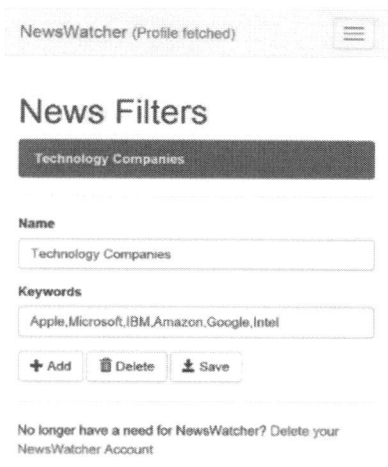

*Figure 99: NewsWatcher News Filter dialog*

```
<h1>News Filters</h1>
<div class="list-group">
   <button ng-repeat="filter in user.newsFilters" type="button"
class="list-group-item" ng-click="selectOne($index)" ng-class="{active:
$index == selectedIdx}"><strong>{{ filter.name }}</strong></button>
</div>
<hr />
<form role='form'>
   <div class="form-group">
      <label>Name</label>
      <input id="nameTxt" class="form-control" maxlength="30" type="text"
ng-model="user.newsFilters[selectedIdx].name">
   </div>
```

```
<div class="form-group">
  <label>Keywords</label>
  <input id="keywordTxt" class="form-control" maxlength="100"
type="text" ng-model="user.newsFilters[selectedIdx].keywordsStr">
  </div>
  <div class="btn-group btn-group-justified" role="group" aria-
label="...">
    <span>
      <button id="btnAdd" type="button" class="btn btn-default" ng-
click="addFilter()">
        <span class="glyphicon glyphicon-plus"></span>
        Add
      </button>
      <button id="btnDelete" type="button" class="btn btn-default" ng-
click="deleteFilter()">
        <span class="glyphicon glyphicon-trash"></span>
        Delete
      </button>
      <button id="btnSave" type="button" class="btn btn-default" ng-
click="saveProfile()">
        <span class="glyphicon glyphicon-save"></span>
        Save
      </button>
    </span>
  </div>
</form>
```

Lastly, there is a link to allow the user to delete their account. The HTML provides a modal dialog like you have used before. Here are the image and HTML:

*Figure 100: NewsWatcher unregister dialog*

```
<hr />
<p>No longer have a need for NewsWatcher? <a id="deleteLink"
href="javascript:void(0)" ng-click="openDelModal()">Delete your NewsWatcher
Account</a></p>
<div class="modal fade" id="myDelModal" role="dialog">
  <div class="modal-dialog">
```

```html
<div class="modal-content">
    <div class="modal-header" style="padding:35px 50px;">
        <button type="button" class="close" data-dismiss="modal">
            &times;
        </button>
        <h4>
            <span class="glyphicon glyphicon-lock"></span> UnRegister
        </h4>
    </div>
    <div class="modal-body" style="padding:40px 50px;">
        <form role="form">
            <div class="checkbox">
                <label>
                    <input id="chkUnRegister" type="checkbox" value=""
                    checked ng-model="deleteOK">Check if you are sure you
want to delete your NewsWatcher account
                </label>
            </div>
            <button id="btnUnRegister" ng-disabled="!deleteOK"
             type="submit" class="btn btn-success btn-block"
             data-dismiss="modal" ng-click="deleteRegistration()">
                <span class="glyphicon glyphicon-off"></span> Delete
NewsWatcher Account
            </button>
        </form>
    </div>
    <div class="modal-footer">
        <button id="btnCancelRegister" type="submit" class="btn btn-
danger btn-default pull-left" data-dismiss="modal">
            <span class="glyphicon glyphicon-remove"></span> Cancel
        </button>
    </div>
    </div>
  </div>
</div>
```

## ProfileCtrl controller
All of the functions necessary to provide the functionality behind the button clicks is made available and should look very similar to code you have in the test files.

```javascript
.controller('ProfileCtrl', ['$rootScope', '$scope', '$http', '$location',
'$window', function ($rootScope, $scope, $http, $location, $window) { //
Retrieve a NewsWatcher user profile
  $http({
    method: 'GET',
    url: "/api/users/" + $rootScope.session.userId,
    cache: false,
    headers: {
      'Cache-Control': 'no-cache',
      'Pragma': 'no-cache',
      'If-Modified-Since': '0'
    },
```

287

```
  responseType: 'json'
}).then(function successCallback(response) {
  $scope.user = response.data;
  for (var i = 0; i < $scope.user.newsFilters.length; i++) {
    $scope.user.newsFilters[i].keywordsStr =
      $scope.user.newsFilters[i].keyWords.join(',');
  }
  $scope.$emit('msg', "Profile fetched");
}, function errorCallback(response) {
  $scope.$emit('msg', "Profile fetch failed. " + response.data.message);
});

$scope.selectedIdx = 0;

$scope.selectOne = function (index) {
  $scope.selectedIdx = index;
}

$scope.deleteFilter = function () {
  $scope.user.newsFilters.splice($scope.selectedIdx, 1);
  $scope.selectedIdx = 0;
}

$scope.addFilter = function () {
  if ($scope.user.newsFilters.length == 5) {
    $scope.$emit('msg', "No more newsFilters allowed");
  } else {
    $scope.user.newsFilters.push({
      name: 'New Filter',
      keyWords : ["Keyword"],
      keywordsStr : "Keyword",
      enableAlert : false,
      alertFrequency : 0,
      enableAutoDelete : false,
      deleteTime : 0,
      timeOfLastScan : 0
    });
    $scope.selectedIdx = $scope.user.newsFilters.length - 1;
  }
}

$scope.saveProfile = function () {
  // Take the comma separated words and turn back into array.
  for (var i = 0; i < $scope.user.newsFilters.length; i++) {
    $scope.user.newsFilters[i].keyWords =
      $scope.user.newsFilters[i].keywordsStr.split(',');
  }

  $http({
    method: 'PUT',
    url: "/api/users/" + $rootScope.session.userId,
    cache: false,
    headers: {
```

```
          'Content-Type': 'application/json'
        },
        responseType: 'json',
        data: $scope.user
    }).then(function successCallback(response) {
        $scope.$emit('msg', "Profile saved");
    }, function errorCallback(response) {
        $scope.$emit('msg', "Profile save failed. " +
            response.data.message);
        });
    }

    $scope.deleteRegistration = function () {
      $http({
        method: 'DELETE',
        url: "/api/users/" + $rootScope.session.userId,
        headers: {
            'Content-Type': 'application/json'
        },
        responseType: 'json'
    }).then(function successCallback(response) {
        $rootScope.loggedIn = false;
        $rootScope.session = null;
        $http.defaults.headers.common["x-auth"] = null;
        $window.localStorage.removeItem("userToken");
        $scope.$emit('msg', "Account deleted");
        $location.path('/').replace();
    }, function errorCallback(response) {
        $scope.$emit('msg', "Account delete failed. " +
            response.data.message);
    });
    }

    $scope.openDelModal = function () {
        angular.element('#myDelModal').modal('show');
    }
}])
```

Notice the addFilter() function. You can see that there is code there to limit the number of filters to five. What do you suppose would happen if the user used the browser developer tools to mess with that code and then added 1000 filters? It could create a document so large that it would fail to be updated in MongoDB. Thus you cannot ever rely on your UI side bounds-checking code to do the right thing, as it is subject to tampering. Thus you have to place code in your service layer that will only take the first five filters and also only match on the first 10 stories for any filter.

That completes the discussion of each of the HTML files and their corresponding controller code. Everything can be zipped up and deployed to the AWS Elastic Beanstalk environment and used. On windows you would select the folders and files as shown before and then right click and select **Send to->Compressed (zipped) folder**.

# Chapter 17: UI Testing of NewsWatcher

With the NewsWatcher application actually up and running, you will want to run it through every conceivable scenario. Manually doing this is great for your entertainment, but it will soon grow tedious if you do that as your only way of finding bugs. For example, what happens if you make any changes to your code base? You have the function and load tests, but you still need to run the UI through its paces to exercise the Angular JavaScript code. Not to fear, there is a great solution to this problem and I will present that as well as general tips for debugging as you proceed.

# 17.1 Debugging UI Issues

To locally debug you server side node.js code is very simple, since you are writing it inside of VS Code, you have the capability to host it locally and set break points. However, the Angular code runs in the browser and browsers have their own debugging capabilities. For example, with the Microsoft Edge browser, you can press **F12** and open up a debug console.

Once open, you can click on the **Console** tab and see errors that happen in your code. This image shows a null reference bug I was able to find in my code:

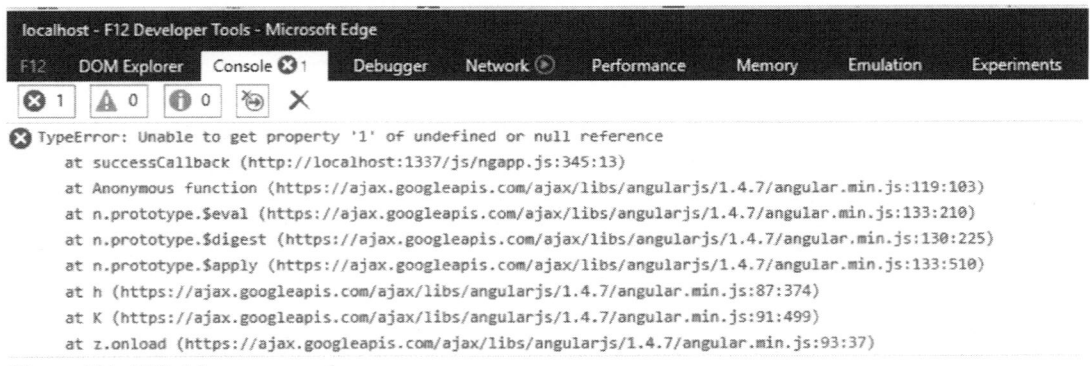

*Figure 101: F12 debugger console*

This window is very handy to have open as you run into problems and many times it is quite easy to just go and fix the bugs you find. Other times, you will need to step through the lines of code. Simply click the **Debugger** tab and you can browse your code and set breakpoints in the browser. The experience is typical of any debugger in that you can inspect variables and set watches on them. Chrome and Firefox also have great debuggers.

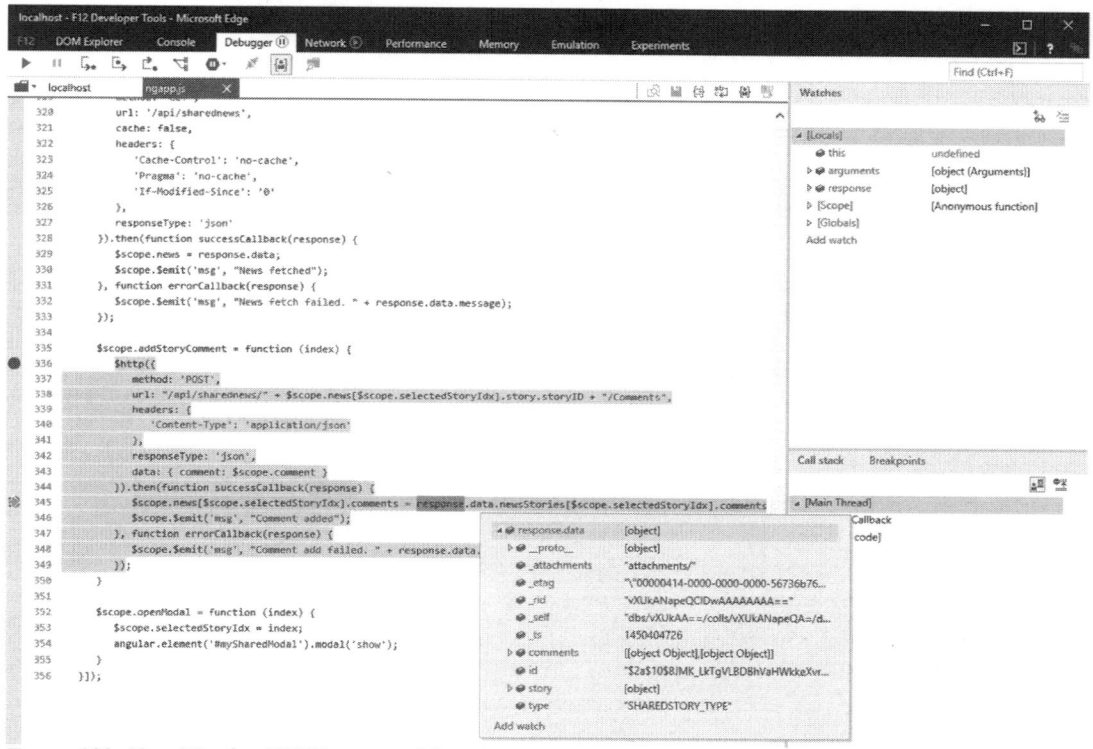

*Figure 102: NewsWatcher HTTP request debugging*

If you have written HTML, you know the capabilities of the browser developer tools and will certainly know how to inspect the DOM elements and their associated CSS. Click the **DOM Explorer** tab to try this out. For example, you might find that an element is not styled or functioning as expected. A quick inspection can usually turn up the issue. The **Network** tab shows you the HTTP traffic going back and forth similar to what you see using Fiddler.

# 17.2 UI Automation Testing

There are tools you can use to record your interactions within a browser session and then play it back. Some actually record screen locations of clicks and then rely on the UI elements to be in that exact same location later for the interaction to work. Other tools actually understand the DOM and can find elements you specify to click on.

# PART III: The Presentation Layer (AngularJS/HTML)

The tool I prefer to use to do automation testing of a UI is a tool created a while a while ago named Selenium. It was built so long ago that it did not support JavaScript directly. Luckily, someone did the work to write a node.js module that exposes its capabilities.

The first step towards accomplishing your UI automation testing will be to install the "selenium-webdriver" from NPM to have it local in your project. Be aware that this might not be as simple as it sounds. Pay attention to the output window as you install it. It might fail because of dependencies. I had to install the JDK, Python tools, and even a more complete Visual Studio install with some of the C++ tools that I would not have dreamed would be required. Your experience might be different on a different OS.

You might also check out an NPM module named Protractor that is written on top of selenium-webdriver. I found it easy enough to go directly through the selenium-webdriver module.

The selenium-webdriver is just an SDK to access the browser DOM and thus you still need some type of testing framework to organize and run your tests. Mocha is perfect for doing this. This is what you would run from the command prompt to get your UI automation tests running.

```
.\node_modules\.bin\mocha --timeout 30000 ui_automation_UAT.js
```

You will populate a Mocha test file with code that uses the selenium-webdriver module capabilities. You also need to set up the `require` statements for asserts and for making HTTP request to do some needed cleanup after a test run. Here are the require statements:

```
var assert = require('assert');
var webdriver = require('selenium-webdriver');
var request = require('supertest')('http://localhost:3000);
```

You use the usual Mocha `describe` and `it` code blocks. You need to first set up some code that runs before any tests in a `before` block. This code initializes Selenium and sets up which browser you want it to use. The `after` block does the cleanup.

Using the driver object, you can get access to any element in the DOM, to inspect it or affect it in some way. For example, with a text control, you can send it keystokes to enter values as a user would. Buttons can be clicked, etc.

Many times, you do something like a button click and then need to wait for the UI to respond. The driver has a `wait()` function you use to wait for UI elements to be available. For example, if you were navigating to a new page, you would use a wait to block the test until the page was ready. The `wait()` function takes as a first parameter, what you are waiting for. You can thus wait for an element to be visible. Inside that function you provide the id by using the webdriver object to locate what you set it as in the HTML. There is a time limit set on the wait for how long it should wait. It will wait up to that time, but if the element appears before that, it will immediately move on. Sometimes you just need to put in a `setTimeout()` call to do the delay.

Here is the specifying of an id in your HTML that you then can use to identify a button by.

```
<button id="btnRegister" ng-click="register()">Register</button>
```

As with all Mocha tests, you need to call `done()` when that test is finished and you want to move on to the next test.

The whole point then of putting together a UI automation test with Selenium is to mimic what you would normally do manually and thus have a repeatable test suite that you can run as part of a CI/CD script and save you tons of time. There is the concept of a User Acceptance Test or UAT that basically is the user script that you want to follow to prove that the UI can do everything it is supposed to do. Development teams can create a UAT for each code iteration they go through before a deployment can be approved.

You can set up the test to go against your staging, production or local hosted site. Here is a trimmed back selection of the code for the UI automation testing:

```
describe('NewsWatcher UI exercising', function () {
    var driver;
    var storyID;
    var token;

    // This runs before all tests in this block
    before(function (done) {
        driver = new webdriver.Builder().withCapabilities(
                            webdriver.Capabilities.firefox()).build();
        driver.get('https://www.newswatcherfs.com/');
        driver.wait(webdriver.until.elementLocated(
            webdriver.By.id('registerLink')), 10000).then(function (item) {
            done();
        });
    });

    // This runs after all tests in this block
    after(function (done) {
        driver.quit().then(done);
    });

    it('should create a new registered User', function (done) {
        driver.findElement(webdriver.By.id('registerLink')).click();
        // Wait for the modal to appear and the controls to be visible
        driver.wait(webdriver.until.elementIsVisible(
            driver.findElement(webdriver.By.id('btnRegister'))), 5000);
```

```
      driver.findElement(webdriver.By.id('displayNameRegister'))
      .sendKeys('Testperson');

      driver.findElement(webdriver.By.id('emailRegister'))
      .sendKeys('Testperson@blah.com');

      driver.findElement(webdriver.By.id('passwordRegister'))
      .sendKeys('Testpass');

      driver.findElement(webdriver.By.id('btnRegister')).click();

      // Wait for the status message update
      setTimeout(function () {
        driver.findElement(webdriver.By.id('currentMsgIndex'))
        .getInnerHtml()
        .then(function (value) {
          assert.equal(value, '(Registered)');
          done();
        });
      }, 3000);
  });

  it('should allow a registered user to login', function (done) {
      driver.findElement(webdriver.By.id('btnLogin')).click();

      // Wait for the status message update
      setTimeout(function () {
        driver.findElement(webdriver.By.id('currentMsgIndex'))
        .getInnerHtml()
        .then(function (value) {
          assert.equal(value, '(News fetched)');
          done();
        });
      }, 3000);
  });

  it('should open the news filters user profile', function (done) {
      driver.findElement(webdriver.By.id('profileLink')).click();

      // Wait for the status message update
      setTimeout(function () {
        driver.findElement(webdriver.By.id('currentMsgIndex'))
        .getInnerHtml()
        .then(function (value) {
          assert.equal(value, '(Profile fetched)');
          done();
        });
      }, 3000);
  });
});
```

## Angular service testing

Angular itself has a recommended pattern of testing if you need to do dependency injection or mocking. This is useful if you are creating your own Angular services. Basically, you end up testing the values and checking if they are correct. That is how you would verify that the Angular binding was correct. Here is an example from the Angular documentation:

```
angular.module('app', [])
.controller('PasswordController', function PasswordController($scope) {
  $scope.password = '';
  $scope.grade = function() {
    var size = $scope.password.length;
    if (size > 8) {
      $scope.strength = 'strong';
    } else if (size > 3) {
      $scope.strength = 'medium';
    } else {
      $scope.strength = 'weak';
    }
  };
});

describe('PasswordController', function() {
  beforeEach(module('app'));

  var $controller;

  beforeEach(inject(function(_$controller_){
    // The injector unwraps the underscores (_) from around
    // the parameter names when matching
    $controller = _$controller_;
  }));

  describe('$scope.grade', function() {
    it('sets the strength to "strong" if the password length is >8 chars',
function() {
      var $scope = {};
      var controller = $controller('PasswordController', { $scope: $scope
});
      $scope.password = 'longerthaneightchars';
      $scope.grade();
      expect($scope.strength).toEqual('strong');
    });
  });
});
```

# 17.3 CPU Profiling and Memory Leak Detection

Just as with Node.js, you can accomplish CPU profiling and take snapshots of memory usage of the pages running in the browser. This is because V8 is the engine of the Chrome browser also. You can also use the Edge or IE browsers, as they also have capabilities for this type of analysis. Here are some images of memory profiling with IE.

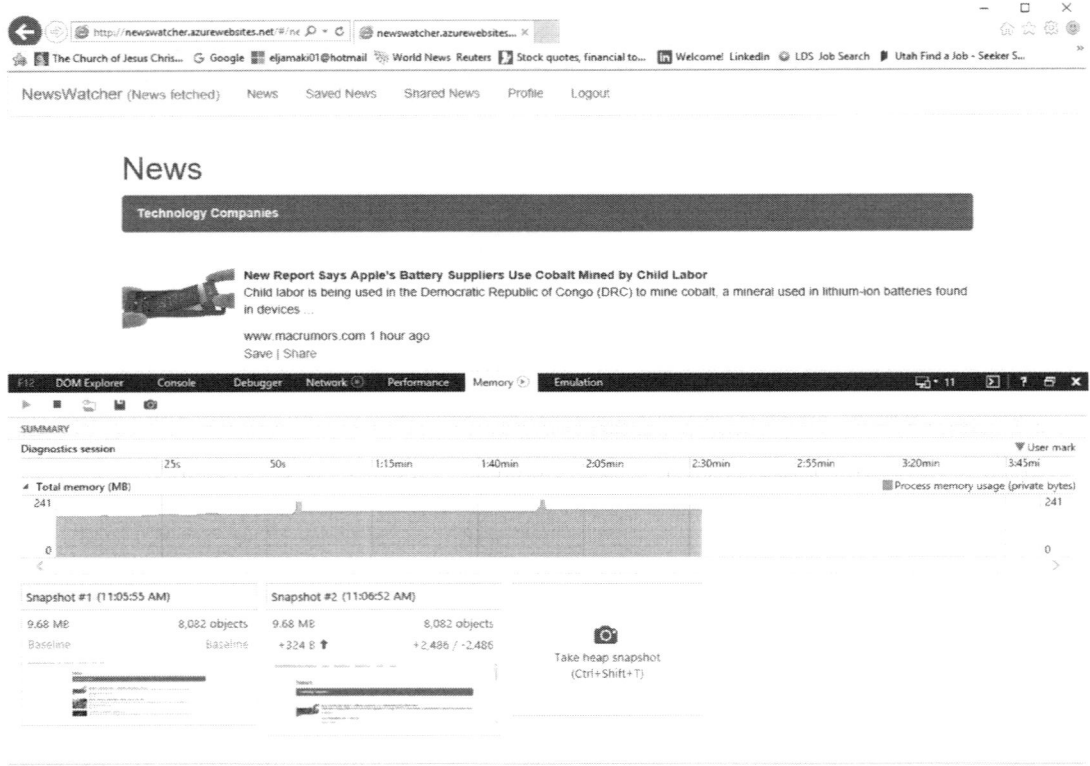

*Figure 103: NewsWatcher IE memory profiling*

# Chapter 17: UI Testing of NewsWatcher

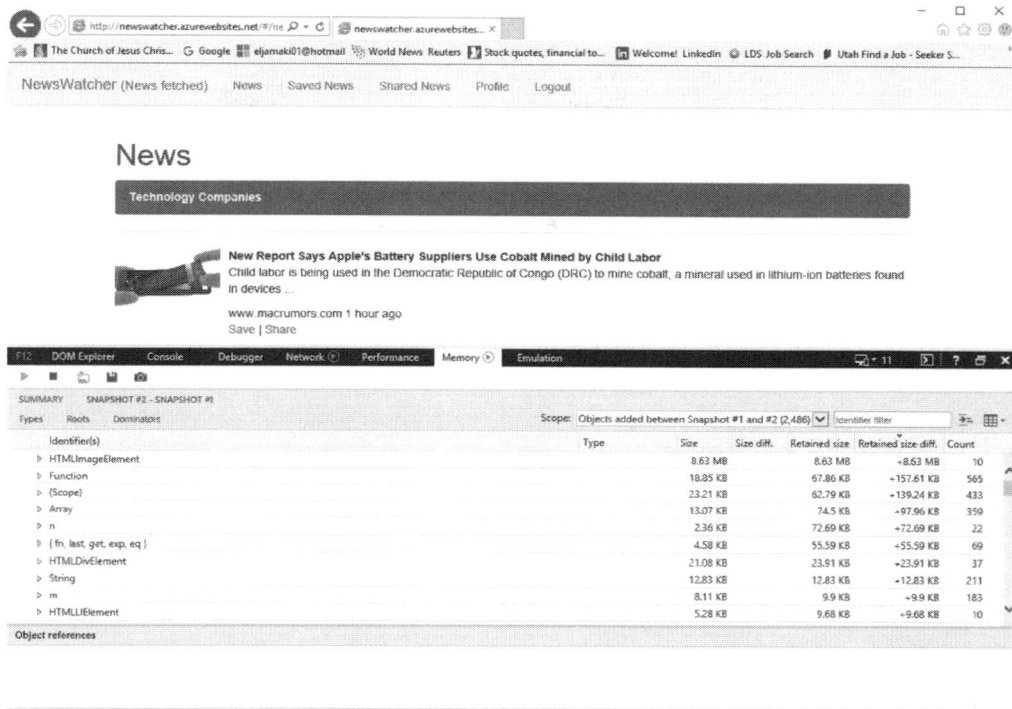

*Figure 104: NewsWatcher IE memory profiling*

Here is Chrome being set up to do CPU profiling:

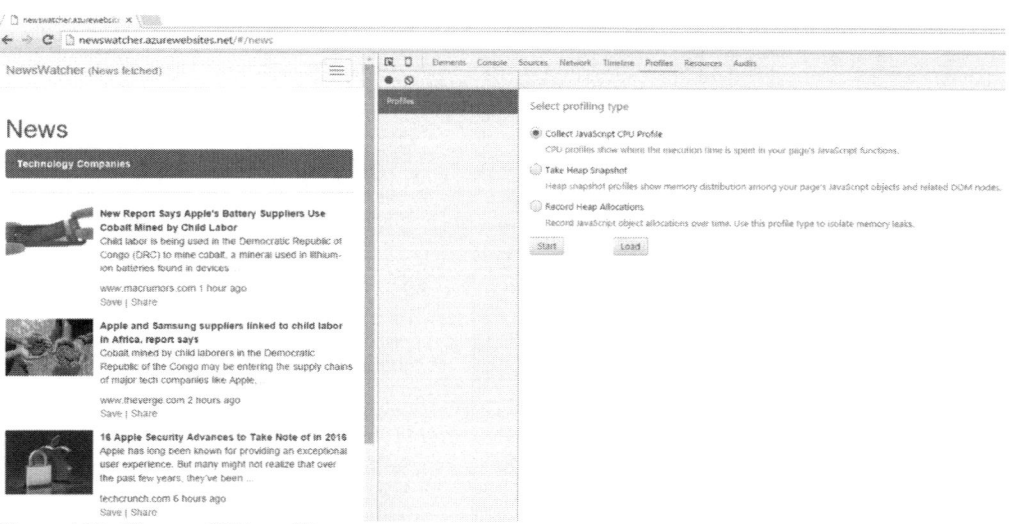

*Figure 105: Chrome CPU profiling*

# Conclusion

A lot of material has now been covered and you should at this time feel really good about your newly acquired knowledge and skills. You started by learning about what a three-tier architecture is and how a MEAN JavaScript full-stack implementation is a great choice for an implementation.

The NewsWatcher sample application was featured throughout the book as a full end-to-end implementation of the architecture you have been learning about. You now have the code that you can refer to and base any of your work off of.

The three parts of the book covered the layers of a three-layer architecture and gave you foundational knowledge about each layer. You also learned about the SDKs to use and specific usage scenarios of everything for the NewsWatcher application.

You can now go forward and do your own learning for your own specific needs and be successful. You may choose to just work in one of the layers, or you may be able to contribute across all layers. It is always good to be knowledgeable overall as you will know better how everything works internally and realize how what you do in one layer affects another layer.

# INDEX

22072101R00173

Printed in Great Britain
by Amazon